THE TRANSLATOR

Professor Jacob Neusner is Unive Professor, Professor of Religious Studies, and The Ungerleider Distinguished Scholar of Judaic Studies at Brown University. He is editor of several scholarly monograph series, including *Studies in Judaism in Late Antiquity* (Brill), *Studies in Judaism in Modern Times* (Brill), *Library of Judaic Learning* (KTAV), and *Brown Judaic Studies* (Scholars Press). He has written *A History of the Mishnaic Law of Purities* (Leiden, 1974-1977) in 22 parts, *A History of the Mishnaic Law of Holy Things* (Leiden, 1978-1979) in 6 parts, *A History of the Mishnaic Law of Women* (Leiden, 1979-1980) in 5 parts, and is currently working on *A History of the Mishnaic Law of Appointed Times* and *A History of the Mishnaic Law of Torts.* His students are now completing *A History of the Mishnaic Law of Agriculture.* Professor Neusner has received the University Medal for Excellence, Columbia University, 1974, and an honorary Doctor of Humane Letters, The University of Chicago, 1978. In 1978 he was appointed by President Carter to serve for six years on the National Council on the Humanities, governing board of the National Endowment for the Humanities.

THE
TOSEFTA

THE TOSEFTA

TRANSLATED FROM THE HEBREW
THIRD DIVISION
NASHIM
(The Order of Women)

BY

JACOB NEUSNER

University Professor
Professor of Religious Studies
The Ungerleider Distinguished Scholar of Judaic Studies
Brown University

KTAV PUBLISHING HOUSE INC.
NEW YORK
1979

Library of Congress Cataloging in Publication Data (Revised)

Tosefta. English.
The Tosefta.

Includes bibliographical references and indexes.
CONTENTS: —division. 3. Nashim.—division 6. Tohorot.
1. Neusner, Jacob, 1932-
BM508.13.E5 1977 296.1'262'05 77-4277
ISBN 0-87068-430-2 (v. 6)
ISBN 0-87068-684-4 (v. 3)

MANUFACTURED IN THE UNITED STATES OF AMERICA

For
Howard Swearer

CONTENTS

THE TOSEFTA
THIRD DIVISION
NASHIM

Preface

I. *Definition of the Document*

Tosefta, redacted about A.D. 400, is a companion to Mishnah and wholly comprehensible only when brought into relationship with Mishnah, redacted about A.D. 200. A collection of materials of a predominately legal character, Mishnah provides for both itself and this associated compilation the principles of organization: a definition of principal divisions, tractates, and of the unfolding agendum of themes and sequences of problems in intermediate divisions ("chapters" for Mishnah) as well. Thus Tosefta is a vine hanging on Mishnah's trellis. It contributes to Mishnah in three ways. First of all, it may cite Mishnah and make some comment or clarify some point of Mishnah's law. Second, while not citing Mishnah, it may complement Mishnah with pericopae able to be fully and completely interpreted only in relationship to Mishnah. Third, it may supplement Mishnah with materials relevant to the theme or general principle of Mishnah, but able to be fully and completely interpreted entirely out of relationship to Mishnah. These three sorts of materials tend to be grouped together by type, with units presenting citation and gloss of Mishnah followed by complementary, and finally, supplementary materials. But that is only a tendency.

II. *The Topic: Women*

The third division of Tosefta and of Mishnah treats laws concerning women. While reviewing Tosefta's relevant corpus, we must keep in mind that it is only in relationship to Mishnah that the mind of earlier Rabbinic Judaism, the kind of Judaism revealed in these documents and in cognate collections in the Talmuds and Midrashic compilations, is to be described and interpreted. Taking an isolated phrase of Tosefta as somehow significant for the position of earlier Rabbinic Judaism on women, their rights, role in society, and responsibilities as members of the community of Israel, the Jewish people, will be an unfortunate error. First, as is clear, the document itself is thereby cut off from its frame. Second, even if we bring together Mishnah and Tosefta for the Division of Women, describing and interpreting their ideas on women will be suitably accomplished only within the larger context of the entire system of which our division forms only one principal part. Mishnah-Tosefta do, after all, constitute a complete and whole system, a statement of the way in which a sacred society is formed upon a Holy Land and by a holy people. Only when we have a clear picture of the encompassing traits of the system as a whole shall we make some sense of its particular conceptions of women (or of Purities or Holy Things, the divisions already laid forth).

Still, even at this point we may make a preliminary observation. There can be no doubt that for Mishnah and Tosefta—that is, for nascent Rabbinic Judaism—women form a subordinated caste. They are in a caste system which, top to bottom, consists of priests, Levites, Israelites, women (with their legal counterparts, e.g., minors, slaves), *Netins, Mamzers,* and other castes of an impaired genealogical character, and, outside the whole, gentiles. Now what is clear is that all other castes are male. Women are not differentiated along genealogical lines, forming, as they do, a caste unto themselves. But men are. That is, the daughter of a priest (here translated: "priest-girl") does not retain her status and transmit it to her children. Only the son of a priest does so. The daughter is part of the priest's household only so long as she has not married, at which point she adopts the caste of her husband.

Why it is that women should constitute a caste and yet shift in relationship to their antecedent (birth) caste, how it is that for women no important sacred role should be defined within the system of Mishnah-Tosefta, and why it is that, of all the systems produced by Judaism, this one (and two others) known to us in late antiquity should reveal the traits, *vis à vis* women, just now specified, I cannot say. When we reflect upon the important social, political, and religious role open to women in the times of ancient Israel, with its women-prophets, queens, and other kinds of religious and political figures who were women, the significant role open to women later on, for instance, in the Hasmonean court, and the prominence of women in the art of synagogues of this very period, we must find it anomalous that only three groups of this period are unable to provide for women an equivalently distinguished role. These are, first, the Essenes of Qumran, who have no place for women in the leadership of the commune; second, the priests of the Temple, who keep women outside of the main sanctuary and allow them no role whatsoever in the conduct of the cult, and, finally, the rabbis of Mishnah-Tosefta, who carry forward the legacy of the Pharisees, scribes, and priests of the period before A.D. 70.

These three groups, of course, have much in common. They are the ones in ancient Judaism which take most seriously the legacy of the Priestly Code and the related priestly literature. The Essenes of Qumran and the Pharisees who stand behind early strata of Mishnah-Tosefta of course draw upon the Priestly Code and the Temple for their principal, generative metaphors. Both groups translate holiness into everyday life, pretending at their tables at home to eat their meals in a state of cultic cleanness as if they were priests in the Jerusalem laboring at the table of the Lord, the altar. So in the end, I am inclined to think, the attitudes toward women which lie at the foundations of Mishnah-Tosefta and which form the fundamental traits of the system of Rabbinic Judaism from its beginnings, in the late first and second century, to the present day, are likely to originate in priestly circles. These will long antedate the period before 70. They must go back to the time of Ezra, when the Priestly Code was given its ultimate structure and shape. Seeking to organize the world so that all things relate to all other things in a great chain of orderly being, the priests have no choice, once women are going to be treated as a distinct caste, but to place their caste in relationship to the others within the larger hierarchical framework to which we have alluded. The alternative is not to treat women as a distinct caste at all, but to include women and men together within the existing caste system. Self-evidently, that is not the choice which was made.

But that is not why we have a division of Women as one of the six divisions of Mishnah-Tosefta. For in our system women remain an anomaly: they are the *only* caste to receive a whole division of Mishnah-Tosefta. Indeed, one of the striking omissions of our document is its failure to provide a significant and well-organized division devoted to the priesthood. Since Mishnah in so many ways expresses the world-view of priests and devotes one-half of its whole to specifically priestly concerns—cultic laws, in Holy Things, cultic cleanness, in Purities, and cultic taxes, in Seeds—the considerable attention paid to women presents a striking and surprising fact. Women both are excluded in deed and occupy disproportionate attention in the system of holiness.

What our system clearly wishes to say about women is that they are to be treated with great respect and protected in their persons and in their property. But in no way are women accorded rights and responsibilities enjoyed by men. They cannot testify in court, for example, against the testimony of men, and they are expected to live only as dependents, first of their fathers, then of their husbands. Obviously, the world-view constructed by Mishnah-Tosefta is hardly distinctive in the attitudes just now outlined. But Mishnah remains particular when we ask, first, Why is it that Mishnah has given one-sixth of the whole to women? and, second, how is it that a caste is defined by sex, as distinct from, and as opposed to, genealogy (birth into a family of priests, Levites, Israelites, *Netins, mamzers,* and so on)? The task is to define, describe, and interpret the system in its own context, not to condemn or apologize for it. But, as is clear from these casual observations, thus far even the work of definition, description, and interpretation, is at its beginnings.

III. *The Tractates*

The principal themes of the seven tractates of the third division are as follows:

Yebamot
Levirate marriage, that is, marriage between a childless deceased man's widow and his brother, as required by Deut. 25:5–10; or the performance of the rite of *ḥaliṣah* ("unloosening the shoe") in lieu of such a marriage. MS Cambridge also calls the tractate, "Women," since other matters beside Levirate marriage are treated, e.g., the right of a priest's daughter to eat food in the status of heave-offering so long as she has not wed a nonpriest; cases of erroneous remarriage of a woman (e.g., after a false report of her husband's death).

Ketubot
The property rights of a woman entering marriage, embodied in a marriage contract which guarantees her a year's maintenance in the event of a divorce or death, as well as the return of dowry; the rights of children produced by this marriage to inherit their mother's property; the matter of claims of virginity (Deut. 22:13–21); the loss of the right to collect what is owing in the marriage contract.

Nedarim
Vows, with special reference at the end to the power of the husband or father of a woman to annul her vows, in line with Num. 30:2–17, accounting for the inclusion of the tractate in our division; euphemisms for vows, vows which are not binding, grounds for the absolution of vows; vows not to derive benefit from one's fellow; vows not to eat a given sort of food; vows for a particular period of time; a sage's absolution of a vow; the power of the husband or father to annul a vow (as above).

Nazir
The vow to become a Nazir, described at Num. 6:1–21; euphemisms for Nazirite-vows, Nazirite vows of a special character; a woman's Nazirite-vows and how they are abrogated by her husband or father; violations of the Nazirite-vow through corpse-uncleanness and drinking wine; the Nazirite's sacrifice and purification-rite.

Sotah
The wife accused of adultery and how she is subjected to the ordeal described at Num. 5:11–31; the draft-exemptions of Deut. 20:1–9; the neglected corpse, Deut. 21:1–9.

Gittin
Writs of divorce, how they are written, delivered, and effected, in line with Deut. 24:1–4; writs of divorce brought from overseas and confirming their validity; preparing a writ for the use of a particular woman and not for any other; the use of an agent for delivering or receiving a writ of divorce; agents for the writing of a writ of divorce; delivering a writ to a woman's domain; signing a writ of divorce.

Qiddushin
The laws of betrothal, lacking Scriptural foundations entirely, deal with the means by which a woman is sanctified for a particular man; effecting a betrothal through an agent; betrothals made upon the fulfillment of a particular condition; the castes who came up to the Holy Land from Babylonia and marriages among and between them.

IV. *Text and Translation*

The text translated here is the Vienna manuscript, as printed and revised by Saul Lieberman, *The Tosefta. According to Codex Vienna, with Variants from Codices Erfurt, Genizah MSS., and Editio Princeps (Venice, 1521). Together with References to Parallel Passages in Talmudic Literature . And a Brief Commentary. The Order of Nashim. Yebamoth. Kethubuth. Nedarim. Nazir* (N.Y., 1967), and *The Order of Nashim. Sotah. Gittin. Kiddushin* (N.Y. 1973). Further information on commentaries systematically consulted is at *Tosefta in English* VI, p. xi.

For Tosefta Sotah Chapters Three through Fifteen, Lieberman prints

MS Erfurt in a column alongside MS Vienna. I did not translate the former, because there are no really material differences between the two, except that Erfurt is much briefer. I considered translating Erfurt and presenting it alongside Vienna, but the result, after a couple of chapters, was a nearly identical translation, with only trivial and unimportant differences in wording. The one significant difference is that Vienna is a great deal fuller and simply contains more material than Erfurt. Nearly everything in Erfurt is in Vienna, but not everything in Vienna is in Erfurt. Since no one to whom this book will be useful will miss a translation of the parallel manuscript, I did not think it worthwhile to present it here.

An exegesis of each pericope, together with an explanation both of the text as translated and its meaning, is found for each tractate in the relevant volumes of my *History of the Mishnaic Law of Women.* These are I. *Yebamot. Translation and Explanation;* II. *Ketubot. Translation and Explanation;* III. *Nedarim, Nazir. Translation and Explanation;* and IV. *Sotah, Gittin, Qiddushin. Translation and Explanation.* There is also V. *The Mishnaic System of Women: History and Meaning* (all: Leiden, 1980 f.).

The translation aims at a literal representation of the order and meaning of the Hebrew words as well as of the formal and formalized character of the language—morphology and syntax—of our document. While, self-evidently, form-analysis is not possible other than in the original language of the document, still it should be possible for readers to form an accurate impression of the highly formalized literature constituted by Mishnah-Tosefta.

In italics are passages in which Mishnah is cited verbatim, or nearly verbatim, as well as citations of biblical verses. In square brackets are inserted the identification of a Mishnah-pericope cited verbatim, or nearly verbatim, by Tosefta. This procedure makes it easy to discern Tosefta's additional observation or gloss of Mishnah. Further explanation of the purpose and character of this translation is at *Tosefta in English* VI, pp. xiv–xvii. The letters marking each stich of a pericope are merely for ready reference in form-analysis and bear no technical significance.

V. *Conclusion*

The reader is referred to the discussion of the character of Tosefta at VI, pp. ix–xvii, and at V, pp. ix–xi. Progress on *The First Division. The Order of Agriculture,* under the editorship of my colleague, Professor Richard S. Sarason, is gratifying. Two-thirds of the tractates already have been translated, and all are now in hand. We hope that the remainder of the work will not be much postponed. When *A History of the Mishnaic Law of Women* is completed, my plan is to proceed to the second division, the Order of Seasons, to take advantage of the availability of Lieberman's text of Tosefta and extensive commentary on Tosefta and, inevitably, on Mishnah (and much else). Hopefully, we shall yet see his edition of, and commentary on, the fourth division of Tosefta, the Order of Torts.

Now completing his second year as president of Brown University, Howard Swearer has won the respect, admiration, and deep affection of the entire community formed by our University. The reason may be adduced in the evidence of his own words, written to me on April 18, 1978, when he kindly accepted the dedication of this project: "I am aware of my several limitations, and I know that I shall make mistakes. But of one thing I can assure you: I am giving all the energy and experience I can muster to Brown University. The University deserves it, and with the positive response of faculty and students, I am encouraged about our collective future." President Swearer represents everything sound and healthy in American higher education and brings hope and vitality to our University in particular. I know of no university more fortunate in the quality and calibre of its administrative and academic leadership than Brown. I offer this dedication as a token of esteem and friendship. Now we know what a president can and should be. It remains to live up to the fresh opportunities for teaching and for learning which open up in this new age of Brown University.

J.N.

Providence, Rhode Island
May 24, 1978
17 Iyyar 5738, *the thirty-third day of the 'omer.*

List of Abbreviations and Glossary

[ ]	= Words supplied by translator.
( )	= To be deleted from the Hebrew text.
[?]	= Translation uncertain.
Amah	= See *handbreadth.*
Ar.	= Tractate ʿArakhin.
Aṣeret	= Pentecost; the Feast of Weeks. *Shabuʿot.*
Bekh.	= Tractate Bekhorot.
Bespeak	= The ordinary marriage takes place in two stages, betrothal (*qiddushin*) and consummation (*nissuʾin*). In the case of levirate marriage, the parallel stages are a declaration of intent to take the deceased childless brother's widow in levirate marriage (Hebrew: ʿŚH MʾMR) and the act of sexual relations which consummates the marriage. The former is translated *bespeak.* Bespeaking in a levirate marriage is thus parallel to betrothal under ordinary circumstances.
Bet kor	= an area sown by a *kor* of seed; 75,000 square cubits.
Chron.	= Chronicles
Dan.	= Daniel
Deut.	= Deuteronomy
Ephah	= Three *seʾahs* or eighteen *qabs* equal one *ephah.*
Ex.	= Exodus
Ez.	= Ezekiel
Festival	= The Festival, without further qualification, refers to the Feast of Tabernacles. *Sukkot.*
Gen.	= Genesis
Git.	= Tractate Giṭṭin
HD	= *Ḥasdé David,* by David Pardo.
HY	= Ḥazon Yeḥezqel, by Yeḥezqel Abramsky.
Hab.	= Habakkuk
Habdalah	= The ceremony which marks the end of the Sabbath or of a festival day and the beginning of an ordinary weekday.

Hag.	= Haggai
Ḥallal[in]	= One unfit for the priesthood because of his father's illegitimate connection (Lev. 21:7, 14ff.).
Hallel	= Psalms 113–118.
Ḥaluṣah	= A woman who has carried out the *Ḥaliṣah*-rite described at Deut. 25:7–9.
Handbreadth	= Four fingerbreadths equal one handbreadth.
Hegemon	= A Roman magistrate.
Hekhal	= The Temple hall containing the golden altar.
Hin	= A liquid measure, equal to twelve *logs*.
Hos.	= Hosea.
Hul.	= Tractate Ḥullin.
Iron-flock slaves	= Slaves or other property brought into a marriage by a wife are dealt with in one of two ways. In the category of 'iron-flock' is property for which the husband bears full responsibility, so that, in the case of loss, he must make up the value. This is equivalent to a fixed income security, in which full payment must be made for the original value of the invested capital. But any rise in value accrues to the husband. See *Melog-slaves*.
Is.	= Isaiah
Issar	= eight *peruṭot*. A *peruṭah* is the smallest copper coin.
Jastrow	= Marcus Jastrow, *A Dictionary of the Targumim, the Talmud Babli and Yerushalmi, and the Midrashic Literature*.
Jer.	= Jeremiah
Josh.	= Joshua
Jud.	= Judges
Kel.	= Tractate Kelim.
Ker.	= Tractate Keritot.
Ket.	= Tractate Ketubot.
Koy	= A cross between a goat and some species of gazelle, neither a cattle nor a wild animal, neither entirely domesticated nor wholly undomesticated.
Land	= The Land of Israel. The Holy Land.
Lev.	= Leviticus.
Lieberman	= Saul Lieberman, *Tosefta Kipshutah. Yebamot Ketubot* (N.Y., 1967); *Nedarim, Nezirut* (N.Y., 1967); *Sotah, Gittin, Qiddushin* (N.Y., 1973).

Log = Twenty-four *qortabs* equal one *log*. Four *logs* equal one *qab*. Three *qabs* equal one *hin*.

M. = Mishnah.

M'ŚH B = A fixed form, *ma'aśeh b-* introduces a precedent. It may be translated, "The story is told concerning . . . ," but is best left untranslated, as a fixed particle.

Ma'aseh = See above.

Mal. = Malachi.

Mamzer = The offspring of a man and woman who by the law of the Torah are not permitted to marry; or the offspring of a marriage forbidden under the penalty of extirpation.

Me. = Tractate Me'ilah.

Melog-slaves = Property brought into a marriage of which the husband has full use and benefit is called *melog* property (here: slaves). The husband is not responsible to make up any loss, damage, or deterioration attendent upon his use of the property. But any rise in value also accrues to the wife. This is like a variable annuity or common stock. See *Iron-flock slaves*.

Men. = Tractate Menaḥot.

Meṣora' = See *Ṣara'at*

Mid. = Middot.

Min. = An Israelite apostate.

Miq. = Tractate Miqva'ot.

Nah. = Nahum

Naz. = Tractate Nazir.

Nazir = A Nazirite, one who keeps the rules of Num. 6:3f.

Ned. = Tractate Nedarim.

Neg. = Tractate Nega'im.

Neh. = Nehemiah

Netin = Descendent of Gibeonites whom Joshua made into Temple slaves, Josh. 9:27.

Nid. = Tractate Niddah.

Num. = Numbers

Oh. = Tractate Ohalot.

'Omer = The barley-sheaf required by Lev. 23:10 to be reaped, and the flour of which is baked and offered

as a meal-offering in the Temple before the new harvest is reaped. Only after the offering of the *'omer* is the produce of the new harvest permitted for ordinary use.

'Orlah-fruit = The fruit of trees in the first three years after they are planted is forbidden, Lev. 10:23. This is called *'orlah*-fruit. In the fourth year the fruit of the trees enters the status of second tithe and is to be sold, with the money paid for it brought to Jerusalem and spent there.

Peruṭah = The smallest copper coin in circulation.

Piggul = Refuse. When the officiating priest, at the time of the tossing of the blood, conceives of the intention to eat the meat of the sacrifice or to burn the sacrificial parts outside of the proper time or place at which he is required to do so, but at some other time, or outside of the Temple courtyard, by said intention he imparts to the sacrifice at the time of the tossing of the blood the status of *piggul,* translated refuse. It is ruined. When the priest does not form such an improper intention, the language used is, "slaughter . . . toss the blood in silence," meaning, without improper intention.

Prosbul = Deut. 15:2 states that all loans are remitted in the seventh year. If, however, the creditor declares before a court of law that the loan in question is under the court's jurisdiction, it is not remitted under the seventh year law; a writ to this effect, signed by witnesses, annuls the effect of the law. Said writ is called a *prosbul.*

Prov. = Proverbs

Ps. = Psalms

Qab = Four *logs* equal one *qab.* Six *qabs* equal one *se'ah.* Three *se'ahs* equal one *ephah.*

Qarṭob = Sixty-four *qarṭobs* equal one *log.* A *qarṭob* is the volume of somewhat more than six eggs (six eggs equal one *log*).

Qid. = Tractate Qiddushin

Qin. = Tractate Qinnim.

Qoh. = Qohelet.

R. = Rabbi.
Refuse = See *piggul*.
Sam. = Samuel
Ṣara'at = Disease referred to at Lev. 13–14.
Se'ah = Six *qabs* equal one *se'ah*. Three *se'ahs* equal one *ephah*. Thirty *se'ahs* equal one *kor*.
Shema' = Deut. 6:4ff.
Shofar = Ram's horn.
Ṣiṣit = Fringes
Song = Song of Songs
Sot. = Soṭah.
T. = Tosefta.
TR = Saul Lieberman, *Tosefet Rishonim*.
Tebul Yom = That which has been immersed in an immersion-pool during the very day on which the immersion has taken place, before sunset is in the status of *Tebul Yom*, a diminished state of uncleanness. It is not wholly clean until sunset.
Tefillin = Phylacteries
Teqi'ot = Sounds of the *Shofar*.
Ṭerefah = The meat of a beast which has been injured so that it cannot survive for twelve months; the meat of a beast which has suffered from some abnormality; the meat of a beast which is not validly slaughtered. This is distinct from carrion, a clean beast which has not died through proper slaughter but either died violently or been slaughtered improperly.
Ulam = The hall leading to the interior of the Temple.
Y. = *Yerushalmi*. Palestinian Talmud.
Yeb. = Yebamot.
Zeb. = Zebaḥim.
Zech. = Zechariah.

Transliterations

א	=	ʼ
ב	=	B
ג	=	G
ד	=	D
ה	=	H
ו	=	W
ז	=	Z
ח	=	Ḥ
ט	=	Ṭ
י	=	Y
כ ך	=	K
ל	=	L
מ ם	=	M
נ	=	N
ס	=	S
ע	=	ʻ
פ ף	=	P
צ ץ	=	Ṣ
ק	=	Q
ר	=	R
שׁ	=	Š
שׂ	=	Ś
ת	=	T

YEBAMOT

1:1 A. Under what circumstances did they rule: *If they died or were divorced, their co-wives are permitted* [to enter into levirate marriage] [M. Yeb. 1:1J–K]?

B. [If this happened] during the lifetime of the husband.

C. But [if] after the death of the husband [they died or were divorced], their co-wives are prohibited [from entering into levirate marriage].

D. [If] they exercised the right of refusal [M. Yeb. 1:1J] during the lifetime of the husband, their co-wives are permitted.

E. [If they did so] after the death of the husband, their co-wives perform the rite of *ḥaliṣah* but do not enter into levirate marriage [cf. M. Yeb. 1:2J].

1:2 A. And any of them who turned out to be barren [M. Yeb. 1:1J],

B. or who was [legally] married to someone else—

C. whether this is in the lifetime of the husband or after the death of the husband—

D. their co-wives are permitted.

E. *Any [young girl] who can exercise the right of refusal and has not exercised the right of refusal and* [the husband of whom] dies [childless]—

F. *her co-wife performs the rite of ḥaliṣah and does not enter in levirate marriage* [M. Yeb. 1:2J].

1:3 A. *How [do we define a case in which] if their co-wives died, they are permitted* [M. Yeb. 1:2G, M. 1:1J]?

B. *[If] his daughter or any one of all those forbidden degrees was married to his brother, and he [the brother] had another wife, and his daughter died, and afterward his brother died—*

C. *her co-wife is permitted.*

D. [If] his brother died, and afterward his daughter died, her co-wife is prohibited.

1:4 A. *[If] the co-wife of his daughter went and married another of his brothers, and he [the other brother] had another wife* [M. Yeb. 1:2D],

B. [if] the co-wife died, and afterward his brother died,

C. even though his daughter is alive,

D. the co-wife of her co-wife is permitted.

E. [If] his brother died and afterward the co-wife died,

F. even though his daughter is exempt [better: *deceased*]

G. the co-wife of her co-wife is prohibited,

H. even if they are a hundred [M. Yeb. 1:2A–F].

1:5 A. You turn out to rule: So long as the brothers are many, the co-wives are many. [If] the brothers are few, the co-wives are few.

B. Just as, *if they died or exercised the right of refusal or were divorced or turned out to be barren* or were married to others, *their co-wives are permitted* [M. Yeb. 1:1J–K],

C. so the co-wife of their co-wives who died or exercised the right of refusal or were divorced or turned out to be barren or married others—their co-wives are permitted.

1:6 A. Just as they exempt [the co-wives] from marriage, so they exempt [them] from betrothal.

B. Under what circumstances?

C. In the case of a woman in which he has no right of consecration.

D9But in the case of a woman in whom he has the right of consecration,

E. "their co-wives perform the rite of *ḥaliṣah* and do not enter into levirate marriage," the words of the House of Hillel.

F. And the House of Shammai permit the co-wives [to marry] the brothers [in a levirate marriage].

1:7 A. *Six forbidden degrees are subject to a more strict rule than these* [the fifteen women referred to in M. Yeb. 1:1].

B. *For they are married [only] to outsiders, [and] their co-wives are permitted* [M. Yeb. 1:3A–B]:

C. For the law of the co-wife applies only [to widows of] the brother.

D. [If] they married brothers not as a transgression [but legally], their co-wives are exempt [from *ḥaliṣah* or levirate marriage].

1:8 A. [If] these co-wives went and got married,

B. the House of Shammai say, "They are invalidated [M. Yeb. 1:4D–E], and the offspring is invalid."

C. And the House of Hillel say, "They are valid, and the offspring is valid."

1:9 A. *[If] they entered into levirate marriage,*

B. *the House of Shammai say, "They are valid* and the offspring is valid."

C. *And the House of Hillel say, "They are invalid,* and the offspring is a *mamzer*" [M. Yeb. 1:4F–H].

D. Said R. Yoḥanan b. Nuri, "Come and observe how this [version of the] law is prevalent among the Israelites: to act in deed in accord with the opinion of the House of Shammai [so entering into levirate marriage], [but to treat the offspring as] a *mamzer* in accord with the opinion of the House of Hillel.

E. "If it is to act in deed in accord with the opinion of the House of Hillel, the offspring is blemished in accord with the opinion of the House of Shammai.

F. "But: Come and let us impose the ordinance that the co-wives should perform the rite of ḥaliṣah and not enter into levirate marriage."

G. But they did not have a moment in which to complete the matter, before the times prevented it.

1:10 A. Said Rabban Simeon b. Gamaliel, "What shall we do with the former co-wives?"

B. They asked R. Joshua, "What is the status of the children of the co-wives?"

C. He said to them, "On what account do you push my head between two high mountains, between the House of Shammai and the House of Hillel, who can remove my head!

D. "But, I hereby give testimony concerning the family of the House of 'Aluba'i of Bet Ṣeba'im and concerning the family of the house of Qipa'i of Bet Meqoshesh,

E. "that they are children of co-wives, and from them have been chosen high priests, and they did offer up sacrifices on the Temple altar."

F. Said R. Ṭarfon, "I crave that the co-wife of the daughter should come my way, and I should [so rule as to] marry her into the priesthood."

G. Said R. Eleazar, "Even though the House of Shammai disputed with the House of Hillel regarding the co-wives, they concur that the offspring is not a *mamzer*.

H. "For the status of a *mamzer* is imposed only on the offspring of a woman who has entered into a marriage prohibited on account of licentiousness [one of those listed at Leviticus Chapter Eighteen], and on account of which they [who enter into such a marriage] are liable to the penalty of extirpation."

I. Even though the House of Shammai and the House of Hillel disputed concerning the co-wives, concerning sisters, concerning the married woman, concerning a superannuated writ of divorce, concerning the one who betrothes a woman with something of the value of a *perutah,* and concerning the one who divorces his wife and spends a night with her in an inn,

J. the House of Shammai did not refrain from taking wives among the women of the House of Hillel, and the House of Hillel from the House of Shammai [M. Yeb. 1:4I].

K. But they behaved toward one another truthfully, and there was peace between them,

L. since it is said, *They loved truth and peace* [Zech. 8:19].

1:11 A. Even though these prohibit what the others permit, they did not refrain from preparing foods requiring cleanness depending upon one another,

B. thereby fulfilling that which is said, *Every way of a man is right in his own eyes, but the Lord weighs the heart* [Prov. 21:2].

1:12 A. r. Simeon says, "They did not refrain from collaboration concerning something which was subject to doubt.

B. "But they most certainly did refrain from collaboration concerning something which was not subject to doubt."

1:13 A. Under all circumstances does the decided law follow the opinion of the House of Hillel.

B. He who wishes to impose upon himself a more stringent rule,

C. to follow the rule in accord with both the House of Shammai and the House of Hillel,

D. concerning such a person the following verse is said: *[The wise man has his eyes in his head,] but the fool walks in darkness* [Qoh. 2:14].

E. He who latches on to the lenient rulings of the House of Shammai and to the lenient rulings of the House of Hillel is an evil man.

F. But if it is to be in accord with the opinions of the House of Shammai, then let it be in accord with both their lenient rulings and their strict rulings.

G. And if it is to be in accord with the opinions of the House of Hillel, then let it be in accord with both their lenient rulings and their strict rulings.

2:1 A. *How [is it so that] the wife of his brother who was not a contemporary [exempts her co-wife from the requirement of levirate marriage or ḥaliṣah* [M. Yeb. 1:1] [M. Yeb. 2:1A]?

B. Two brothers [living] at the same time,

C. and one of them died without offspring,

D. and the second survived, but did not complete bespeaking his levirate wife before a brother was born to them [the first two brothers],

E. and then he [the second brother] died—

F. the first [brother's wife, that is, the sister-in-law of the second brother] goes forth on the grounds of being the wife of his brother who was not a contemporary.

G. The second [brother's wife] either undertakes a rite of *ḥaliṣah* or enters into levirate marriage.

H. [If the second brother, before he died, did complete] bespeaking [the sister-in-law], but he did not complete effecting the marriage before a brother was born to them,

I. and [then] he [the second brother] died,

J. or a brother was born to them and afterward he did complete bespeaking [the sister-in-law] but did not complete effecting the marriage before the first brother died,

K. [the second brother's] second wife [=his first brother's widow] goes forth [without *ḥaliṣah* let alone levirate marriage] on the grounds of being the wife of his brother who was not a contemporary, and the [second brother's] first wife undertakes the rite of *ḥaliṣah* but does not enter into levirate marriage [M. Yeb. 2:1I].

L. R. Simeon says, "The act of intercourse [effecting levirate marriage] or the act of *ḥaliṣah* of one of them exempts her co-wife [M. Yeb. 2:2H–J].

M. "If one has effected the rite of *Ḥaliṣah* with a woman who is bespoken [but not by intercourse], he performs the rite of *ḥaliṣah* with the wife of the first brother."

N. "[If] he married her and then died and thereafter another brother was born to them,

O. "or [if] another brother was born to them and afterward he married her and then died,

P. "both of them [both wives of the second brother] are exempt from the requirement of effecting the rite of *ḥaliṣah* or from levirate marriage.

Q. "[If] he married her and then a brother was born to him and afterward he died, they are exempt from the requirement to perform *ḥaliṣah* and from that of levirate marriage," the words of R. Meir.

R. R. Simeon says, "Since one of them [the women] was not forbidden to him, and he came and found both of them subject to permission [to enter into levirate marriage with him], either the act of intercourse [in levirate marriage] or the rite of *ḥaliṣah* of one of them exempts her co-wife.

S. What is "bespeaking" [M'MR]?

T. [If the levirate husband says,] "Lo, thou art sanctified to me by money" or "by something worth money" or "by a writ."

U. What is [the language to be used in a] writ?

V. "I, So-and-so, the son of So-and so, take upon myself responsibility for Miss So-and so, my deceased childless brother's wife, to care for her and to supply maintenance for her in an appropriate way. This is with the proviso that the payment of her marriage-contract is the obligation of the estate of her [deceased] first husband."

W. Just as the act of sanctification effects acquisition in the case of a woman only when both of them are agreed, so a statement of bespeaking effects acquisition of a sister-in-law only when both of them are agreed.

X. What is the difference between an act of sanctification betrothal and bespeaking?

Y. The act of sanctification completes the transaction. The bespeaking does not complete the transaction

2:2 A. The women of forbidden degrees of whom they spoke are not equivalent to his wife in any respect.

B. They have no right to a marriage-contract, to disposition of the return on their property, to sustenance, or to indemnity [the provision of the replacement of clothing].

C. And he [the husband] does not retain the right to possess things which she finds or the fruit of her labor, or to annul vows which she may make.

D. He does not inherit her estate.

E. Nor is he permitted to make himself unclean in burying her [should he be a priest otherwise forbidden to have contact with the dead].

F. He has no power of sanctification over her.

G. And she does not require a writ of divorce from him.

H. She is invalid, and the offspring is a *mamzer*.

2:3 A. A widow [married to] a high priest, a divorcee or a woman who has undergone the rite of *ḥaliṣah* to an ordinary priest [M. Yeb. 2:4B1–3]—lo, these are deemed as his legal wife in every respect.

B. They have a right to a marriage-contract, to the disposition of the return on their property, to nourishment, and to indemnity [the provision of replacement of clothing which is worn out].

C. And he [the husband] does retain right to possess things which she finds and the fruit of her labor, and to annul vows which she may make.

D. He does inherit her estate.

E. But he does not make himself unclean in burying her.

F. He does have the power of sanctification over her.

G. And she does require a writ of divorce from him [to annul the marriage].

H. But she is invalid, and the offspring [of such a marriage] is invalid.

2:4 A. *A secondary grade [of forbidden degrees] on account of the rulings of scribes* [M. 2:4A]—

B. [such women] are not deemed as his legal wife in every respect.

C. They have no right to a marriage contract, to disposition of the return of their property, to sustenance, or to indemnity [provision of the replacement of worn-out clothing].

D. But he [the husband] does not retain the right to possess things which she finds or the fruit of her labor or to annul vows which she may make.

E. [Nonetheless] he does inherit her estate and he makes himself unclean for her in burying her [if he is a priest and otherwise prohibited from doing so].

F. He does have power of sanctification over her.

G. And she does require a writ of divorce from him.

H. She is valid, and the offspring [of such a union] is valid.

I. [Nonetheless] they force him to divorce her.

J. R. Judah says, "A widow wed to a high priest or a divorcee or a woman who has undergone the rite of *ḥaliṣah* wed to an ordinary priest—these constitute *prohibitions on account of a commandment* [M. Yeb. 2:3C]. A secondary grade of forbidden degrees [listed at Leviticus Chapter Eighteen] on account of the rulings of scribes constitutes a prohibition on account of sanctity" [*vs.* M. Yeb. 2:4].

K. Said R. Simeon b. Leazar, "On what account did they rule that a widow married to a high priest has the right of a marriage-contract [T. 2:3B]? Because he [the husband] is fit [to marry her], but she is invalid [to marry him].

L. "And in every case in which the male is valid and the female is invalid, they [sages] have imposed a fine on him, requiring him to pay her marriage-contract.

M. "On what account did they rule that those [women] prohibited to a man as a secondary grade of forbidden degrees [T. 2:4C] do not receive a marriage contract? Because he is valid to marry her, and she is valid to marry him. They [sages, therefore] imposed a fine on her, denying her a marriage contract, so that it will be easy in his view to divorce her."

N. Rabbi says, "This rule [K] is a restriction deriving from the teachings of the Torah itself, and the teachings of the Torah do not require a backup. But this other [M] is prohibited by reason of the teachings of scribes, and the teachings of scribes most certainly do require a backup.

O. "Another matter: This one has responsibility for getting the woman ready to marry him. But this woman has responsibility for getting herself ready to marry him."

2:5 A. There are women who [1] either effect the rite of *ḥaliṣah* or undergo levirate marriage, [2] undergo levirate marriage but do not effect the rite of *ḥaliṣah,* [3] effect the rite of *ḥaliṣah* but do not undergo levirate marriage, [4] neither effect the rite of *ḥaliṣah* nor undergo levirate marriage.

B. [1] The forbidden degrees of whom we have spoken [at M. 1:1, 3: the women prohibited at Leviticus Chapter Eighteen] neither enter into levirate marriage nor effect the rite of *ḥaliṣah.*

C. In addition to them, the wife of a man who is a eunuch by nature, the wife of a man who bears sexual traits of both sexes, the wife of a brother from the same mother, the wife of a proselyte, the wife of a freed slave, and a barren woman,

D. do not effect the rite of *ḥaliṣah* and do not enter into levirate marriage [A4].

E. The deaf-mute and the idiot enter into levirate marriage but do not effect a rite of *haliṣah* [A2].

F. A woman prohibited by reason of a commandment and one prohibited by reason of sanctity [M. Yeb. 2:3C, 2:4] effect *ḥaliṣah* and do not enter into levirate marriage [A3].

G. A woman who cannot bear children and one past menopause and all other women either effect a rite of *ḥaliṣah* or enter into levirate marriage [A1].

2:6 A. There are men who [1] either undergo a rite of *ḥaliṣah* or enter into levirate marriage, [2] enter into levirate marriage but do not undergo a rite of *ḥaliṣah,* [3] undergo a rite of *ḥaliṣah* but do not enter into levirate marriage, [4] neither enter into levirate marriage nor undergo a rite of *ḥaliṣah.*

B. With the forbidden degrees of whom we have spoken [at M. Yeb. 1:1, 3] men do not undergo the rite of *ḥaliṣah* nor do they enter into levirate marriage [A4].

C. In addition to them, a eunuch by nature, a man who bears sexual traits of both sexes, a brother from the same mother, a proselyte, and a freed slave neither undergo the rite of *ḥaliṣah* nor enter into levirate marriage.

D. The deaf-mute and the idiot enter into levirate marriage but do not undergo a rite of *ḥaliṣah* [A2].

E. Those who are subject to doubt undergo a rite of *ḥaliṣah* but do not enter into levirate marriage [A3].

F. A man with crushed testicles and one whose penis is cut off, a eunuch by human action, [and] an old man either undergo a rite of *ḥaliṣah* or enter into levirate marriage [A/1].

3:1 A. The secondary grade of forbidden degrees on account of rulings of scribes [M. Yeb. 2:4A] [includes the following]:

[1] The mother of his mother, [2] the mother of his father, [3] the wife of his father's father, [4] the wife of his father's mother, [5] the wife of his mother's brother by the same father, [6] the wife of his father's brother by the same mother, [7] the wife of the son of his son, and [8] the wife of the son of his daughter.

B. A man is permitted to marry the wife of his father-in-law and the wife of his step-son, but is prohibited to marry the daughter of his step-son.

C. And his step-son is permitted to marry his wife and his daughter.

D. This woman [the wife of the step-son] says, "I am permitted to you, but my daughter is prohibited to you."

E. *His sister who also is his deceased childless brother's wife*—[as to *her* sister, coming to him from a different brother] *either effects a rite of ḥaliṣah or enters into levirate marriage* [M. Yeb. 2:3D].

F. How so?

G. His daughter by a woman whom he has raped, married to his brother, and she has a sister from the same mother but by a different father, married to his other brother,

H. and he [the brother] dies without children—

I. she either performs the rite of *ḥaliṣah* or enters into levirate marriage.

J. [If] the daughter of his daughter is married to his brother, and the daughter of his wife is married to another of his brothers, and the daughter of the daughter of his wife is married to another of his brothers, and she has a sister by the same father and a different mother, married to another of his brothers,

K. and he dies without children—

L. she either performs the rite of *ḥaliṣah* or enters into levirate marriage.

M. The daughter of his son who is married to his brother, and the daughter of the son of his wife who is married to his brother, and she has a sister by the same mother but by a different father, married to his other brother,

N. and he dies without children—

O. she either performs a rite of *ḥaliṣah* or enters into levirate marriage.

P. His mother-in-law and the mother of his mother-in-law and the mother of his father-in-law married to his brother, and she has a sister, whether of the same father or of the same mother, married to his other brother,

Q. and he dies without children—

R. she either performs a rite of *ḥaliṣah* or enters into levirate marriage.

S. His sister by the same mother, the sister of his mother by the same mother, the sister of his wife by the same mother, married to his brother, and she has a sister by the same father but by a different mother, married to his other brother,

T. and he dies without children—

U. either performs the rite of *ḥaliṣah* or enters into levirate marriage.

V. The sister of his mother on her father's side, and the sister of his wife on her father's side, married to his brother, and she has another sister from her mother but with a different father, married to the same brother,

W. and he dies without children—

X. she either performs the rite of *ḥaliṣah* or enters into levirate marriage.

Y. The wife of his brother on his mother's side, and the wife of his brother who was not a contemporary, and his daughter-in-law, married to his brother [after the death of his son], and she has a sister, whether from on her father's side or on her mother's side, married to his other brother,

Z. and he dies without children—

AA. she either performs the rite of *ḥaliṣah* or enters into levirate marriage.

BB. They asked R. Eliezer, "Does a *mamzer* inherit?"

CC. He said to them, "Does he undergo a rite of *ḥaliṣah* [with his deceased childless brother's widow] [M. Yeb. 2:5]?"

DD. "Does he undergo a rite of *ḥaliṣah*?"

EE. He said to them, "Does he inherit?"

FF. "Does he inherit?"

GG. He said to them, "Does one plaster his house [as a sign of his status as a *mamzer*]?"

HH. "Does one plaster his grave?"

II. "Does one plaster his grave?"

JJ. He said to them, "May one raise dogs?"

KK. "May one raise dogs?"

LL. He said to them, "May one raise pigs?"

MM. "May one raise pigs?"

NN. He said to them, "May one raise chickens?"

OO. "May one raise chickens?"

PP. He said to them, "May one raise small cattle?"

QQ. "May one raise small cattle?"

RR. He said to them, "May one rescue a shepherd from a wolf?"

SS. "May one rescue a shepherd from a wolf?"

TT. He said to them, "It appears to me that you have asked only about a female-sheep."

UU. "And what is the law as to saving the female-sheep?"

VV. He said to them, "It appears to me that you have asked only about the shepherd."

WW. "What is the fate of Mr. So-and-so as to the world to come? What is the fate of Mr. Such-and-such as to the world to come?"

XX. He said to them, "It appears to me that you have asked only about Mr. So-and-so."

YY. "And what *is* the fate of Mr. So-and-so as to the world to come?"

ZZ. And it was not that R. Eliezer meant to put them off, but the reason is that he never in his entire life stated a rule which he had not heard.

4:1 A. *Two* unrelated *men who betrothed two sisters,*

B. *this one does not know which one of them is betrothed, and that one does not know which one of them is betrothed—*

C. *this one gives two writs of divorce, and that one gives two writs of divorce* [M. Yeb. 2:7A–C].

D. [If] one of them died, the second man is prohibited [to marry] either one of the women.

E. [If] one of the women died, both of the men are prohibited [to enter into levirate marriage with the] second, [surviving sister].

F. [If both] men died, and one of them had one brother, he effects a rite of *ḥaliṣah* with both of them.

G. [If there survived] two brothers, they effect a rite of *ḥaliṣah* with both women.

H. If they went ahead and married [the two sisters], they must put them out.

4:2 A. He who betrothed one of two unrelated women, and does not know which of them he betrothed, marries both of them.

B. [If] he died and left behind one brother, he marries both of them.

C. [If he left] two brothers, they marry the two women.

4:3 A. *Two brothers who betrothed two sisters,*

B. *this one does not know which one of them he betrothed, and that one does not know which one of them he betrothed,*

C. *this one gives two writs of divorce, and that one gives two writs of divorce* [M. Yeb. 2:7A–C].

D. [If] one of them died, the second one is prohibited [from entering into levirate marriage] with either one of them.

E. [If] one of them died, both of the brothers are prohibited [to enter into marriage] with the second sister.

F. [If] they died and left yet one more brother, he performs a rite of *ḥaliṣah* with both sisters.

G. [If they left] two brothers, they perform a rite of *ḥaliṣah* with both sisters.

H. If they went ahead and married the two women, they must put them away.

I. Two unrelated men who betrothed two unrelated women

J. this one does not know which one of them he betrothed, and that one does not know which one of them he betrothed—

K. this one gives two writs of divorce, and that one gives two writs of divorce.

L. [If] one of them died, the second is permitted [to enter into ordinary marriage] with either one of the women.

M. [If] one of the women died, either one of the two men is permitted [to enter into marriage with] the second woman.

N. What should they then do [to make this possible (M)]?

O. One of them gives a writ of divorce, and one of them marries her.

P. [If] they died—

Q. this one has a brother, and that one has a brother—

R. this one performs a rite of *ḥaliṣah* with this woman, and the other enters into levirate marriage with that woman,

S. and this one performs a rite of *ḥaliṣah* with that woman, and the other enters into levirate marriage with that woman.

T. If they went ahead [without following the stated procedure] and married them, they must put them away.

U. *It is a religious duty for the oldest [surviving brother] to enter into levirate marriage [with the deceased, childless brother's widow*] [M. Yeb. 2:8A],

V. but not for the oldest [widow] to be taken into levirate marriage.

W. But [the levir] effects levirate marriage with whichever widow [of his deceased, childless brother] he wishes.

4:4 A. A well which is nearer to the water-course is to be filled first.

B. If the second [person, whose well is farther away] went ahead and filled his, lo, this one is prompt and rewarded on that account.

C. [If] this one went ahead and moved the water-coese over to the well of his fellow, lo this one is prompt and rewarded on that account.

D. A creditor and an heir, one of whom went ahead and took over movable goods—lo, this one is prompt and rewarded on that account.

E. He who says to his fellow, "Go and betroth for me Miss Such-and-so," [and] he went and betrothed her for himself,

F. "Go and buy me such and such an object," [and] he went and bought it for himself,

G. what he has done is done. But he has behaved deceitfully.

H. He who redeems a woman taken into captivity is permitted to marry her.

I. He who testifies concerning a captive woman [that she has not been raped], lo, this one may not marry her.

J. But if he married her, he does not have to put her away.

4:5 A. *He who delivers a writ of divorce from overseas and stated, "In my presence was it written and in my presence was it sealed" may not then marry his [the man's] wife [to whom he brought the writ of divorce].*

B. *[If he testified,] "He [the husband] has died," "We killed him," "I killed him," he may not marry his wife.*

C. *R. Judah says, '[If he stated,] 'I have killed him," his wife may not remarry.*

D. *"[But if he stated,] 'We killed him,' his wife may remarry"* [M. Yeb. 2:9].

E. They said to him, "[M'ŚH B] A certain thug was caught in Qapotqia [Cappodocia] and was being taken out to be executed. He said, 'Go tell the wife of Simeon b. Kahana': I murdered him when he came into Lud.'

F. "And the case came to sages, who permitted his wife to remarry."

G. He said to them, "Is there proof from that case? But in that case, the doomed man said only, 'We murdered him.'"

H. He who is suspected [of having intercourse] with a married woman who then was divorced by the other [after being divorced by her first husband, she remarried, and then was divorced again]—

I. lo, this one [even now] may not marry her.

J. But if he did marry her, he does not have to put her away.

K. He who is suspected [of having intercourse] with a woman may not marry her mother, her daughter, or her sister.

L. But if he did marry one of these, he need not put her away.

4:6 A. A gentile or a slave who had sexual relations with an Israelite woman, even though the gentile went and converted, or the slave was freed,

B. lo, such a one may not marry the woman.

C. But if he married her, he need not put her away [cf. M. Yeb. 2:8C–E].

D. An Israelite who had sexual relations with a slave girl or with a gentile woman, even though the slave was freed, or the gentile woman converted,

lo, this one may not marry her.

E. But if he married her, he need not put her away.

F. *A sage who forbade a woman to her husband by reason of [her] vow against her husband, lo, this one may not marry her* [M. Yeb. 2:10A].

G. Said R. Judah, "Under what circumstances? When he [the sage] was not married, or when he was married but divorced her [his wife] on account of this woman in particular [cf. M. Yeb. 2:10D].

H. "But if he had a wife who died, he is permitted to marry her [of F]."

I. *And in the case of all of them who were married to other men who died,* [M. Yeb. 2:10E], they [such widows] are permitted to be married to them [the sages of F].

J. And in the case of all of them [the judges, agents] who were married and [whose wives] died, they are permitted to be married to them [M. Yeb. 2:10E].

K. R. Eliezer says, "All of them who were married to their [the judges' or agents'] brothers, and whose [husbands, the brothers] died—they are permitted to enter into levirate marriage with them [the judges, agents]."

L. But him who affixes his seal on a deed of sale for a field or on a writ of divorce for a woman have the sages not brought under suspicion [to begin with].

4:7 A. A sage who judged a case, declaring something unclean or clean, prohibited or permitted,

B. and so witnesses who participated in a case—

C. lo, these are permitted to purchase [the object which was under judgment].

D. But sages have said, "Keep distant from what is ugly and from what looks ugly."

4:8 A. There is he who is prompt and rewarded on that account, who is prompt and loses out on that account, who is restrained [in the exercise of what is permitted] and is rewarded on that account, and who is restrained and loses out on that account:

B. He exercises restraint on the eve of the Sabbath, on the Sabbath, and after the Sabbath,

C. on the eve of the seventh year, in the seventh year, in the year after the seventh year,

D. during the intervening days of a festival,

E. and all who are anxious about transgression,

F. lo, such a one exercises restraint and is rewarded on that account .

5:1 A. *Four brothers—*

B. *two of them married to two sisters—*

C. *and those who are married to the sisters died—*

D. *lo, these [surviving, childless widows] perform a rite of ḥaliṣah but do not enter into levirate marriage [with the other two brothers].*

E. *And if they went ahead and married [the two widows], they must put them away.*

F. *R. Leazar says, "The House of Shammai say, 'They may remain wed.'*

G. *"And the House of Hillel say, 'They must put them away'"* [M. Yeb. 3:1A–G].

H. R. Simeon says, "They may remain wed."

I. Abba Saul says, "In this matter, the House of Hillel took the lenient position [and in fact ruled that they remain wed, with the Shammaites then are in the position that they must put them away]."

5:2 A. [If] one of the women was the mother-in-law of one of the men,

B. he is prohibited [to marry] her but permitted to marry her sister.

C. And the second [brother] is prohibited from marrying either one of them.

D. It turns out that the one who is prohibited is permitted, and the one who is permitted is prohibited.

E. [If] one of the women was the mother-in-law of this one, and the second was the mother-in-law of that one—

F. this one is prohibited to marry the mother-in-law of his own, but permitted to marry the mother-in-law of his brother.,

G. and that one is prohibited to marry the mother-in-law of his own, but permitted to marry the mother-in-law of his brother.

H. This is the sort of case concerning which they have stated: The one who is prohibited to this one is permitted to that one, and the one who is prohibited to that one is permitted to this one.

5:3 A. [If] one of them was the mother-in-law of both of them,

B. this one is prohibited to marry her, but permitted to marry her sister, and that one is prohibited to marry her but permitted to marry her sister.

C. [If] two of the women were the mother-in-law of one of them, the second is permitted [Better: *prohibited*] to marry both of them.

D. This is the general principle: So long as they are suitable for him, they are prohibited from marrying him by reason of *not taking a woman in marriage with her sister* [Lev. 18:18].

E. But if they were prohibited to him by reason of a forbidden degree of some other sort, he is prohibited from marrying her and permitted to marry her sister [M. Yeb. 3:3C].

5:4 A. *Three brothers—*

B. *two of them married to two sisters—*

C. *or to a woman and her daughter,*

D. *or to a woman and the daughter of her son—*

E. *lo, these women perform the rite of ḥaliṣah and do not enter into levirate marriage.*

F. *And R. Simeon declares* both of them *exempt* both from the rite of *ḥaliṣah* and from levirate marriage [M. Yeb. 3:4A–F].

G. *Three brothers—*

H. *two of them married to two sisters—*

I. *and one of them is unmarried—*

J. *one of the husbands of the sisters died,*

K. *and the one who was unmarried went* and married her [the childless widow of his brother],

L. *and afterward his second brother died—*

M. *his wife [remains] with him, and this one [the widow of the just-now-*

perished brother] goes forth [without ḥaliṣah or levirate marriage] on the grounds of being the sister of his wife [M. Yeb. 3:5A–F].

N. *Three brothers—*

O. *two of them married to two sisters,*

P. *and one of them is unmarried—*

Q. *one of the husbands of the sisters died—*

R. *this one who was unmarried* [M. Yeb. 3:5] went and did not suffice to bespeak his levirate sister-in-law before the wife of the surviving brother died, and afterward he [the unmarried one] died—

S. [or] he bespoke her but did not suffice to marry her until the wife of the surviving brother died, and afterward he died—

T. [or] he married her, and the wife of the surviving brother died, and afterward he died—

U. lo, this one [the surviving sister] is exempt from *haliṣah* and from levirate marriage.

5:5 A. *Three brothers—*

B. *two of them married to two sisters—*

C. *and one of them married to an unrelated woman—*

D. *one of the husbands of the sisters died* [M. Yeb. 3:6A–C],

E. and he did not suffice to bespeak his levirate sister-in-law before he died—

F. this unrelated woman either performs the rite of *ḥaliṣah* or enters into levirate marriage.

G. [If] he bespoke her but did not suffice to marry her before he died, this unrelated woman performs the rite of *ḥaliṣah* but does not enter into levirate marriage.

H. [If] he married her and afterward he died, this unrelated woman is exempt from the rite of *ḥalisah* and from levirate marriage.

I. [If] the one who was married to the unrelated woman died,

J. [if] one of the husbands of the sisters went and did not suffice to bespeak his levirate sister-in-law before he died,

K. this unrelated woman either effects the rite of *ḥaliṣah* or is taken in levirate marriage.

L. [If] he bespoke her but did not suffice to marry her before he died, this unrelated woman performs the rite of *ḥaliṣah* and does not enter into levirate marriage.

M. [If] he married her and afterward died, this unrelated woman is exempt from the rite of *ḥaliṣah* and from the requirement of levirate marriage.

5:6 A. *Three brothers—*

B. *two of them married to two sisters,*

C. *and one of them married to an unrelated woman—*

D. the husband *of one of the sisters died* [M. Yeb. 3:6A–D]—

E. and the one married to the unrelated woman went but did not suffice to bespeak his levirate sister-in-law before the wife of the surviving brother died—

F. and afterward he died—

G. this unrelated woman either performs the rite of *ḥaliṣah* or is taken in levirate marriage.

H. [If] he bespoke her, but did not suffice to marry her [cf. Lieberman, p. 15 to 1.31] before the wife of the surviving brother died, and afterward he died—

I. this unrelated woman performs the rite of *ḥaliṣah* but is not taken in levirate marriage.

J. [If] he married her, and the wife of the surviving brother died, and afterward he died,

K. both of them are exempt from the rite of *ḥaliṣah* and from levirate marriage.

L. [If] the one married to the unrelated woman died,

M. [and] one of the husbands of the sisters went and did not suffice to bespeak his levirate sister-in-law before the wife of the surviving brother died, and afterward he died,

N. both of the women perform the rite of *ḥaliṣah* or enter into levirate marriage.

O. [If] he bespoke her but did not suffice to marry her before the wife of the surviving brother died, and afterward he died,

P. both of these women perform the rite of *ḥaliṣah* and do not enter into levirate marriage.

Q. [If] he married her, and the wife of the surviving brother died, and afterward he died, the act of sexual relations or the rite of *ḥaliṣah* of one of the women exempts her co-wife [from the requirement of either].

5:7 A. What is a case of doubt concerning betrothal [M. Yeb. 3:8]?

B. [If] a man betrothed a woman with something which may or may not be worth a *peruṭah*.

C. *Three brothers married to three unrelated women—*

D. *and one of the [brothers] died—*

E. *and the second brother bespoke her [the widow of his deceased, childless brother],*

F. *and then he too died—*

G. *lo, these [women] perform the rite of ḥaliṣah* and do not enter into levirate marriage [M. Yeb. 3:9A–E].

H. "This is the case of the co-wife of the wife of the brother from the same father, who performs the rite of *ḥaliṣah* and does not enter into levirate marriage," the words of R. Yosé.

I. R. Leazar b. *R. Simeon says, "He enters into levirate marriage with any one he wants and performs the rite of ḥaliṣah with the other"* [M. Yeb. 3:9H].

J. But this is on the condition that the act of intercourse comes before the rite of *ḥaliṣah.*

K. [If] he married her and afterward died,

L. the act of intercourse or the rite of *ḥaliṣah* of one of the women exempts her co-wife.

5:8 A. *Two brothers married to two sisters—*

B. *and one of the brothers died,*

C. *and afterward the wife of the second died—*

D. *lo, this one is prohibited to him for all time, since she was prohibited to him for a single moment* [M. Yeb. 3:9I–L].

E. "If he had sexual relations with her, he is liable on her account on the grounds of having sexual relations with the wife of his brother and on the grounds of her being the sister of his wife," the words of R. Meir.

F. R. Yośe and R. Simeon say, "He is liable only on account of having sexual relations with the wife of his brother."

G. "A non-priest who participated in the sacrificial service in the sanctuary or a blemished priest who participated in the sacrificial service in a state of uncleanness is liable on grounds of being a non-priest and on grounds of uncleanness, on grounds of being a blemished priest and on grounds of uncleanness," the words of R. Yosé.

H. R. Simeon says, "He is liable only on grounds of being a non-priest or on grounds of being blemished."

5:9 A. *Two men who betrothed two women,*

B. *and at the time of their entry into the marriage-canopy, the two women [inadvertently] were exchanged for one another* [M. Yeb. 3:10A–B]—

C. lo, these [four parties, in all] are liable for sixteen sin-offerings:

[1] on the count of being brothers, and [2] on the count of being sisters, and [3] on the count of having intercourse with menstruating women, and [4] on account of intercourse with a married woman.

D. If they are not brothers, they are liable for twelve sin-offerings.

E. If they are not sisters, they are liable for eight,

F. If they are not menstruating, they are liable for four.

G. [If] the men were adult and the girls were minor, they are liable for only two.

H. [If] the women were adult and the males minors, the women are liable for two.

I. If their father married them off, they are liable for eight.

5:10 A. If one of them was adult, and the other male was a minor, the one who is subject to sexual relations with the minor is liable, for she is the wife of the adult.

B. But the one who has sexual relations with the adult is exempt, for she is the wife of the minor.

6:1 A. He who bespeaks his deceased childless brother's wife and she turns out to be pregnant and gives birth—

B. when the offspring is timely [viable and apable of surviving],

C. his act of bespeaking is no bespeaking.

D. [It therefore follows that] *he is permitted to marry her relatives, and she is permitted to marry his relatives.*

E. *And he has not invalidated her from marrying into the priesthood.*

F. *[If] the offspring is not timely [and cannot have survived],*

G. his act of bespeaking is bespeaking.

H. *He is prohibited from marrying her relatives, and she is prohibited from marrying his relatives.*

I. *And he has invalidated her from marrying into the priesthood* [M. Yeb. 4:1].

6:2 A. *He who marries his deceased childless brother's widow,*

B. *and it turns out that she is pregnant and gives birth—*

C. *when the offspring is timely,*

D. *he must put her away, and they are liable for a sacrifice.*

E. *[If] the offspring is not timely,*

F. *he may confirm [the marriage*] [M. Yeb. 4:2A–G].

G. [If] it is a matter of doubt whether or not the offspring is timely, they assign to the case two stringent rules [that is, he cannot keep the marriage going, and he divorces the woman both with a writ of divorce and with a rite of *ḥaliṣah*].

H. *[If] it is a matter of doubt whether the offspring is born at nine months, therefore assigned to the first husband, or born at seven months, therefore assigned to the second* [M. Yeb. 4:2H],

I. the first [of two such offspring] is suitable to be made high priest, but the second is deemed a *mamzer* by reason of doubt.

J. R. Liezer b. Jacob says, "The second is not a *mamzer,* by reason of doubt."

6:3 A. He who bespeaks his deceased childless brother's wife and she turns out to be pregnant—

B. lo, in such a case her co-wife should not be married until it is clear that it is a foetus capable of surviving.

C. For the offspring does not exempt [the co-wife from levirate connection] until it comes forth into the world's light.

D. A woman awaiting levirate marriage who died—

E. [the levir] is permitted to marry her mother.

F. What is her status as to maintenance and support?

G. So long as the husband is liable, the levirate brothers are liable.

H. [If] the husband is not liable, then the levirate brothers are not liable.

I. *He who marries his deceased childless brother's widow acquires the estate of his brother.*

J. *R. Judah says, "One way or the other: If the father is alive, the property reverts to the father* [M. Yeb. 4:7D–E].

K. "If the father is not alive, the estate goes to the brothers."

6:4 A. Four [relatives of a man] are liable [to extirpation for marrying the sister-in-law with whom the man performed *ḥaliṣah*], on the authority of the Torah, and four are secondary to them:

B.His father, and his son, his brother, and the son of his brother—lo, these are liable on her account.

C. The father of his father, the father of his mother, the son of his son, and the son of his daughter—lo, these are secondary to them [M. Yeb. 4:7J].

D. A strict rule applies to a divorcee which does not apply to a woman with whom he has performed the rite of *ḥaliṣah,* and to the woman with whom he has performed the rite of *ḥaliṣah* which does not apply to the divorcee.

E. The divorcee is permitted to return to the one who has divorced her [if she does not in the meanwhile remarry].

F. Therefore he is liable for punishment for marrying her kinswomen.

G. A woman with whom he has performed the rite of *ḥaliṣah* is prohibited from returning to the man with whom she has performed the rite of *ḥaliṣah.*

H. Therefore he is exempt from punishment if he marries one of her kinswomen.

I. *A woman awaiting marriage with a levir, the brother of whom betrothed her sister—*

J. *in the name of R. Judah b. Betera did they say, "They instruct him: "Wait until your older brother does a deed"'* [M. Yeb. 4:9A–B]—

K. either until she performs the rite of *ḥaliṣah,* or until she is taken in levirate marriage.

L. [If] the one who has betrothed the sister died, the levir effects the rite of *ḥaliṣah* with both of them.

M. [If] the levir dies, the one who betrothed the sister divorces his wife with a writ of divorce and the wife of his [deceased] brother with *ḥaliṣah* [M. Yeb. 4:9F–G].

N. In the name of R. Eliezer they said, "[If] his wife died, he performs the rite of *ḥaliṣah* with the deceased childless brother's widow [who is the sister of his now-deceased wife].

O. "[If] his deceased chidless brother's widow died, he may complete the marriage to his wife."

6:5 A. *He who was married to two women and who died—*

B. *the act of sexual relations [in levirate marriage] or the rite of ḥaliṣah of one of them exempts her co-wife* [from the requirement to do the same] [M. Yeb. 4:11C–D].

C. [If] one of them was prohibited to one of the brothers by reason of a prohibition of a forbidden degree, and he [nonetheless] performed a rite of *ḥaliṣah* with her, he has done nothing whatsoever.

D. He has not exempted her co-wife.

E. But either she or her co-wife enters into levirate marriage with one of the other brothers.

F. [If] she was prohibited by reason of a commandment [of scribes (M. 2:3–4)] or by reason of sanctity [of the priesthood (M. 2:4)],

G. [if] he performed the rite of *ḥaliṣah* with her or had sexual relations with her [as levir], her co-wife is exempt [from doing the same].

H. *He who remarries a woman whom he has divorced after she had remarried, and he who marries a woman with whom he has performed the rite of ḥaliṣah, and he who marries the kinswoman of a woman with whom he has performed ḥaliṣah* [M. Yeb. 4:12A]—

I."he has no power of betrothal over her, and she does not require a writ of divorce from him.

J. "She is invalid [for marriage into the priesthood], and the offspring [of such a union] is invalid," the words of R. 'Aqiba [*cf.* M. Yeb. 4:12C].

K. And sages say, "He does have the power of betrothal over her, and she does require a writ of divorce from him.

L. "She is valid [for marriage into the priesthood], and the offspring [of such a union] is valid.

M. "But they force him to put her away."

6:6 A. [If] she was yearning to go home to her father's house,

B. or she was subject to her husband's wrath,

C. or her husband was old or sick,

D. or her husband had gone overseas,

E. or her husband was imprisoned,

F. and she who aborts after her husband's death,

G. and the barren woman,

H. and the old woman,

I. and the woman who does not exhibit the signs of femininity,

J. and a minor who is not yet ready to give birth—

K. "[all of the above] must wait three months [before remarrying]," the words of R. Meir.

L. R. Judah permits betrothal and remarriage forthwith.

M. Said R. Ishmael b. R. Yoḥanan b. Beroqa, "I heard in the vineyard in Yabneh that no woman may remarry or be taken in betrothal until three months have passed."

N. "The female convert, the female captive, and the freed slave-girl must wait three months [before entering into betrothal or marriage, lest they be left pregnant from the former status]," the words of R. Judah.

O. R. Yosé permits them to wed forthwith.

P. And so did R. Yosé, say, "*All women may be betrothed* [forthwith] *except for a widow,* during the period of thirty days from the death of her husband, *on account of the period of mourning* [M. Yeb. 4:10I–K].

Q. "And none of them may be married before three months will have passed."

6:7 A. The deceased childless brother's widow with whom her levir has performed the rite of *ḥaliṣah* in a period of three months [from the death of her husband] must wait [from that time] for three months.

B. [If] this took place three months after [the death of the husband], she does not have to wait for three [more] months.

C. The three months of which they have spoken are three months after the death of her husband, and not three months after the rite of *ḥaliṣah* with her levir.

D. He who deposits a writ of divorce for his wife and says, "Do not deliver it to her before three months have passed,"

E. as soon as the writ of divorce reaches her hand, she is permitted to remarry forthwith.

F. And one does not take account of the possibility that it is a superannuated writ of divorce [after the issuance of which the couple has had sexual relations].

G. The daughter of a priest who was married to an Israelite and the husband of whom has died eats heave-offering in the evening [of the same day].

H. And one does not take account of the possibility that she is pregnant [and therefore not permitted to do so].

I. The widow of a childless brother, for the first three months after his death, is supported from the estate of her husband.

J. After three months she is not supported either from her husband's estate or from her levir's property.

K. If her levir went to court and [then] fled, lo, she is supported from his property.

L. M'ŚH B: A certain party came before R. Yosé. He said to him, "What is the law as to performing the rite of *ḥaliṣah* during the three months [of the husband's death]?"

M. R. Yosé cited to him the following verse: *And if the man is not willing to take his deceased childless brother's widow* (Deut. 25:7).

N. [And the meaning, he said, is this:] "She who is appropriate for marriage with the levir is appropriate for performance of the rite of *ḥaliṣah*.

O. "Since she is not suitable for levirate marriage [during three months of the husband's death], she also is not suitable for the rite of *ḥaliṣah*."

P. The deceased childless brother's widow should not engage in the rite of *ḥaliṣah* nor enter into levirate marriage until three months have passed from the death of her husband.

Q. And just as they do not say to him to enter into levirate marriage, so they do not say to him to perform the rite of *ḥaliṣah*.

R. M'SH B: In Piga a certain person was going overseas, and had a deceased childless brother's widow awaiting marriage, and also had a little brother.

S. In the name of R. Leazar b. R. Ṣadoq they said, "Let her go through the rite of *ḥaliṣah*, lest some ill-chance happen to him, and she turn out to be subject to levirate marriage with a minor [and therefore have to wait for many years]."

T. And sages say, "Just as they do not say to him to enter into levirate marriage, so they do not say to him to perform the rite of *ḥaliṣah*."

U. As to a beautiful captive [Deut. 21:13]: The Torah gave her thirty days, but sages have ruled that she has to wait three months, for the welfare of a possible offspring.

V. R. Simeon b. Leazar indeed brought proof for this proposition from the Scripture, since it says, "*A month of days and afterward . . .*" (Deut. 21:13).

6:8[–9] A. He who has sexual relations with his deceased childless brother's widow for the sake of her beauty [or] for the sake of her property—they regard him [for having acted with improper motive] as if he has entered into contact with a woman of prohibited degree.

B. And the offspring of such a union is near unto being a *mamzer*.

C. R. Meir did say, "A man should not have sexual relations with his deceased childless brother's wife until she reaches her time of [sexual] maturity,

D. "and so in the case of co-wives, and so in the case of forbidden degrees: they should not be married or betrothed until they will reach their time of maturity,

E. "lest these [minor co-wives] be found to be sexually neuter, and these [remarriages] should turn out to be invalid."

F. And sages say, "Lo, they are adjudged in accord with the presumption which pertains to them and remain valid."

G. R. 'Aqiba concedes in the case of a widow wed to a high priest or a divorcee or a woman who has performed the rite of *ḥaliṣah* wed to an ordinary priest, that, even though these come under the negative rule, *He shall not come,* the offspring is not a *mamzer.*

H. For a *mamzer* derives only from near of kin.

I. R. Simeon of Teman concedes in the case of a man who had sexual relations with his wife while she is menstruating that, even though the act is subject to extirpation, the offspring is not a *mamzer,* for an offspring is a *mamzer* only in the case of a union of near of kin.

7:1 A. He who bespeaks his deceased childless brother's widow and dies—

B. she performs the rite of *ḥaliṣah* and does not enter into levirate marriage [M. Yeb. 3:9].

C. R. Simeon says, "She either performs the rite of *ḥaliṣah* or enters into levirate marriage,

D. "for if his bespeaking is valid, she should enter into levirate marriage, for she is now the wife of the second brother [to die].

E. "[If] the bespeaking is not valid, she should enter into levirate marriage, for she is the wife of the first [brother to die]."

7:2 A. How is the duty of levirate marriage [carried out]?

B. They bespeak her and afterward marry.

C. [If] one has married her before bespeaking her, he has acquired [her as his wife].

D. He who bespeaks his deceased childless brother's widow has acquired her for himself and invalidated her for marrying any of the other surviving brothers.

E. [If] any of the other brothers had sexual relations with her, bespoke her, gave her a writ of divorce, or performed the rite of *ḥaliṣah* with her,

F. he has spoiled her for him [the brother who had originally bespoken the widow].

7:3 A. He who bespeaks his deceased childless brother's widow—her co-wife is invalid.

B. He who gives a writ of divorce to his deceased childless brother's widow—both she and her co-wife are invalid.

C. [If] he performed a rite of *ḥaliṣah* with her [after a writ of divorce], her co-wife is exempt [from doing so].

D. *And sages say, "There is a writ of divorce after a writ of divorce, and a bespeaking after a bespeaking"* [M. Yeb. 5:1E–F].

E. Rabban Gamaliel concedes to sages that there is a writ of divorce after a bespeaking, and a bespeaking after a writ of divorce, a writ of divorce [to the third widow after] intercourse with the second widow which took place after the bespeaking of the first, and a bespeaking [of the third widow] after intercourse with the second widow which took place after the writ of divorce of the first.

F. How [under what circumstances] did Rabban Gamaliel rule that there is no writ of divorce after a writ of divorce?

G. Two deceased childless brother's widows and a single levir—

H. [if] he gave a writ of divorce to this one and went and gave a writ of divorce to the other—

I. Rabban Gamaliel says, "He performs the rite of *ḥaliṣah* with the first. But he is permitted to marry the kinswomen of the second."

J. And sages say, "He is prohibited from marrying the kinswomen of either one of them. And one of them requires a rite of *ḥaliṣah.*"

K. [If] he bespoke one of them and then went and bespoke the other,

L. Rabban Gamaliel says, "He gives a writ of divorce to the first and [also] performs the rite of *ḥaliṣah* with her, and he is permitted to marry the kinswomen of the second."

M. And sages say, "He is prohibited to marry the kinswomen of either one of them.

N. "And both of them require a writ of divorce from him, and one of them performs the rite of *ḥaliṣah* with him."

O. And so is the rule in the case of two levirs and a single deceased brother's childless widow.

7:4 A. *[If the levir] had sexual relations with this one and had sexual relations with that one,*

B. *had sexual relations with this one and bespoke that one* [M. Yeb. 5:5D–E],

C. had sexual relations with this one and gave a writ of divorce to that one,

D. had sexual relations with this one and performed the rite of *ḥaliṣah* with that one,

E. *nothing whatsoever is valid after the rite of ḥaliṣah.*

F. *[If] he performed the rite of ḥaliṣah with this one* and performed the rite of *ḥaliṣah* with that one,

G. performed the rite of *ḥaliṣah* with this one and *bespoke that one* [M. Yeb. 5:5A–B],

H. *performed the rite of ḥaliṣah with this one and gave a writ of divorce to that one,*

I. performed the rite of *ḥaliṣah* with this one and had sexual relations with that one—

J. nothing whatsoever is valid after sexual relations.

7:5 A. Even though they have said, *"Nothing whatsoever is valid after sexual relations,"*

B. nonetheless a rite of *ḥaliṣah* after an act of sexual relations still invalidates the widow for marriage into the priesthood [as a woman with whom a valid rite of *ḥaliṣah* has been performed].

C. How so?

D. Three childless deceased brother's widows and one levir—

E. [if] he bespoke this one and had sexual relations with the other one and went and bespoke the third—

F. R. Neḥemiah says, "The first requires a writ of divorce. But after the act of sexual relations there is no valid effective procedure.

G. "[This is so] by an argument *a fortiori:* Now if performing a rite of *ḥaliṣah* invalidates a woman for marriage into the priesthood [even] in the case of rite of *ḥaliṣah* which takes place after an act of sexual relations, [and after sexual relations] there is no effective procedure whatsoever,

H "then an act of sexual relations which does not invalidate the woman from marrying into the priesthood,

I. "in the case of sexual relations after a rite of *ḥaliṣah*—

J. "is it not logical that there should be nothing valid after it [an act of sexual relations]?"

K. And sages say, "They require three writs of divorce and a single performance of *ḥaliṣah* with one of them [M. Yeb. 5:3].

L. "Under what circumstances did they rule, 'There is nothing whatsoever after sexual relations'?

M. "This is the case when it is *de novo.* But if it is not *de novo* [but *de facto*], lo, this is deemed equivalent to an act of bespeaking."

8:1 A. A nine-year-and-one-day-old boy of Ammonite, Moabite, Egyptian, Edomite, Samaritan origin, a *Netin,* or *Mamzer* [of that age or older] who had sexual relations with the daughter of a priest, with the daughter of a Levite, or with the daughter of an Israelite, has rendered her invalid for marrying into the priesthood.

B. R. Yosé says, "Anyone whose seed is valid—she is valid [for marrying into the priesthood]. And any whose seed is invalid—she is invalid [thus the Egyptian is delisted]."

C. Rabban Simeon b. Gamaliel says, "Any whose daughter you are permitted to marry—you are permitted to marry his widow, and any whose daughter you are not permitted to marry—you are not permitted to marry his widow [thus Ammonites and Moabites are delisted]."

8:2 A. A Levite woman who is taken captive—her daughter is valid to marry into the priesthood.

B. Levites, who became unfit from the priesthood by their mothers—sages did not scruple concerning them.

C. A Levite who was taken captive and who was raped—they give her tithe [to eat].

D. The daughter of a Levite born from a *Netin*-mother or from a *mamzeret*-mother—they do not give her tithe to eat.

8:3 A. An ordinary priest who married a sterile woman—lo, this one feeds her heave-offering [M. Yeb. 6:5A].

B. A high priest may not marry a woman whom he has raped or seduced.

C. But he may marry a girl who has exercised the right of refusal.

D. A high priest whose brother has died performs the rite of *ḥaliṣah* [M. Yeb. 6:41].

E. If there are other brothers available for the task, he does not perform the rite of *ḥaliṣah*.

F. On what account did they rule, *A high priest who has bespoken his deceased childless brother's widow should not marry her* [M. Yeb. 6:4G–H]?

G. Because bespeaking does not effect a complete [and unambiguous] act of acquisition.

8:4 A. *A man should not desist from having sexual relations unless he has children* [M. Yeb. 6:6A].

B. Grandchildren are deemed [for the purposes of the present rule] to be equivalent to children.

C. [If] one of them died or one of them was made into a eunuch, he then is not permitted to desist from sexual relations.

D. A man has no right to live without a woman, and a woman has no right to live without a man.

E. A man has no right to drink a contraceptive drink so that he should not impregnate a woman,

F. and a woman has no right to drink a contraceptive drink so that she should not become pregnant.

G. A man has no right to marry a barren woman, an old woman, a sterile woman, or a minor, or any who cannot bear children.

H. A woman has no right to be married even to a eunuch [sterile but capable of sexual relations].

I. R. Judah says [regarding D–E], "He who renders males eunuchs is liable [for doing so], but he who does so to females is exempt."

J. R. Nathan says, "*The House of Shammai say, 'Two sons*—just as Moses had two sons, as it is said, *And the sons of Moses, Gershom and Eliezer* [I Chron. 23:15].

K. "And the House of Hillel say, '*A son and a daughter,* as it is said, *Male and female he made them*" [M. Yeb. 6:6B–C].

L. R. Jonathan says, "The House of Shammai say, 'A male and a female.'

M. "And the House of Hillel say, 'A male or a female.'"

8:5 A. *[If] a man married a woman and lived with her ten years and she did not give birth, he has no right to desist [from sexual relations*] [M. Yeb. 6:6E],

B. but he should put her away and pay off her marriage contract,

C. lest it was because he did not merit being reproduced through her.

D. And even though there is no proof for that proposition, there is at least Scriptural indication for it, as it is said, *At the end of ten years*

E. *of Abram's dwelling in the land of Canaan* [Gen. 16:3].

F. As is our way, we learn that living abroad does not count.

8:6 A. A woman whose husband was old or sick, or who herself was sick, or whose husband was imprisoned, or whose husband went abroad—

B. [the years with such husbands] do not count for her.

C. [If] he divorced her, she should go and remarry someone else, lest it was because she did not merit being reproduced through him.

D. And to what extent is she permitted to remarry?

E. Up to three husbands.

F. Beyond that point she should marry only someone who already has a wife and children.

G. Lo, if she should marry someone who has no wife and children, she goes forth without the payment of her marriage contract,

H. because her marriage is in error.

8:7 A. R. 'Aqiba says, "Whoever spills blood, lo, such a one diminishes the divine image, since it says, *He who shed the blood of man by man his blood will be shed* [Gen. 9:6]."

B. R. Eleazar b. 'Azariah says, "Whoever does not engage in reproductive sexual relations, lo, such a one sheds blood and annuls the divine, diminishes the divine image,

C. "since it says, *For in the image of God he made man,*

D. "and it says, *And you, be fruitful and multiply* (Gen. 9:6, 9:7)."

E. Ben 'Azzai says, Whoever does not engage in reproductive sexual relations, lo, such a one sheds blood and diminishes the divine image,

F. "since it says, *For in the image of God he made man.*

G. "And it says, *And you, be fruitful and multiply* (Gen. 9:6, 9:7)."

H. Said to him R. Eleazar b. 'Azariah, "Ben 'Azzai, words are nice when they come from someone who does what they say.

I. "Some people expound nicely but do not nicely do what they say, or do what they say but do not expound nicely.

J. "Ben 'Azzai expounds nicely but does not nicely do what he says."

K. He said to him, "What shall I do? My soul thirsts after Torah. Let other people keep the world going."

9:1 A. An Israelite girl who married a priest and brought him *melog*-slaves and iron-flock-slaves—

B. *melog*-slaves eat by virtue of her rights.

C. But iron-flock-slaves eat by virtue of his rights [M. Yeb. 7:2].

D. What are *melog*-slaves?

E. Loss or profit, lo, both accrue to her.

F. And what are iron-flock slaves? Loss or profit, lo, either accrues to him [M. Yeb. 7:1F–K].

G. [If] they are brought at fixed value, they are taken out at fixed value.

H. [If] they come in as boys, they are taken out as young men.

I. [If] they are brought in as young men, they are taken out as old men.

J. In the case of both of them, the fruit of their labor belongs to the husband.

K. In the case of both of them, the husband is liable to maintain them.

L. In the case of both of them, they [husband or wife separately] cannot sell them.

M. The husband cannot sell them, because they are mortgaged to his wife.

N. And the wife cannot sell them, because the husband enjoys the fruit of their labor.

O. [If he, the husband] died and left her as she was [childless],

P. the *melog*-slaves do not eat [heave-offering, if the master is a priest], just as she does not [eat heave-offering any longer].

Q. The iron-flock slaves do eat [heave-offering] because they are in the possession of the [husband's] heirs until they are returned to her.

R. [If] he left her children, these and those [types of slaves] continue to eat [heave-offering].

S. [If] he left her pregnant, these and those [types of slaves] do not eat.

T. [If] he left her with children and left her pregnant, the *melog*-slaves eat [heave-offering] just as she eats heave-offering.

U. But the iron-flock slaves do not eat heave-offering, on account of the share of the foetus in them [M. Yeb. 7:3B].

V. R. Ishmael b. R. Yosé says in the name of his father, "The daughter validates eating heave-offering.

W. "But the heirs do not validate eating heave-offering."

X. R. Simeon says, "All of them in the case of male heirs eat heave-offering. In the case of female heirs, they do not eat heave-offering, perchance the foetus may be male, and the daughter gets nothing when there is a son."

9:2 A. A priestly girl who married an Israelite, and brought to him [in her dowry] *melog*-slaves and iron-flock-slaves—

B. he died and left her as she was [childless]—

C. the *melog*-slaves do [not] eat heave-offering, just as she does [not] eat heave-offering.

D. The iron-flock-slaves do not eat heave-offering, because they are in the presumptive possession of the heirs until they are returned to her.

E. A priest who was a deaf-mute, an idiot, or a minor who purchased slaves—

F. they do not eat heave-offering.

G. But [if] a court acted in their behalf, or [if] a court appointed guardians for their estates, or [even if] the slaves came to them in an inheritance from some other source [than the priestly father],

H. lo, these slaves do eat heave-offering.

I. A priest who bought a slave, and an Israelite owns even one-hundredth of him—

J. [the slave] does not eat heave-offering.

K. The wife of a priest who bought slaves,

L. or her slaves who bought slaves—

M. lo, these eat heave-offering.

N. The slave of a priest who ran away, and the wife of a priest who rebelled against him—[even if they do not know whether or not the priest is still alive] lo, these eat heave-offering.

O. The man guilty of manslaughter should not go outside of the borders of the city of his refuge, in the assumption that the high priest still is alive.

9:3 A. *The foetus, the levir, betrothal, a deaf-mute, a boy nine years and one* *day old invalidate a woman from eating heave-offering but do not validate her to do so* [M. Yeb 7:4A–B].

B. Said R. Simeon, "In this case the rule of justice is smitten.

C. "For if a fact serves to invalidate, that fact should serve to validate. If a fact does not serve to validate, that fact also should not serve to invalidate."

D. [If] his daughter of sound senses is married to his brother who was a deaf-mute, her co-wife is exempt from *ḥaliṣah* and from levirate marriage,

E. on the strength of an argument *a fortiori:*

F. Now if the marriage of her daughter is valid, the marriage of her co-wife should be valid. If the marriage of her daughter is not valid, then the marriage of her co-wife should not be valid.

G. [If] his daughter who was a deaf-mute was married to his brother who was of sound senses, her co-wife should perform a rite of *ḥaliṣah* but not enter into levirate marriage.

H. A deaf-mute whose father married her off, lo, she is deemed equivalent to a woman of sound senses for all purposes.

9:4 A. An Israelite girl of sound senses who was married to a priest who was a deaf-mute does not eat heave-offering.

B. [If] she became pregnant, she does not eat heave-offering.

C. An Israelite girl who was a deaf-mute who was married to a priest of sound senses does not eat heave-offering.

D. [If] she became pregnant, she does not eat heave-offering.

E. [If] she gave birth [to a sound foetus], she then does eat heave-offering.

F. A priestly girl of sound senses who married an Israelite idiot immerses out of the embrace of her husband and then eats heave-offering in the evening [when the purification is complete].

G. [If] she became pregnant, she no longer eats heave-offering.

H. [If] she gave birth, she does not eat heave-offering.

I. Anyone who has seed of a priest, whether male or female, even seed of his seed, lo, such a woman eats heave-offering.

J. [If] her daughter from an Israelite was married to a priest, she [the daughter] does not eat heave-offering,

K. until she has seed from a priest first.

9:5 A. A priestly woman, the foetus of whom died in her womb—lo, this one eats heave-offering.

B. *A woman who is in difficult labor—*

C. *they cut the foetus out of her womb*—even on the Sabbath—*and remove it limb by limb*

D. *because her life takes precedence.*

E. *If, however, the foetus's head emerged,* even on the second day [of hard labor],

F. *they do not touch it*

G. *for they do not set aside one life on account of another life* [M. Ohalot 7:6].

10:1 A. An Israelite girl of sound senses who was betrothed to a priest of sound senses,

B. but he did not suffice to marry her before he was made a deaf-mute—

C. she does not eat heave-offering.

D. [If] he died and left her before his levir, even though he [the levir] was a deaf-mute, she eats heave-offering.

E. Greater is the power of the levir to permit her to eat heave-offering than the power of the husband to do so.

F. An Israelite girl of sound senses who was betrothed to a priest of sound senses,

G. but he did not suffice to marry her before she was made a deaf-mute—

H. she does not eat heave-offering.

I. [If] he died and left her before his levir, even though he [the levir] was a deaf-mute, she eats heave-offering.

J. Greater is the power of the levir to permit her to eat heave-offering than the power of the husband to do so.

K. An Israelite girl of sound senses who was married to a priest who was a deaf-mute does not eat heave-offering.

L. [If] he died and left her before a levir, [if] he was of sound senses, she eats heave-offering. [If] he was a deaf-mute, she does not eat heave-offering.

M. She does not eat heave-offering until she enters the marriage-canopy for the sake of consummation of the marriage and has sexual intercourse with her husband for the sake of the marital relation.

N. An Israelite girl who was a deaf-mute who was married to a priest of sound senses does not eat heave-offering.

O. [If] he died and left her before a levir, even though he [the levir] is of sound senses, she does not eat heave-offering.

10:2 A. An Israelite girl of sound senses who was betrothed to a priest of sound senses,

B. and who entered the marriage canopy for the sake of marriage, but he [the husband] did not suffice to have sexual relations with her before his testicles were crushed or his penis was cut off [M. Yeb. 8:1]—

C. lo, this one eats heave-offering,

D. since she had entered the category of one permitted to do so, even for a single moment [M. Yeb. 8:4E–G].

E. [If] she was still betrothed when his testicles became crushed or his penis was cut off, lo, this one does not eat heave-offering.

F. A widow betrothed to a high priest, a divorcee or a woman who had performed the rite of *ḥaliṣah* with an ordinary priest, who entered the marriage-canopy for the purpose of marriage,

G. and [the priestly husband] did not have time to complete the act of sexual relations before he died,

H. is valid for marriage into the priesthood and valid for eating heave-offering.

I. [If] he actually had sexual relations with her, he has rendered her invalid for marriage into the priesthood and invalid for eating heave-offering.

J. A [priest] does not exhibit defined sexual traits does not eat heave-offering. His wife and slaves do eat it.

K. One who has his prepuce drawn forward and one who is born circumcised—lo, these eat heave-offering.

L. A [priest] who bears the sexual traits of both sexes eats heave-offering but not Holy Things [M. Yeb. 8:6B].

M. A [priest] who does not exhibit defined sexual traits does not eat heave-offering [=J] or Holy Things.

N. *Said R. Eleazar, "I heard concerning a person who exhibits the traits of both sexes that they are liable for having sexual relations with him to stoning, as they are liable for having sexual relations with a male*" [M. Yeb. 8:6E].

O. Under what circumstances?

P. When he had sexual relations at the place of the male genitals. But if he did not have sexual relations at the place of the male genitals, he is exempt.

10:3 A. *Who is he who has crushed testicles?*

B. *Any one whose testicles are crushed* [M. Yeb. 8:2–B]—

C. which are punctured or perforated, or one of which is lacking.

D. Said R. Ishmael b. R. Yoḥanan b. Beroqa, "I heard in the Vineyard at Yabneh: He who has only one testicle, lo, such a one is a eunuch by nature."

E. Said R. Yose, "M'ŚH B: A man in Kefar Mendon went up to the top of an olive tree and fell down, and one of his testicles was crushed. He came and had sexual relations with his wife and died.

"They came and asked R. Yoḥanan b. Nur, 'May his wife enter into levirate marriage?'

"He said to them, 'Before you ask me about the law as to her entering levirate marriage, ask me the law as to her eating heave-offering?

"'For she has been rendered invalid for marriage into the priesthood and invalid for eating heave-offering'" [M. Yeb. 8:1, 4].

10:4 A. *Who is one whose penis is cut off?*

B. Any one whose sexual organ is cut off from the crown and below.

C. But if so much as a hair-thread of the crown remained [M. Yeb. 8:2C–E]—

D. near the head and going around the top, he is valid.

E. [If] it is perforated at the bottom, he is invalid, because it [the semen] pours out.

F. [If] the hole is closed up, he is valid, because he can impregnate.

G. This is one who is invalid and who once more returns to his state of validity.

10:5 A. *That which is bruised or crushed or broken or cut [you shall not offer to the Lord*] (Lev. 22:24)—

"all of them refer to the testicles," the words of R. Judah.

B. R. Eliezer b. Jacob says, "All of them refer to the penis."

C. R. Yosé says, "*Bruised or crushed* refers to the testicles, *broken or cut* to the penis."

10:6 A. Who is a eunuch by nature?

B. Any male who survived for twenty years without producing two pubic hairs.

C. Even if he produced two pubic hairs thereafter, lo, he is deemed a eunuch for all purposes.

D. What are the indications thereof?

E. Any who has no beard and whose skin is smooth [and not hairy].

F. Rabban Simeon b Gamaliel says in the name of R. Judah b. Yair, "Any whose urine does not produce a froth."

G. And some say, "Any whose urine is sour."

H. And some say, "Any whose semen is watery."

I. And some say, "Any who urinates without producing an arch."

J. And others say, "Any who bathes in cold water in the rainy season and whose flesh does not steam."

K. R. Simeon b. Eleazar says, "Any whose voice croaks, so one cannot tell whether it is male or female."

10:7 A. Who is a sterile woman?

B. Any female who survived for twenty years without producing two pubic hairs.

C. Even if she produced two pubic hairs thereafter, lo, she is deemed sterile for all purposes.

D. What are the indications thereof?

E. Any who has no breasts, and whose hair is abnormal, and who finds sexual relations painful.

F. R. Simeon b. Gamaliel says, "Any who has no *mons veneris* like other women."

G. R. Simeon b. Eleazar says, "Any who has a deep voice, so one cannot tell whether it is a male or a female."

11:1 A. A person lacking clearly defined sexual traits who effected an act of betrothal—his act of betrothal is valid.

B. [If] he was betrothed, his act of being betrothed is valid.

C. He performs the rite of *ḥaliṣah* and they perform the rite of *ḥaliṣah* with his wife.

D. If there are brothers available, however, he does not perform the rite of *ḥaliṣah* or enter into levirate marriage.

E. But in any event they enter into levirate marriage with his wife.

F. R. Yosé b. R. Judah says, "He does not perform the rite of *ḥaliṣah* and they do not perform the rite of *ḥaliṣah* [with his wife]. He does not enter into levirate marriage and they do not enter levirate marriage with his wife.

G. "For it is possible that he may be torn open and turn out to be a eunuch by nature."

11:2 A. A eunuch by nature, a person exhibiting the traits of both sexes, a brother born of the same mother, a proselyte, and a freed slave do not perform the rite of *ḥaliṣah* and do not enter into levirate marriage.

B. How so?

C. [If any of these] died and left wives and had surviving brothers,

D. [and if] the surviving brothers went and bespoke the wife, gave her a writ of divorce, or performed a rite of *ḥaliṣah,* they have done nothing whatsoever.

E. [If] they have had sexual relations with her, they have invalidated her [from marrying into the priesthood] and are liable for a sacrifice.

F. [If] the brothers [of any of these] died and left childless widows, and they had brothers,

G. and [if] the surviving brothers went and bespoke the wife, gave her a writ of divorce and performed a rite of *ḥaliṣah* they have done nothing whatsoever.

H. And if they had sexual relations, they have rendered her invalid [for marrying into the priesthood], and they are liable for a sacrifice.

I. A man with crushed testicles or whose penis is cut off or a eunuch by act of man and an old man either perform the rite of *ḥaliṣah* or enter into levirate marriage.

J. How so?

K. [If] they died and left wives and had surviving brothers,

L. [and if] the surviving brothers came and bespoke the widow, gave her a writ of divorce or performed the rite of *ḥaliṣah,* what they have done is valid.

M. [If] they had sexual relations with the widow, they have acquired her and freed her co-wives [from the obligation of levirate connection].

N. [If] the brothers died and left wives, and they had surviving brothers,

O. [and if] they came and bespoke the widow, gave her a writ of divorce, or performed the rite of *ḥaliṣah*, what they have done is valid.

P. And if they had sexual relations with the widow, they have acquired her and exempted the co-wives [from the obligation of levirate connection].

Q. But they are prohibited to confirm the marriage [if the woman may come into the congregation], since it is said, *One with crushed testicles or a cut off penis shall not enter into the congregation of the Lord* (Deut. 23:2).

11:3 A. And in both of these instances the brothers do not have the right to inherit her.

B. R. Eleazar says, "The first inherits her" [M. Yeb. 10:1M, P.]

11:4 A. A woman whose husband went overseas, and whom they came and told, "Your husband has died,"

B. and whom the court instructed to remarry—

C. and who went and remarried [M. Yeb. 10:2G–I]

D. as a widow to a high priest or a divorcee or one who has performed the rite of *ḥaliṣah* to an ordinary priest,

E. "is liable for a sacrifice for each and every act of sexual relations [with the husband whom she was not legally permitted to marry]," the words of R. Eliezer.

F. And sages say, "One offering covers all."

G. And sages concede to R. Eliezer that if she was married to five men, she owes a sacrifice for each and every one.

H. R. Simeon says, "If the court gave instruction on their own, [the marriage is deemed] a willful [act of adultery between] a man and a [married] woman.

I. "[If] she remarried on her own, [it is deemed a case in which] a man unintentionally [has committed an act of adultery with] a married woman."

11:5 A. A woman who went overseas with her husband,

B. and who came and reported, "My husband has died,"

C. [and] remarried on her own testimony,

D. and again she went overseas and came and said, "My husband has died,"

E. [and] she remarried on her own testimony,

F. and again went overseas and came and said, "My husband has died,"

G. and remarried on her own testimony,

H. and lo, all of them in fact are coming back—

I. she goes forth from all of them.

J. But she is permitted to remain married to the first [M. Yeb. 10:15, 5].

K. The act of sexual relations or of *ḥaliṣah* on the part of the brother of the first exempts her co-wives.

L. Those of [the brother of the] second and third do not exempt her co-wives.

M. If the second had sexual relations with her for the purpose of marriage after the death of the first, the act of sexual relations or of *ḥaliṣah* on the part of the brother of second exempts her co-wives.

N. Those of the third and the fourth do not exempt her co-wives.

11:6 A. "*A woman whose husband and son went overseas.*

B. "*and whom they came and told, 'Your son died, and afterward your husband died,'*

C. "*and who entered into levirate marriage,*

D. "*and whom they afterward told, 'Matters were reversed'* [M. Yeb. 10:3G]—

E. "since she was not appropriate for levirate marriage but for remarrying,

F. "all offspring which she produced, lo, they are *mamzerim.*

G. "If they said to her, 'Your husband died and afterwards your son died,' and she went and remarried, and afterward they said to her, 'Matters were reversed'—

H. "since she was not appropriate for remarrying, but for levirate marriage,

I. "all the offspring which she produced [delete: during the life time of her levirate husband], lo, they are *mamzers,*" the words of R. Meir which he stated in the name of R. 'Aqiba.

J. And sages say, "The status of *mamzer* is not applicable to the offspring of a levirate marriage [which is invalid]."

K. *If they said to her, "Your husband has died," and she remarried, and afterward they said to her, "Your husband was alive, but then he died"* [M. Yeb. 10:3J]

L. *lo, this one goes forth* with a writ of divorce.

M. And all the offspring which she produced while her husband was yet alive, lo, they are *mamzers.*

N. Those produced after the death of her husband are valid [M. Yeb. 10:3L].

O. If they said to her, "Your husband has died," and she was betrothed [better: entered into levirate marriage], and afterwards they said to her, "He was alive, but he has died,"

P. lo, this one puts her away with a writ of divorce and a rite of *ḥaliṣah.*

Q. All the offspring which she produced while her husband was yet alive are *mamzers.*

R. Those which she produced after the death of her husband are valid.

S. If they said to her, "Your levirate brother-in-law has died," and she went and got married, and afterward they told her, "He was alive, but he now has died"—

T. since she was not appropriate for remarriage but for levirate marriage—

U. lo, this one goes forth with a writ of divorce.

V. "All the offspring which she produced while her levirate brother-in-law was yet alive are *mamzers,*" the words of R. Meir which he stated in the name of R. ʿAqiba.

W. And sages say, "The status of *mamzer* is not applicable to the offspring of a levirate marriage."

11:7 A. *He whose wife went oversaeas, and whom they came and told, "Your wife has died,"*

B. *and [who] married her sister,*

C. *and whom they afterward told, "She was then alive, but now she has died,"*

D. lo, this one remains wed to the sister.

E. *And the former offspring is a mamzer, but the latter offspring is not a mamzer.*

F. *R. Yosé says, "Anyone who invalidates [his wife for marriage] with others invalidates her for marriage for himself, and anyone who does not invalidate his wife [for marriage] with others does not invalidate her for himself"* [M. Yeb. 10:4G–I].

G. [If] they told him, "Your wife has died," and he married her sister, and she went overseas, and they told him, "Your wife has died,"

and he married her sister, and she went overseas, and they told him, "Your wife has died,"

and he married her sister, and she went overseas,

H. and lo, all of them are coming along—

I. the first is his wife, and she exempts her co-wives.

J. And all of the rest of them are not his wives.

K. And if he has sexual relations with the second for the purposes of marital coition after the death of the first,

L. the second is his wife, [and] exempts her co-wife,

M. and all the rest of them are not his wives.

11:8 A. "[If] they told him, 'Your daughter died first, and then your brother died?' and he went and entered into levirate marriage with her co-wife,

B. "and afterward they told him, 'Matters were reversed,'

C. "since she was not appropriate for levirate marriage, but for ordinary marriage—

D. "all the offspring which she produced, lo, they are *mamzers.*

E. "[If] they said to him, 'He died first, and then your daughter died,' and her co-wife went and married someone else, and afterward they told him, 'Matters were reversed'—

F. "since she was not appropriate to be married in an ordinary way but only to enter into levirate marriage,

G. "all the offspring which she produced while her levirate husband was yet alive, lo, they are *mamzers,*" the words of R. Meir, which he said in the name of R. 'Aqiba.

H. And sages say, "The status of *mamzer* is not applicable to the offspring of levirate marriage."

11:9 A. A deaf-mute with whom the rite of *ḥaliṣah,* was performed, a deaf-mute who performed the rite of *ḥaliṣah,* she who performs the rite of *ḥaliṣah* with an idiot, so too: an idiot-girl who performed the rite of *ḥaliṣah,* and she who performed the rite of *ḥaliṣah* with a minor

B. goes forth.

C. "And thirteen rules apply to her," the words of R. Meir, which he stated in the name of R. 'Aqiba.

D. And sages say, "The status of *mamzer* is not applicable to the offspring of levirate marriage."

11:10 A. A boy nine years and one day old who had sexual relations with his deceased childless brother's widow and then died—

B. she performs the rite of *ḥaliṣah* but does not enter into levirate marriage,

C. for the act of sexual relations by a boy nine years and one day old is equivalent to the act of bespeaking of an adult.

D. R. Simeon says, "She either performs the rite of *ḥaliṣah* or enters into levirate marriage.

E. "For if his act of sexual relations is valid, she may enter into levirate marriage, since she is the wife of the first.

F. "If his act of sexual relations is not valid, she enters into levirate marriage,

G. "since she is deemed the wife of the second [brother]."

H. *A boy nine years and one day old spoils [the deceased childless brother's widow] for the other brothers* in one way, *and the brothers spoil her for him* [M. Yeb. 10:6A–C] in four ways:

I. He spoils her for the brothers through an act of sexual relations.

J. But they spoil her for him through an act of sexual relations, a writ of divorce, an act of bespeaking, and a rite of *ḥaliṣah* [all of which, done by them, is valid] [M. Yeb. 10:6G–I].

K. And just as he does not invalidate her for the brothers by means of an act of bespeaking, a writ of divorce, and *ḥaliṣah,* so brothers [nine years old] do not spoil her for one another through a writ of divorce, an act of bespeaking, or a rite of *ḥaliṣah.*

L. How so?

M. Two brothers nine years and one day old—

N. this one went and bespoke her,

O. and that one went and bespoke her—

P. this one went and gave her a writ of divorce,

Q. and that one went and gave her a writ of divorce—

R. this one went and performed the rite of *ḥaliṣah,*

S. and that one went and performed the rite of *ḥaliṣah*—

T. he has done nothing whatsoever.

U. R. Meir says, "[If] she performed the rite of *ḥaliṣah* with a minor, she is invalidated for marriage with either one of them."

V. [If] she this one went and had sexual relations with her, and that one went and had sexual relations with her,

W. she is invalid for marriage with either one of them [M. Yeb. 10:7A–C].

X. R. Simeon says, "The first one may keep her as his wife, and the second one must put her away.

Y. "If the act of sexual relations of the first is valid, the act of sexual relations of the second is not valid.

Z. "For a valid act of sexual relations [acquiring the woman as wife] cannot follow another such act.

AA. "[If] the act of sexual relations of the first is not valid, then the act of sexual relations of the second is also not valid."

11:11 A. *A boy nine years and one day old who had sexual relations with his deceased childless brother's widow and went and had sexual relations with her co-wife*

B. *spoils her for himself.*

C. *R. Simeon says, "He has not spoiled her for himself* [M. Yeb. 10:8A–D].

D. "For if his act of sexual relations with the first is valid, his act of sexual relations with the second is not valid.

E. "For a valid act of sexual relations cannot follow another such act.

F. "If his act of sexual relations with the first is not valid, his act of sexual relations with the second is not valid."

G. Under what circumstances?

H. In the case of an act of sexual relations of a boy nine years and one day old.

I. But a deaf-mute, an idiot, and a minor who have had sexual relations have effected an act of acquisition.

J. And they have freed the co-wives [from the obligation of levirate marriage].

K. An idiot or a minor who married wives and who died—

L. their wives are exempt from the requirement of performing the rite of *ḥaliṣah.*

M. This is the general principle: Any act of sexual relations [performed by them] which requires articulated consciousness is not a valid act of sexual relations.

N. But any which does not require articulated consciousness—lo, this is a valid act of sexual relations.

12:1 A. *R. Judah prohibits [marrying the kinswomen] of the one whom one's father has raped and the one whom one's father has seduced* [M. Yeb. 11:1D],

B. since it is said, *The nakedness of the wife of your father you shall not uncover. It is the nakedness of your father* (Lev. 18:8).

C. And further on it is said, *A man shall not take the wife of his father and shall not uncover the garment of his father* (Deut. 23:1).

D. And it says, "*And she shall be a wife to him* (Deut. 22:29)."

12:2 A. *The convert whose sons converted with her—they neither perform the rite of ḥaliṣah nor enter into levirate marriage* [M. Yeb. 11:2A].

B. [If] their conception was not in a state of sanctity and their birth was not in a state of sanctity, they neither perform the rite of *ḥaliṣah* nor enter into levirate marriage.

C. And they are not liable [to observe the prohibition against marrying] the wife of one's brother.

D. [If] her conception was not in a state of sanctity but her giving birth was in a state of sanctity, then they neither perform the rite of *ḥaliṣah* nor enter into levirate marriage.

E. But they are liable on account of [the prohibition against marrying] the wife of one's brother.

F. [If] her conceiving and giving birth were in a state of sanctity, lo, she is equivalent to an Israelite for all purposes.

12:3 A. *Five women whose offspring were confused with one another* [M. Yeb. 11:3A]—

B. some of them are brothers, and some of them are not brothers—

C. those who are brothers perform the rite of *ḥaliṣah,* and those who are not brothers enter into levirate marriage.

D. Some of them are priests and some of them are not priests—

E. the priests perform the rite of *ḥaliṣah* and those who are not priests enter into levirate marriage.

F. Some of them are brothers and some of them are priests—

G. they perform the rite of *ḥaliṣah* and do not enter into levirate marriage.

H. [If] there is a doubt whether a woman is his mother or his daughter or his sister—

I. they perform the rite of *ḥaliṣah* and do not enter into levirate marriage.

J. This is the general rule: In all cases of doubt having to do with the deceased childless brother's widow, they perform the rite of *ḥaliṣah* and do not enter into levirate marriage.

12:4 A. What is the sort of case in which a man performs the rite of *ḥaliṣah* with his mother by reason of doubt?

B. His mother and another woman have two males—

C. they went and had two male sons in hiding [and the offspring are confused by reason of lack of access to light]—

D. the first two[B] went and married the mother of one another—

E. and they died without offspring—

F. this one performs the rite of *ḥaliṣah* with both of the widows, and that one performs the rite of *ḥaliṣah* with both of them.

G. It turns out that this one performs the rite of *ḥaliṣah* with his mother by reason of doubt.

H. What is the sort of case in which a man performs the rite of *ḥaliṣah* with his sister by reason of doubt?

I. His mother and another woman—

J. and they have two male offspring—

K. they went and produced two female offspring in hiding—

L. and they [K] married two brothers from the same father but not from the same mother—

M. and they [the brothers] died without offspring—

N. this one performs the rite of *ḥaliṣah* with both of them, and that one performs the rite of *ḥaliṣah* with both of them.

O. It turns out that a man performs the rite of *ḥaliṣah* with his sister by reason of doubt.

12:5 A. What is the sort of case in which a man performs the rite of *ḥaliṣah* with his daughter by reason of doubt?

B. His wife and another woman produced two female offspring in hiding—

C. and the two were married to two brothers from the same father [delete: but a different mother]—

D. and they died without offspring—

E. he performs the rite of *ḥaliṣah* with both of them.

F. It turns out that this man performs the rite of *ḥaliṣah* with his daughter by reason of doubt.

12:6 A. *A priest-girl whose offspring was confused with the offspring of her slave-girl* [M. Yeb. 11:5A]—

B. they do not eat that which is heaved out of Most Holy Things [for the use of the priesthood],

C. for slaves of priests do not eat from it.

D. But they eat from that which is heaved out of Lesser Holy Things.

E. for slaves of priests eat it.

F. Both of them go out to the threshing floor and take a single portion [M. Yeb. 11:5C].

G. For they do not give [heave-offering] to a slave unless his master is with him.

H. R. Yosé says, "He may say to him, 'If I am subject to the authority of my master, give me by reason of the authority of my master, and if not, give me by reason of my own authority.'"

I. *If the confused sons grew up and freed one another* [M. Yeb. 11:5G], they do not eat of that which is heaved out of Lesser Holy Things.

J. For non-priests do not eat it.

K. R. Judah says, "He sells heave-offering and purchases unconsecrated food with the proceeds [M. Yeb. 11:5N–O].

L. "For whoever does not eat the Holy Things of other people also does not eat the Holy Things belonging to himself."

12:7 A. *She who did not delay three months after her husband [divorced her* *or died] and remarried and gave birth* [M. Yeb. 11:6A]—

B. and it is not known [whether the offspring is of the first husband or the second]—

C. if it falls within the range of probability of the first husband [if the woman gave birth seven months after the death of the first husband and the pregnancy was recognized a month after the remarriage, it is in the range of probability of the first husband],

D. lo, it is the son of the first husband.

E. [If] it falls within the range of probability of the second husband [if the woman gave birth nine months after the death of the first husband and was not known to be pregnant four months after his death],

F. lo, it is the son of the second husband.

G. *If it is a matter of doubt whether it is nine months old, belonging to the first, or seven months, belonging to the second* [M. Yeb. 11:6B],

H. [if] the son hit this [man] and then went and hit that one, [or] cursed this one and then went and cursed that one—

I. he is exempt from punishment.

J. [But] if he hit both of them simultaneously [or] cursed both of them simultaneously, he is liable to punishment.

K. R. Judah says, "He who hits his father and someone else simultaneously is liable. He who curses his father and someone else simultaneously is liable."

L. *[If] she had children from the first husband and children from the second, they perform the rite of ḥaliṣah and do not enter into levirate marriage.*

M. *And so he too performs the rite of ḥaliṣah for them, but does not enter into the levirate marriage* [M. Yeb. 11:6C–E].

N. *If he had brothers from the first marriage and brothers from the second, not from the same mother,*

O. *he performs the rite of ḥaliṣah with them or enters into levirate marriage, and they for him: these perform the rite of ḥaliṣah and those enter into levirate marriage* [M. Yeb. 11:6F–H].

12:8 A. A woman concerning whom a bad name goes around—

B. the offspring are valid,

C. for children are in the presumptive paternity of [her] husband.

D. R. Judah says, "*[If] both of them are from a single watch,* [or] both of them are from a single paternal origin, *he takes a single portion*" [M. Yeb. 11:7U].

12:9 A. *The proper way to carry out the rite of ḥaliṣah is before three judges* [M. Yeb. 12:1A]—

B. and this is on condition that they know how to pronounce [Scriptures read in the rite].

C. R. Judah says, "Before five."

D. Said R. Leazar b. R. Simeon, M'ŚH W: "A woman performed the rite of *ḥaliṣah* before R. Ishmael when he was by himself, at night."

12:10 A. If she performed *ḥaliṣah* with a sandal which was damaged but held the larger part of the foot,

B. with a slipper which was torn but which covered the larger part of the foot,

C. with a sandal of cork, with a sandal of bast, with one of felt, and with the artificial leg of a cripple,

D. and with a support for the feet,

E. or with a leather sock—

F. and she who performs the rite of *ḥaliṣah* with a sandal which is too big—

G. whether he is standing or sitting or lying—

H. and she who performs the rite of *ḥaliṣah* with a blind man—

I. her performance of *ḥaliṣah* is valid.

J. [If she does so] with a sandal which is damaged and does not hold the larger part of the foot,

K. with a slipper which was torn and does not cover the larger part of the foot,

L with a hand-support,

M. with a sock of cloth,

N. and she who performs the rite of *ḥaliṣah* with a shoe which is too small—

O. her performance of *ḥaliṣah* is invalid.

12:11 A. Said R. Judah, "If R. Eliezer could see the wooden sandal of our own day, he would say concerning it, 'Lo, it is equivalent to a proper sandal for all purposes.'"

B. Said R. Simeon, "I came across a certain elder from Nisibis. I remarked to him, 'Was R. Judah b. Betera an authority for you?'

C. "He said to me, 'Yes. And he was constantly at my money-changing stall.'

D. "I said to him, 'Did you ever see him perform the rite of *ḥaliṣah*?'

E. "He said to me, 'Yes.'

F. "I said to him, 'With what did you see him do it, with a slipper or with a sandal?'

G. "He said to me, 'And do they perform the rite of *ḥaliṣah* with a slipper?'

H. "I said to him, 'If so, on what account did R. Meir rule that they perform the rite of *ḥaliṣah* with a slipper?'"

I. R. Jacob says in his name, "R. Meir conceded that they do not perform the rite of *ḥaliṣah* with a slipper."

12:12 A. *A minor who performed the rite of ḥaliṣah should perform the rite of ḥaliṣah again when she grows up.*

B. "*If she did not perform the rite of ḥaliṣah, her performance of ḥaliṣah is invalid,*" the words of R. Eliezer [M. Yeb. 12:4E–F].

C. And sages say, "If she did not perform the rite of *ḥaliṣah,* her performance of the rite of *ḥaliṣah* is valid."

D. [If] the straps of the slipper or of the sandal came out,

E. or [if] the greater part of the foot came out,

F. her performance of *ḥaliṣah* is invalid.

G. If he wanted to revert [and marry her as his levirate wife], he does not revert.

H. [If] she removed the foot but did not spit and did not pronounce the required formula, her performance of *ḥaliṣah* is valid [M. Yeb. 12:3].

I. If he wanted to revert, he reverts.

J. [If] she spit but did not pronounce the required formula and did no t remove the shoe, her performance of *ḥaliṣah* is invalid.

K. [If] she pronounced the required formula but did not spit and did not remove the shoe, she has done nothing whatsoever.

L. And he may retract.

12:13 A. A rite of *ḥaliṣah* done under a false assumption is valid.

B. [If] one performed the rite of *ḥaliṣah* with a woman—

C. he with proper intention, and she not with proper intention,

D. she with proper intention, and he not with proper intention,

E. her rite of performance of *ḥaliṣah* is invalid.

F. A rite of *ḥaliṣah* imposed by an Israelite court is valid. One imposed by a gentile court is invalid.

G. Among gentiles they bind him and instruct him, "Do precisely what Rabbi So-and-So tells you to do!"

12:14 A. They perform the rite of *ḥaliṣah* with a woman, even though they do not know her.

B. They execute the right of refusal with a woman, even though they do not know her.

C. A woman who claimed, "I have performed the rite of *ḥaliṣah*," brings evidence of her claim.

D. [If she claimed,] "I have exercised the right of refusal," she brings evidence of her claim.

12:15 A. At first they wrote out a writ of *ḥaliṣah*: She came before us and removed his shoe from his right foot and she spit before us spit which was visible, and she said, *Thus will be done,* etc. (Deut. 25:9).

B. R. Simeon says in the name of R. ʿAqiba, "The act of removing the shoe is essential, and the act of spitting is not essential [M. Yeb. 12:3]."

C. R. Simeon b. Eleazar says, "Since he did not want to raise up a name for his brother in Israel, let him come and take a name for himself instead of that name: *And his name will be called in Israel,* etc."

D. *It is a duty for the judges and not a duty for the disciples* [M. Yeb. 12:6L–M].

E. *R. Judah says, "It is a duty for all the bystanders to say, 'The man whose shoe has been removed! The man whose shoe has been removed!'"*

F. Said R. Judah, "MʿŚH W: We were in session before R. Ṭarfon, and he said to us, 'All of you respond: 'The man whose shoe has been removed! The man whose shoe has been removed!'"

13:1 A. Aforetimes they would write writs of refusal:

B. "She is not suitable for him or fond of him, nor does she wish to be married to him."

C. *The House of Hillel say, "In a court and not in a court"*—

D. but on condition that there should be three [suitable witnesses].

E. R. Yosé b. R. Judah and R. Eleazar b. R. Simeon say, "Even before two."

F. How is the duty of refusal appropriately carried out?

G. She testified, "I do not care for So-and-so, my husband. I reject the betrothal effected for me by my mother or my brothers."

H. Even if she is sitting in a palanquin and went to the one who betrothed her to him, and said to him, "I do not care for this man, So-and-So, my husband"—

I. there is no statement of refusal more powerful than that [statement].

J. R. Judah says, "Even if she went to buy something in a store and said to him [the store-keeper], 'I do not care for this man, So-and-So, my husband,' there is no statement of refusal more powerful than that statement."

K. More than this did R. Judah say, "Even if there are guests gathered around the table, and she said to them, 'I do not care for this man, So-and-So, my husband,' there is no statement of refusal more powerful than that statement."

13:2 A. A minor who effected a betrothal in her own behalf,

B. or who married herself off,

C. while her father was yet alive—

D. her betrothal is null, and her act of marriage is null [M. Yeb. 13:2A].

13:3 A. She who exercises the right of refusal against a man does not collect a marriage-contract.

B. [If] he gave her a writ of divorce, she has the right to collect a marriage-contract.

C. *R. Eliezer says, "The deed of a minor is null* [M. Yeb. 13:2F].

D. "He has no right to take over things which she finds nor to the fruit of her labor, nor to abrogate her vows.

E. "He does not inherit her and does not become unclean for her [if he is a priest and she should die].

F. "And she is not deemed to be his wife for any purpose whatsoever,

G. "except that she goes forth [from this relationship] by her exercise of the right of refusal."

H. R. Joshua says, "He has the right to take over things which she finds, and to the fruit of her labor, and to abrogate her vows.

I. "He does inherit her, and he does become unclean for her.

J. "And lo, she is deemed to be his wife for all purposes,

K. "except that she goes forth by her exercise of the right of refusal."

13:4 A. Said R. Ishmael, "I have reviewed all the rulings of sages, and I have found not a single one but R. Eliezer whose rulings are consistent with respect to minor girls.

B. "And I therefore prefer the ruling of R. Eliezer to the ruling of R. Joshua.

C. "For R. Eliezer rules consistently, and R. Joshua is inconsistent [at K]."

13:5 A. She who exercises the right of refusal against a man who took her back and who died either performs the rite of *ḥaliṣah* or enters into levirate marriage.

B. [If] he divorced her and then took her back to him and died, she either performs the rite of *ḥaliṣah* or enters into levirate marriage.

C. R. Eliezer says, "She performs the rite of *ḥaliṣah* but does not enter into levirate marriage,

D. "for she was prohibited to him for a single moment" [M. Yeb. 13:6A–B].

E. Sages concede to R. Eliezer in the case of *a minor whose father married her off, and whose husband divorced her, then took her back, and died,* that she performs the rite of *ḥaliṣah* and does not enter into levirate marriage,

F. for she has been prohibited to him for a single moment.

G. The reason is that the act of divorce is completely valid, but the act of remarriage is not completely valid [M. Yeb. 13:6E–F].

H. This ruling holds true in the case in which he divorced her while she was a minor and took her back while she was a minor.

I. But if he divorced her while she was a minor and took her back while she was a minor and she grew up with him and then he died,

J. then she performs the rite of *ḥaliṣah* or enters into levirate marriage.

K. R. Eliezer says, "She performs the rite of *ḥaliṣah* but does not enter into levirate marriage,

L. "for she was prohibited to him for a single moment."

M. *This is the general principle: In the case of a writ of divorce following the exercise of the right of refusal she is prohibited from returning to him* [M. Yeb. 13:4M]. *In a case of the exercise of the right of refusal after a writ of divorce, she is permitted to go back to him* [M. Yeb. 13:4N].

N. Rabban Simeon b. Gamaliel, R. Ishmael b. R. Yoḥanan b. Beroqa, and R. Joshua b. Qorḥa say, "One way or the other, since she has gone forth from him with a writ of divorce, she is prohibited from returning to him."

O. M'ŚH B: A certain girl was married while an orphan and then divorced, and then he took her back to him, and she exercised the right of refusal against him, and married another man. And he [the second husband] died.

P. And they came and asked R. Judah b. Baba, "What is the law as to her returning to the first husband?"

Q. And he ruled for them, "One way or the other, since she went forth from him [the first husband] with a writ of divorce, she is prohibited from returning to him [without regard to the intervening right of refusal]."

13:6 A. *Rabban* Simeon b. *Gamaliel says, "If she exercised the right of refusal, she exercised the right of refusal [without instruction to do so, and it is valid]. But if not, let her wait until she reaches maturity* [M. Yeb. 13:7L–M],

B. "and then he should consummate the marriage,

C. "and this one [the widow] goes forth on grounds of being the sister of his wife [M. Yeb. 13:7M]."

D. Two brothers married to two [sisters who were] orphans, one a minor and the other a deaf-mute—

E. the husband of the minor dies—

F. the deaf-mute goes forth through a writ of divorce.

G. And the minor waits until she grows up, and then she performs the rite of *ḥaliṣah.*

H. [If] the husband of the deaf-mute dies, the minor goes forth through a writ of divorce.

I. And the deaf-mute is prohibited [from entering into levirate marriage].

J. But if he [the levir in any case] had sexual relations with her, she goes forth with a writ of divorce and is permitted [to remarry].

13:7 A. *He who was married to two minor orphans and who died—*

B. *[If] the levir went and had sexual relations with the first, and then he went and had sexual relations with the second—*

C. both of them are prohibited to him.

D. *And so is the rule with two deaf-mutes* [M. Yeb. 13:9A–E].

E. *A minor and a deaf-mute—*

F. *[If] the levir went and had sexual relations with the minor, then he went and had sexual relations with the deaf-mute—*

G. *or one of the brothers had sexual relations with the deaf-mute—*

H. both of them are prohibited for him [M. 13:9F–I].

I. The deaf-mute goes forth with a writ of divorce, and the minor goes forth with a writ of divorce and with the rite of *ḥaliṣah.*

J. She waits until she grows up and then she performs the required rite of *ḥaliṣah.*

K. *A woman of sound senses and a deaf-mute—*

L. *the levir went and had sexual relations with the woman of sound senses, then he went and had sexual relations with the deaf-mute—*

M. *or one of his brothers went and had sexual relations with the deaf-mute—*

N. both of them are prohibited to him [M. Yeb. 13:10A–D].

O. The deaf-mute goes forth with a writ of divorce, and the woman of sound senses with a writ of divorce and a rite of *ḥaliṣah.*

P. *An adult and a minor—*

Q. *[If] the levir went and had sexual relations with the adult, then he went and had sexual relations with the minor—*

R. *or one of his brothers went and had sexual relations with the minor—*

S. *both of them are prohibited to him* [M. Yeb. 13:11A–D].

T. The minor goes forth with a writ of divorce, and the adult goes forth with a writ of divorce and the rite of *ḥaliṣah.*

U. *R. Eliezer says,* "In the case of all of them, *they instruct the minor to exercise the right of refusal against him*" [M. Yeb. 13:11H].

V. *A deceased childless brother's widow who claimed within thirty days of levirate marriage, "I have not yet had sexual relations with my levir"* [M Yeb. 13:12D]—

W. whether the levir claimed, "I did have sexual relations with her," or whether he said, "I did not have sexual relations with her,"

X. *they force him to perform the rite of ḥaliṣah for her* [M. Yeb. 13:12E].

Y. [*If she so claimed*] *after thirty days [of the levirate marriage had passed], they request him to perform the rite of ḥaliṣah for her* [M. Yeb. 13:12F–G].

Z. [If] she claims, "I have had sexual relations," and he claims, "I did not have sexual relations with her," lo, this one goes forth with a writ of divorce.

AA. [If] he claims, "I had sexual relations with her," and she claims, "I did not have sexual relations with him,"

BB. even though he retracts and claims, "I did not have sexual relations with her,"

CC. lo, this one goes forth with a writ of divorce.

DD. R. Judah says, "[If] she vowed not to enter into levirate marriage [with her husband's brother, should her husband die without children], even if this is in the lifetime of her husband [who then dies]—

EE. "they request [the levir, after the brothers has died childless] to perform the rite of *ḥaliṣah* with her" [M. Yeb. 13:13E–F].

FF. How does he put her away with a sign-language?

GG. He makes a sign and then gives to her her writ of divorce.

HH. A woman of sound senses married to a man of sound senses, who has a brother of sound senses—

II. a woman of sound senses married to a deaf-mute, who has a brother of sound senses—

JJ. he either performs the rite of *ḥaliṣah* or enters into levirate marriage.

KK. A woman of sound senses married to a man of sound senses who has a brother who is a deaf-mute—

LL. he marries her and does not put her away for all time.

MM. A woman of sound senses married to a deaf-mute, who has a brother who is a deaf-mute,

NN. a deaf-mute woman married to a man of sound senses who has a brother of sound senses—

OO. a deaf-mute woman married to a man of sound senses who has a brother of sound senses—

PP. a deaf-mute woman married to a deaf-mute man who has a brother of sound senses—

QQ. a deaf-mute woman married to a deaf-mute man who has a deaf-mute brother—

RR. [in all these cases] he marries the woman. And if he wants, he may put her away. If he wants to confirm the marriage, he confirms the marriage.

13:8 A. Two brothers who were deaf-mutes married to two sisters of sound senses [M. Yeb. 14:3B]—

B. or to two sisters who were deaf-mutes [M. Yeb. 14:3A]—

C. *or two sisters, one of sound senses and one a deaf-mute,*

D. *and so: two sisters who were deaf-mutes married to two brothers of sound senses—*

E. *or two brothers who were deaf-mutes,*

F. *or two brothers, one of sound senses and one a deaf-mute* [M. Yeb. 14:3C–F]—

G. and so: two brothers, one of sound senses and one a deaf-mute, married to two sisters, one a deaf-mute and one of sound senses—

H. a deaf-mute married to a man of sound senses and a woman of sound senses married to a deaf-mute—

I. neither the rite of *ḥaliṣah* nor levirate marriage applies here [M. Yeb. 14:3G].

J. But the [levir's] wife remains with him.

K. And the other goes forth as the sister of his wife.

L. *But if the women were unrelated to one another, he takes them in marriage.*

M. *If he wanted to put her away, he puts her away* [M. Yeb. 14:3H–J].

N. And if he wanted to confirm the marriage, he confirms the marriage.

14:1 A. The woman who said, "My husband has divorced me," [or] "My levir has performed the rite of *ḥaliṣah* with me,"

[or] "My levir has entered into levirate marrage with me and then died"—

B. lo, this woman is not believed.

C. All those who are not believed to testify concerning a woman [M. Yeb. 15:4A]—she too is not believed to testify concerning them.

D. *[If] one witness says, "He has died," and one witness says, "He has not died,"*

E. *a woman says, "He has died," and a woman says, "He has not died,"*

F. *lo, this one should not remarry* [M. Yeb. 15:5E–G].

G. R. Menaḥem b. R. Yosé says, "[If] one witness says, 'He has died,' and she remarried, and another witness came along and said, 'He has not died,' lo, this woman should not go forth [M. Yeb. 15:4D].

H. "But if to begin with one witness says, 'He has died,' and one witness says, 'He has not died,'

I. "a woman says, 'He has died,' and a woman says, 'He has not died,'

J. "even though he has she has remarried, she must go forth."

K. If one woman says, "He has died," and two women say, "He has not died," lo, the two women are deemed equivalent to one man.

L. R. Neḥemiah says, "In any situation in which the sages have declared valid the testimony of a woman as equivalent to the testimony of a single man, all things follow the number of opinions."

M. Two women [who contradict] one woman are like two male witnesses [who contradict] a single male witness.

N. If two witnesses say, "He has died," and a hundred say, "He has not died," lo, the hundred are deemed equivalent [merely] to the two witnesses.

14:2 A. *[If] a man betrothed one of five girls, and it is not known which one of them he betrothed, and each of them says, "Me did he betrothe"* [M. Yeb. 15:7E–F]—

B. [if] he made a purchase from one of five men, and it is not known from which of them he made the purchase, and each and every one of them says, "From me did he make the purchase"—

C. Said R. Simeon b. Leazar, "R. Ṭarfon and R. 'Aqiba did not dispute concerning a man who betrothed one of five girls, and it is not known which of them he betrothed, that he deposits the proceeds of the marriage-contract among them and takes his leave.

D. "Concerning what did they dispute? Concerning a case in which he had actually had sexual relations.

E. "And they did not dispute concerning a case in which he made a purchase from one of five people, and it is not known from which one of them he made the purchase, that he deposits the proceeds of the purchase among them and takes his leave.

F. "Concerning what did they dispute? Concerning a case in which he stole [the object]."

G. R. Ṭarfon concedes in the case in which a man says to two, "I stole a *maneh* from one of you, but it is not known from which one of you I stole it,"

H. or, "The father of one of you deposited a *maneh* with me, and it is not known to me the father of which one of you it was,"

I. that he gives a *maneh* to this one and a *maneh* to that one, since he himself confessed the matter on his own."

14:3 A. The woman whose husband went overseas—

B. and whom they came and told, "Your husband died,"

C. and he had a brother, who entered into levirate marriage with her, and [the levir] died—

D. and afterward her husband returned home—

E. he [the husband] is prohibited from marrying her [M. Yeb. 10:1] but permitted to marry her co-wife,

F. he is prohibited from marrying her, but permitted to marry the wife of his brother [=E].

G. The woman who went—she and her husband—overseas,

H. and who came home and said, "My husband died,

I. "and the elder [the husband's father] was here in the country, and he too has died"—

J. lo, this one is not believed [to force her mother-in-law into levirate marriage with her late father-in-law's brother, M. Yeb. 15:4A].

K. The woman who went—she and her husband—overseas,

L. and came and said, "My husband has died"—

M. she is permitted [to remarry] but her co-wife is prohibited [from remarrying] [M. Yeb. 15:4A, 15:6].

N. R. Eliezer says, "Since she is permitted, her co-wife also is permitted."

O. *If they entered into levirate marriage and the levirs died, they are prohibited from remarrying.*

P. *R. Eliezer says, "Since they have been permitted to the levirs, they are not permitted to anyone"* [M. Yeb. 16:2I].

Q. Two women—this one has witnesses [to the effect that her husband has died] and children, and that one has no witnesses and no children [M. Yeb. 16:2E–H]—

R. both of them are permitted [to remarry].

14:4 A. [If] one fell into a lion's pit, they do not give testimony concerning him [in the assumption that he has died].

B. [If] he fell into a furnace of fire, they do give testimony concerning him [in the assumption] that he has died.

C [If] he was crucified, they do not give testimony concerning him [that he has died].

D. [If] he was mortally wounded, they do give testimony concerning him [that he has died].

E. R. Simeon b. Leazar says, "He can be healed and live."

F. [If] he fell into a pit full of snakes or scorpions, they give testimony concerning him [that he has died].

G. R. Judah b. Beterah says, "They scruple, lest he be [take account of the possibility that he is] a wizard."

H. If he fell into an oil-vat or one of wine, they give testimony concerning him.

I. R. Aḥa says, "[If it is one] of oil, they give testimony concerning him. [If it is one] of wine, they do not give testimony concerning him."

J. Eleazar b. Mahaba'i says, "They give testimony on the basis of a mole [that this is a sign that it is the deceased]."

K. [If one hears], "So-and-So is dead," "So-and-So is lost," "So-and-so is frightened to death," "So-and-so is not in the world," "There is nothing whatsoever left of so-and-so, so his wife may remarry"—they do not accept testimony that so-and-so really has died.

14:5 A. *"[If] he fell into water, whether in sight of shore or not within sight of shore, his wife is prohibited,"* the words of R. Meir [M. Yeb. 16:4A–B].

B. And sages say, "[If it is] within sight of shore, she is permitted [to remarry]. [If it is] not within sight of shore, his wife is prohibited from remarrying. For a wave may have picked him up and thrown him back onto dry land."

C. Said R. ʿAqiba, "When I was traveling on the sea, I saw a ship struggling in the waves, and I was saddened for the fate of a disciple of sages who was on board. And when I came to Caesarea-Mazaca in Cappodocia, I saw him in session and asking questions of law before me.

"I said to him, 'My son, how did you escape from the ocean?'

"He said to me, 'One wave tossed me to the next, and the next to the next, until I came up on dry land.'

"I said, 'How great are the words of sages. For they have said:

"'*If it is within sight of shore, his wife is permitted to remarry. If it is not within sight of shore, his wife is permitted*'" [M. Yeb. 16:4A–B].

14:6 A. Said Rabbi, MʿŚH B: "Two men were fishing with traps in the Jordan. And one of them went into an underwater cave of fish. His fellow waited for him long enough for him to have died through drowning and then reported the matter in his home.

B. "At dawn the sun came up, and the man [trapped in the case] saw the way out of the cave and came home and found a mourning party in his house."

C. *Said R. Meir, MʿŚH B: "A certain man fell into a large cistern and came up after thirty days,"* [M. Yeb. 16:4C].

D. They said to him, "They do not adduce a miracle-story in evidence."

14:7 A. Even if one heard the sound of professional mourners mentioning his name among the deceased—

B. there is no more solid evidence than that.

C. [If] one heard an Israelite court declare, "So-and-so, son of So-and-so, is dead," or "has been killed," his wife may remarry.

D. [If] one heard royal bureaucrats (*commentarienses*) saying, "So-and-so, son of So-and-so, is dead," or "has been slain"—his wife should not remarry.

E. *They permit a woman to remarry on the evidence of an echo* [M. Yeb. 16:6B].

F. MʿŚH Bʿ *A certain person stood on top of a mountain and said, "Mr.*

So-and-so, the son of So-and-so [M. Yeb. 16:6C] *has been bitten by a snake and died. And they went* [M. 16:6F–G] and found that his face was swollen up [so they did not recognize him], but they [nonetheless] permitted his wife to remarry.

G. *And in the case of a gentile, if he intended to give testimony, his testimony is not valid* [M. Yeb. 16:5D].

H. Abba Yudan of Ṣidon says, M'ŚH B: "A certain gentile and an Israelite were going along, and that certain gentile said, 'Oh woe for a certain Israelite who perished here, and I lamented and buried him here.'

I. "And the case came before sages, who permitted his wife to remarry."

J. Said Rabban Simeon b. Gamaliel, M'ŚH B: "A band of prisoners went to Antioch, and upon their return they said, 'Of our group only So-and-so, a Jew, was killed.' And the case came before sages, who permitted his wife to remarry."

14:8 A. ŠWB M'ŚH B: Sixty men went down to the fortress at Betar and not a single one of them came back. And the matter came before sages, who permitted their wives to remarry.

B. They give testimony concerning him [the deceased] only by mentioning his name and the name of his father, his name and the name of his town.

C. But if one said, "So and so has gone forth from such and such a town," and they searched in that town—

D. if only he went forth from that town, his wife may remarry.

14:9 A. M'ŚH B: Two were running after a gang and one of them grabbed an olive tree, and tore it off and drove off the gang and came back.

B. And he said to him, "Good for you, Lion."

C. He said to him, "How do you know about me, that I'm a lion. That's just what I'm called in my town—Yoḥanan b. Yonatan, Lion of the town of Shaḥara.

D. Three days later the man [Yoḥanan] got sick and died, and [on the testimony of the man who knew his name and the name of his village], they permitted his wife to remarry.

14:10 A. They do not cross-examine witnesses in matters concerning wives' [remarrying].

B. R. Ṭarfon and R. 'Aqiba say, "They do cross-examine witnesses in matters concerning wives."

C. M'ŚH B: A certain party came before R. Ṭarfon to give testimony concerning a woman [that her husband had died so] she may remarry.

D. He said to him, "My son, how do you know the testimony for this woman?"

E. He said to him, "Rabbi, he was with us on a caravan, and a robber-band fell on us, and he grabbed the branch of a fig-tree and tore it off and drove the gang away.

F. "And I said to him, 'I congratulate you, Lion!'

G. "He said to me, 'Well have you said! You guessed my name. That's just what I'm called in my village, Yoḥanan b. Yonatan, the lion of the town of Shaḥara.'"

H. He [Ṭarfon] said to him, "Well said, my son: Yonatan b. Yoḥanan, the lion of the town of Shaḥara."

I. He said to him, "No, Rabbi. It was Yoḥanan b. Yonatan, the lion of the town of Shaḥara.

J. He said to him, "But did you not just say, Yonatan b. Yoḥanan, of the town of Shaḥara, a lion?"

K. He said to him, "But his name was Yoḥanan b. Yonatan of the town of Shaḥara."

L. So R. Ṭarfon cross-examined him three times, and each time his testimony came out just as before.

M. And he permitted the wife to remarry on the strength of his testimony.

N. From that time forth they became accustomed to cross-examine witnesses in matters concerning women.

O. *Said to them R. 'Aqiba, "When she will be an inn-keeper-woman, she will be believed too*" [M. Yeb. 16:7].

KETUBOT

1:1 A. On what account did they rule, *A virgin is married on Wednesday* [M. Ket. 1:1A]?

B. *So that if he had a complaint against [her] virginity, he goes to court early [on the next morning, when it is in session].*

C. If so, she should [just as well] be married after the Sabbath [on Sunday].

D. But because the husband does his preparations [for the wedding-feast] through the [three] weekdays, they arranged that he should marry her on Wednesday.

E. From the time of the danger [Bar Kokhba's War] and thereafter, they began the custom of marrying her on Tuesday,

F. and sages did not stop them.

G. [If] he wanted to marry her on Monday, they do not listen to him.

H. But if it is on account of constraint [a death in the family], it is permitted.

I. On what account do they keep the husband apart from the bride on the night of the Sabbath for the first act of sexual relations?

J. Because he makes a bruise.

K. On what account did they rule, *A widow is married on Thursday* [M. Ket. 1:1A]?

L. For if he should marry her on any day of the week, he may leave her and go back to work.

M. So they arranged that he should marry her on Thursday, so that he should remain away from work for three successive days,

N. Thursday, the eve of the Sabbath [Friday], and the Sabbath—three days away from work.

O. He turns out to take pleasure with her for three days running.

1:2 A. *An adult male who had sexual relations with a minor female,*

B. *and a minor male who had sexual relations with an adult female,*

C. *and a girl injured by a blow [so that her signs of virginity are destroyed]*—

D. *their marriage-contract [for a marriage] to another is two hundred [zuz]* [M. Ket. 1:3A–D].

E. In the name of R. Judah b. 'Agra' they said, "Who is a minor female and who is a minor male?

F. "A minor male is younger than nine years and one day old.

G. "A minor female is younger than three years and one day old."

H. He who marries into the priesthood and he who gives [his daughter in marriage] into it—

I. an arrangement which they arranged in court:

J. An Israelite girl married to a priest, or a priest-girl married to an Israelite—

K. one pays four hundred *zuz*.

1:3 A. A man of sound senses who married a deaf-mute girl or an idiot—

B. their marriage-contract is two hundred *zuz*,

C. for he wants to gain a hold on their possessions.

D. A deaf-mute or an idiot who married a woman of sound senses,

E. even though the deaf-mute went and became sound in his senses,

F. or the idiot regained his mind—

G. they [these women of sound senses] do not receive a marriage-contract.

H. [If after being healed] they went to confirm the marriage, they pay a *maneh* as the marriage-contract.

I. A gentile or a slave who had sexual relations with an Israelite girl,

J. even though the gentile went and converted,

K. the slave went and was freed,

L. they [the women] do not have a marriage-contract.

M. [If] they [the convert, the freed slave] wanted to confirm the marriage, they pay a *maneh* as the marriage-contract.

N. An Israelite who had sexual relations with a slave-girl or with a gentile woman,

O. even though the slave-girl went and was freed,

P. or the gentile-girl went and converted—

Q. they [the women] do not have a marriage contract..

R. [If] he wanted to confirm the marriage, he gives a *maneh* as the marriage contract.

S. An adult-woman and a barren woman—their marriage contract is two hundred *zuz*.

T. [If] she was married in the assumption that she is suitable and turned out to be barren, she has no marriage-contract.

U. [If] he wanted to confirm the marriage, he gives a *maneh* as the marriage-contract.

V. He who has sexual relations with a deaf-mute girl or with an idiot or with a mature woman or with a girl wounded by a blow—

W. they are not subject to a claim of virginity.

X. In the case of a blind woman or a barren woman, they are subject to a claim of virginity.

Y. Sumkhos said in the name of R. Meir, "A blind girl is not subject to a claim of virginity."

1:4 A. Said R. Judah, "In olden times in Judah they would investigate the character of the wedding, the groom, and the bride, three days before the wedding-celebration. But in Galilee they did not have that custom.

B. "In olden times in Judah they would put the bride and groom off by themselves for an hour before the wedding-celebration so that he should feel confident with her. But in Galilee they did not have that custom.

C. "In olden times in Judah they would appoint two best men, one on the side of the groom, and one on the side of the bride. And even so, they appointed them only for the marriage. But in Galilee they did not have that custom.

D. "In olden times in Judah the best men would sleep in the place in which the bride and groom were sleeping. But in Galilee they did not have that custom.

E. "Anyone who did not follow this custom has no claims against the virginity of the girl."

F. [If] he married her in the assumption that she was suitable and she turned out to have had prior sexual relations,

G. even though she was in private [with him],

H. [or] there are witnesses that she was not alone with him for sufficient time to have sexual relations,

I. the second has no claim of virginity against her.

J. Therefore the marriage-contract on his account is only *maneh.*

K. "The claim of virginity may be brought for thirty days," the words of R. Meir.

L. R. Yosé says, "If she was in private with him [it must be brought] forthwith. If she was not in private with him, [then it may be brought] even after thirty days."

1:5 A. He who accuses [his bride of having had sexual relations with another man before marriage], and his witnesses against her turn out to be conspirators—

B. he is scourged and pays four hundred *zuz* [to the accused woman].

C. And the conspirator-witnesses are taken out for stoning.

D. [If] she was an orphan, he is scourged, and her marriage-contract remains valid, and he pays her four hundred *zuz* [in addition to it].

E. And the conspirator-witnesses are taken out for stoning.

F. [If] he did not tell the witnesses to bear witness, but they came along on their own and testified against the girl [and they turned out to be conspirators]—

G. he [the husband] is not scourged and does not pay her four hundred *zuz*.

H. But the conspirator-witnesses are taken out for stoning.

I. [If] she committed fornication when she was a girl, and after she had matured, he accused her [of having done so],

J. he is not scourged and does not pay four hundred *zuz*.

K. And she or the conspirator-witnesses against her are then taken out for stoning.

1:6 A. *[If] she was pregnant,*

B. *[and] they said to her, "What is the character of this foetus,"*

C. *[and she said], "It is from Mr. So-and-so, and he is a priest,"*

D. *Rabban Gamaliel and R. Eliezer say, "She is believed.*

E. "For this is the sort of a testimony which a woman is valid to give."

F. *R. Joshua says, "She is not believed"* [M. Ket. 1:9].

G. Said R. Joshua to them, "Do you not concede in the case of a girl taken captive by gentiles, who is subject to testimony that she was taken captive, and who says, 'I am pure,' that she is *not* believed?"

H. They said to him, "No. If you have stated that rule in connection with a woman taken captive, who is subject to witnesses as to her having been taken captive, will you say so of this one, who is not subject to witnesses at all?"

I. He said to them, "And what greater evidence is there than this—that her belly is up there between her teeth!"

J. They said to him, "But gentiles are deemed unscrupulous as to prohibited sexual relations, [but Israelites are not]."

K. He said to them, "There is no one appointed as a watchman over prohibited sexual relations [even for Israelites]."

L. Under what circumstances [do the sages accept her testimony]? In the case of testimony which pertains to her own person.

M. But as to the offspring, all concede [Gamaliel and Eliezer to Joshua], that it is held to be of unknown fatherhood [*shetuqi* (M. Qid.1:1)].

2:1 A. Witnesses who said," We testify about So-and-so, that he is the son of a divorcee, or the son of a woman who has performed the rite of *ḥaliṣah*, of a Samaritan, of a *Netin*, or a *Mamzer*"—

B. [if] before their testimony was cross-examined in court, they said, "We were joking,"

C. lo, they are believed.

D. If after their testimony was cross-examined in court, they said, "We are joking," they are not believed.

E. This is the general principle of the matter:

F. Witnesses who testified to declare someone unclean or clean, to bring someone near or to put someone afar, to prohibit or to permit, to exempt or to render liable—

G. [if] before their testimony was cross-examined in court, they said, "We are joking," lo, these are believed.

[If] after their testimony was cross-examined in court, they said, "We are joking," they are not believed.

H. Greater is the power of a writ [document] than the power of witnesses, and [greater is the power of] witnesses than the power of a writ.

I. Greater is the power of a writ, for a writ [of divorce] removes a woman from the domain of her husband, which is not the case with witnesses.

J. Greater is the power of witnesses, for witnesses who said, "So-and-so has died,"—his wife may remarry. But if it was written in a writ, "So-and-so has died," his wife may not remarry.

J. If they said, "What is written in this document we in fact had heard but forgot," his wife may remarry.

L. A man may write down his testimony in a document and give testimony on the strength of that document and continue even a hundred years after [the date of the document].

M. Greater is the power of a document than the power of money, and greater is the power of money than the power of a document.

N. For a document allows one to collect from indentured [mortgaged] property, which is not the case with money.

O. Greater is the power of money, for money serves for the redemption of things which have been given as Valuations and as *ḥerem* [to the sanctuary], things which have been sanctified, and second tithe, which is not the case with a document.

P. Greater is the power of a document and of money than the power of possession, and greater is the power of possession than the power of a document and money.

Q. Greater is the power of a document and money, for a document or money serve to acquire a Hebrew slave, which is not the case with [mere] possession.

R. Greater is the power of possession, for if one sold a man ten fields, as soon as he takes possession of one of them, he has acquired ownership of all of them.

S. But if he gave him only the price of one of them, or wrote him a document only for one of them, he has acquired ownership of that field alone.

2:2 A. The two hundred *zuz* owing to a virgin, the *maneh* owing to a widow, the compensation for damages and half-damages, double payment, and four-and-five-times payment—

B. all of them, even though they are not written in a document, do people collect from indentured property.

C. The woman who said, "I am married," and then went and said, "I am not married" is believed.

D. For the mouth which prohibited is the mouth which permitted [M. Ket. 2:5A–B].

E. [If] she said, "I was taken captive, but I am pure, and I have witnesses that I am pure," they do not say, "Let us wait until the witnesses come and render her permitted." But they permit her [to return to her husband] forthwith [M. Ket. 2:5E–F].

F. If once she has been permitted, witnesses come and say, "She was taken captive," lo, this one should not remarry.

G. [If they say,] "She was taken captive and was contaminated," even though she has children, she should go forth [M. Ket. 2:5I].

H. One witness says, "She was taken captive and has been contaminated,"

I. and one witness says, "She was taken captive but is pure"—

J. One woman says, "She was taken captive and is contaminated,"

K. and one woman says, "She was taken captive but is pure"—

L. lo, this one should not remarry. But if she remarried, she should not go forth.

M. *Two women who were taken captive* [M. Ket. 2:6H]—

N. This one says, "I am unclean, but my girl-friend is clean,"—

O. she is believed.

P. [If] she says, "I am clean, and my girl-friend is unclean," she is not believed.

Q. "I and my girl-friend are unclean"—she is believed concerning herself, but she is not believed concerning her girl-friend.

R. "I and my girl-friend are clean"—she is believed concerning her girl-friend but she is not believed concerning herself [M. Ket. 2:6E].

S. *And so too with two men* [M. Ket. 2:7A]: This one says, "My friend is a priest," and this one says, "My friend is a priest,"—they give them [heave-offering] [M. Ket. 2:7E].

T. But as to confirming that they are priests [for genealogical purposes], they are not believed until there will be three of them,

U. so that there will be two giving testimony about this one, and two giving testimony about that one.

2:3 A. *They raise to the priesthood* [people thought to be] Levites or

Israelites *on the strength of the testimony of a single witness* [M. Ket. 2:8C].

B. But they lower someone from the priesthood only on the evidence of two witnesses.

C. R. Judah says, "Just as they lower someone from the priesthood only on the evidence of two witnesses, so they raise someone to the priesthood only on the evidence of two witnesses" [M. Ket. 2:8A].

D. *R. Eleazar said, "Under what circumstances? When there are those who cast doubt about the matter. But when there is none who casts doubt about the matter, they do raise someone to the priesthood on the evidence of a single witness"* [M. Ket 2:8B].

E. How does one cast doubt about the matter?

F. If they said, "How does Mr. So-and-so jump up into the priesthood, who never raised his hands to give the priestly blessing in his entire life, who never took his share [of heave-offering] in his entire life"—this is not a suitable casting of doubt.

G. [If they said], "He is the son of a divorcee or of a woman who has performed the rite of *ḥaliṣah,* of a Samaritan, a *Netin,* or a *Mamzer,*" lo, this constitutes casting doubt about the matter.

H. Rabbi raised someone to the priesthood on the strength of a single witness.

I. R. Yosé raised someone to the priesthood on the strength of a single witness.

J. A bad story spread around town. Said R. Yosé, "This tale-bearing is no proof. But if anyone has grounds for raising doubt about the matter, let him come and present them."

K. *Rabban Simeon b. Gamaliel says in the name of R. Simeon, son of the Prefect, "They raise someone to the priesthood on the evidence of a single witness* [M. Ket. 2:8C], and not only on the evidence of a single witness, but on the evidence of a woman;

L. "and not that the woman comes to court, but if she merely says, 'Let them give him heave-offering,' [that is adequate evidence]."

3:1 A. There are two presumptive grounds for a person's being deemed to be in the priesthood in the Land of Israel: Raising up hands [in the priestly benediction], and sharing heave-offering at the threshing floor.

B. And in Syria: Up to the point at which the agents announcing the new moon reach, the raising of hands in the priestly benediction [constitutes adequate grounds], but not sharing heave-offering at the threshing-floor.

C. Babylonia is in the same status as Syria.

D. R. Simeon b. Eleazar says, "Also in Alexandria at the outset, because there was a court there."

E. Rabban Simeon b. Gamaliel says, "Just as eating heave-offering is a presumptive evidence that a person is a priest in the case of the dividing of shares at the threshing floor, so is the first tithe a presumptive evidence that a person is a Levite in the case of the dividing of shares at the threshing floor."

F. But a person who takes his share [of heave-offering] in court [at the division of an estate] has no presumption that he is a priest.

3:2 A. All are believed to give testimony about her, even her son, even her daughter—

B. except for her and her husband,

C. *for a man does not give testimony in his own behalf.*

D. *Said R. Zekhariah b. Haqqaṣab, " By this sanctuary! Her hand did not move from mine from the time that the gentiles entered Jerusalem until they left it"* [M. Ket. 2:9F–G].

E. But even so, he set aside a house for her by herself. She was supported by his property. But he never was alone with her except in the presence of her children.

3:3 A. A man is believed to say, "Father told me this family is unclean," "That family is clean," "We ate at the cutting off [ceremony marking the marriage of a man or woman to someone beneath his or her genealogical rank] of Mrs. So-and-so,"

B. "and that his teacher said to So-and-so, 'Go and immerse [to be clean for] your heave-offering,'" "We used to bring heave-offerings and tithes to So-and-so."

C. They are believed so far as allowing the giving of heave-offerings and tithes to So-and-so, but not to confirm him in the priesthood [for genealogical purposes].

D. Or [if he said], "Others brought him [heave-offering and tithes]"—they are not believed.

E. But if he was a gentile and converted, a slave and was freed, lo, these are not believed.

F. They are not believed to say, "I remember about So-and-so that he owes Mrs. So-and-so a *maneh*"—

G. and "Such-and-such a road crosses such-and-such a field"—

H. for this [right of way] is equivalent to property.

I. R. Yoḥanan b. Beroqah says, "They are believed."

J. Said R. Yoḥanan b. Beroqah, "A woman or a minor is believed to say, 'From here this stream went forth.'"

K. Under what circumstances?

L. When they gave testimony on the spot [about their own home-town].

M. But if they went forth and came back, they are not believed,

N. for they may have stated matters only because of enticement or fear.

3:4 A. All the same are men, women, slaves, and minors:

B. they are believed to say, "This place is unclean," and "This place is clean" [M. Ket. 2:10E].

C. R. Judah says, A little Israelite girl who was taken captive, even if she is ten years old, lo, she remains in her status of holiness, and her marriage-contract remains valid [M. Ket. 3:2C]"

3:5 A. He who has sexual relations with a deaf-mute, or with an idiot, or with a mature woman, or with a woman injured by a blow [and so without a hymen]—

B. they do not receive a penalty.

C. A blind girl and a barren girl receive a penalty.

D. R. Neḥuniah b. Haqqaneh says, "*He who has sexual relations with his sister, with the sister of his father, with the sister of his mother, with the sister of his wife, with the wife of his brother, with the wife of the brother of his father, or with a menstruating woman* [M. Ket. 3:1D]—they do not receive a penalty."

E. And so did R. Neḥuniah b. Haqqaneh say, "The Day of Atonement is equivalent to the Sabbath as to payment."

3:6 A. All the same are the one who rapes and the one who seduces [both of them pay fifty *sheqels* as a fine].

B. What is the difference between him who rapes and him who seduces?

C. *The one who rapes pays compensation for pain, and the one who seduces does not pay compensation for pain* [M. Ket. 3:4E–F].

D. R. Simeon says, "Neither one nor the other pays compensation for pain,

E. "for in the end, [it is so] for all women, [whether raped or seduced, to suffer pain when they lose their virginity]."

F. They said to him, "The girl who willingly has sexual relations is not the same as the girl who unwillingly has sexual relations."

G. Even though they said, *The one who rapes pays the penalty immediately* [M. Ket. 3:4G],

H. but if he should put her away, he pays nothing [in addition].

I. R. Yosé b. R. Judah says, "He gives a *maneh* as her marriage-contract."

J. Even though they said, *The one who seduces, if he should divorce her, pays a pentalty* [M. Ket. 3:4H],

K. but the compensation for her shame and her injury he pays forthwith.

L. What is the difference between paying forthwith and paying later on? As to paying forthwith, if the girl dies, her father inherits [her estate, inclusive of the fines]. But if he pays later on, if she should die, her husband inherits [her estate].

3:7 A. All the same are the one who rapes and the one who spreads a bad story about a girl, who divorced [the woman they have raped or maligned, respectively]:

B. they force him to bring her back.

C. [If] they are priests, they incur forty stripes.

D. All the same are the one who rapes and the one who seduces—

E. either she or her father is able to dissent [from the required marriage], since it says, *And if refusing, her father shall refuse* [Ex. 22:16], and it further says, *And she shall be a wife for him* (Deut. 22:29) —with her consent.

F. Him do you force, but you do not force the levir.

3:8 A. "A minor-girl, from the age of one day until she will produce two pubic hairs, is subject to the right of sale and does not receive a fine," the words of R. Meir.

B. For R. Meir did rule, "*In any situation in which there is a right of sale, there is no fine. And in every situation in which there is a fine, there is no right of sale*" [M. Ket. 3:8A].

C. And sages say, "A minor girl from three years and one day of age until she will have completely matured does receive a fine [even though her father has the right of sale]."

4:1 A. Greater is the power of the husband than that of the father, and [greater is] the power of the father than that of the husband.

B. Greater is the power of the husband, for the husband disposes of the fruit of her labor during her lifetime, which is not so for the father [M. Ket. 4:4D].

4:2 A. Greater is the power of the father,

B. for the husband *is liable to maintain her, to redeem her [if she is taken captive], and to bury her* [M. Ket. 4:4F],

C. and, in a place in which it is customary to say a lamentation, to arrange for a lamentation for her,

D. which is not incumbent on the father.

4:3 A. Greater is the power of a wife than the power of the sister-in-law [the deceased, childless brother's wife],

B. and [greater is the power of] the sister-in-law than of the wife.

C. Greater is the power of the wife, for the wife eats heave-offering as soon as she enters the marriage-canopy,

D. even if she has not yet had sexual relations with the husband,

E. which is not the case for the sister-in-law.

F. Greater is the power of the sister-in-law,

G. for he who has sexual relations with his sister-in-law [deceased, childless brother's widow], whether inadvertently or intentionally, whether under constraint or willingly,

H. even if she is in her father's house,

I. has acquired her as his wife,

J. which is not the case with a wife.

4:4 A *[If] the father went along* with her agents or *with the agents of the husband.*

B. *or if the agents of the father went along with the agents of the husband* [M. Ket. 4:5C],

C. if she had a courtyard along the way and went in and spent the night in it,

D. or if [the husband] entered the marriage-canopy not for the purpose of consummating the marriage,

E. and she died,

F. even though her marriage-contract is with her husband, her father inherits it.

G. *If the father gave her over to the agents of the husband, or the agents of the father gave her over to the agents of the husband* [M. Ket. 4:5B–D],

H. or if she had a courtyard on the way and went in there and spent the night in it,

I. or if she entered the marriage-canopy for the purpose of consummating the marriage,

J. and she died,

K. even though her marriage-contract is with her father, her husband inherits it.

L. Under what circumstances?

M. In the case of her marriage-contract.

N. But as to heave-offering, she does not eat heave-offering until she enters the marriage-canopy [M. Ket. 5:3].

4:5 A. [If] she was taken captive, he is not liable to redeem her.

B. Under what circumstances?

C. In the case of a girl taken captive by a government official.

D. If she was taken captive by a thug, he redeems her.

E. If [then] he wants to confirm the marriage, he confirms it. If not, he puts her away and pays her a *maneh* as her marriage-contract [M. Ket. 4:8–9C]

F. [If] she was taken captive after her husband's death, the levirs are not liable to redeem her.

G. And not only so, but even if she is taken captive while her husband was alive, and afterward her husband died, the levirs are not liable to redeem her.

H. [If] she was maintained by his property and required medical attention, lo, that is equivalent to any other aspect of her support [M. Ket. 4:9D–E].

I. Rabban Simeon b. Gamaliel says, "Medical care of fixed cost—she is healed at the expense of her marriage-contract. But as to medical care of unlimited cost—lo, that is equivalent to any other aspect of her support."

J. If there were years of famine, [if] he then said to her, "Take your writ of divorce and your marriage-contract, go and feed yourself," he has that right.

4:6 A. *[If] he did not write for her [in her marriage-contract], "Male children which you will have from me will inherit the proceeds of your marriage-contract in addition to their share with their older brothers," he is liable.*

For this is in all events an unstated condition imposed by the court [on all marriage-contracts] [M. Ket. 4:10].

B. All provinces wrote their marriage-contracts as did the Jerusalemites [M. Ket. 4:12D].

4:7 A. A man marries a woman on condition of not having to maintain her and of not having to support her.

B. And not only so, but he may make an agreement with her that she maintain and support him and teach him Torah.

C. M'ŚH B: Joshua, the son of R. 'Aqiba married a woman and made an agreement with her that she maintain and support him and teach him Torah.

D. They were years of famine. They [the husband and wife] went and divided their property.

E. She began to complain against him to sages.

F. And when he came to court, he said to them, "She is more credible to me than any man."

G. She said to them, "Most assuredly did he covenant with me thus."

H. Sages said to her, "Nothing validly follows the agreement."

4:8 A. It is a religious duty to support the daughters, and one need not say, the sons.

B. R. Yoḥanan b. Beroqah says, "It is an obligation to support the daughters."

4:9 A. Hillel the Elder made an exegesis of ordinary language [of legal documents, and not merely of the text of the Torah].

B. When the Alexandrians would betrothe a woman, afterward someone else would come along and grab her right out of the market.

C. Such an incident came before sages, and they considered declaring the children to be *mamzers.*

D. Hillel the elder said to them, "Show me the marriage-contract of your mothers."

E. They showed them to him, and written in it was the following language:

F. "When you will enter my house, you will be my wife in accord with the law of Moses and Israel" [but not before that time, on the strength of which he decided that they were not *mamzers*].

4:10 A. R. Meir expounded, "He who receives a field [as a share-cropper] from his field, and once he had acquired position of it, he neglected it—

B. "they make an estimate of how much it is suitable to produce and he pays the sum to him.

C. "For thus does he write him, 'If I neglect and I do not work it, I shall pay you from the best produce.'"

4:11 A. R. Judah expounded, "A man brings in behalf of his wife all the offerings which she owes,

B. "even if she ate prohibited fat, or even if she desecrated the Sabbath.

C. "For thus does he write for her in her marriage-contract, 'And obligations which you owe will be mine from before up to now.'

D. "If she gave him a quittance for part of her marriage-contract, she gave him a quittance for the whole.

E. "For thus does she write him, 'Obligations which you owe will be mine from before up to now.'"

4:12 A. R. Joshua b. Qorḥa expounded, "He who lends money to his fellow should not exact a pledge greater than his debt.

B. "For thus does he [the borrower] write to him [in the document of loan].

C. "'You will be paid from my property, from property which I acquire from before up to now.'"

4:13 A. R. Yosé the Galilean expounded, "In a place in which they collect the marriage-contract as a loan, they collect it as a loan, and they do not collect the [full amount] of the marriage-contract.

B. "In a place in which they double the sum of the marriage-contract, they collect only half."

4:14 A. The father of the groom who has made a pledge for the marriage-contract of his daughter-in-law,

B. if there are available possessions belonging to the son, they collect the marriage-contract from the property of the son.

C. And if not, they collect from the property of the father.

D. [If] the father wrote over a house or a field as a surety for the marriage-contract of his daughter-in-law, one way or the other, they collect from them.

E. He who went abroad, and whom they told, "Your son has died,"

F. [and] who went and wrote over all his property as a gift, and afterward who was informed that his son was alive—

G. his deed of gift is valid.

H. R. Simeon b. Menassia says, "His deed of gift is not valid, for if he had known that his son was alive, he would never have made such a gift."

4:15 A. If he was sick in bed, and they said to him, "To whom will your property go," and he said to them, "I had imagined that I should have a son. Now that I do not have a son, my property goes to So-and-so,"

B. and afterward he was informed that he had a son—he has not said anything [to annul the gift].

C. If he was sick in bed, and they said to him, "To whom will your property go?" and he said to them, "I had imagined that my wife would be pregnant, but now that she is not pregnant, my property goes to So-and-so,"

D. and afterward he was informed that his wife was pregnant—

E. he has said nothing.

4:16 A. A proselyte who died, and whose property Israelites took over [assuming he had no Israelite heirs],

B. and afterward it became known that he had had sons, or that his wife was pregnant—

C. they all are liable to restore [to his legitimate heirs the property they took over].

D. [If] they returned it all, and the sons died, or his wife miscarried,

E. he who took possession in the second-go-round has acquired possession, but he who had taken possession in the first go-round has not acquired possession.

4:17 A. The daughters, whether they were married before they reached full maturity, or whether they reached full maturity before they were married, lose their right to sustenance, but do not lose their right to dowry.

B. R. Simeon b. Eleazar says, "Also: they lose their rights to a dowry."

C. What do they do?

D. They hire husbands for themselves who collect their dowry for them.

4:18 A. "All the same is landed property and movable property: they are siezed for the support of the wife and daughters," the words of Rabbi.

B. R. Eleazar b. R. Simeon says,"Landed property do sons remove from the possession of sons, and daughters from daughters, and daughters from sons, but not sons from daughters.

C. "Movable property do sons remove from the possession of sons, and daughters from daughters, and sons from daughters, but not daughters from sons."

D. Whether the father indentured the property while he was alive, or whether the heirs did so after the death of the father, they are not seized for the matter of the marriage-contract.

E. But for maintenance they do collect from that property.

5:1 A. Reaching maturity is equivalent to a demand [on the part of the prospective husband that the betrothed prepare herself for marriage] [M. Ket. 5:2A].

B. [And] they give her twelve months in which to prepare for marriage.

C. If she was a minor, either she or her father can dissent.

D. *R. Ṭarfon says, "They give her all her food as heave-offering"* [M. Ket. 5:2F]. Under what circumstances?

E. At the stage of betrothal.

F. But at the stage of marriage, R. Ṭarfon concedes that they give her half in unconsecrated food and half in heave-offering.

G. Under what circumstances?

H. In the case of the priest-girl married to a priest.

I. But in the case of an Israelite girl married to a priest, all concur that they give her all her food from unconsecrated produce.

J. R. Judah b. Betera says, "Two-thirds heave-offering, and one-third unconsecrated food."

K. R. Judah says, "She sells the heave-offering [to priests] and purchases unconsecrated food with the proceeds."

L. Rabban Simeon b. Gamaliel says, "In any situation in which heave-offering is mentioned, one gives [in heave-offering] twice the amount of unconsecrated produce."

M. *This is the first Mishnah.*

N. Our sages said, "*The* Israelite *girl does not eat heave-offering until she enters the marriage-canopy* [M. Ket. 5:3F–G], and the levirate sister-in-law until she actually has sexual relations.

O. "If she dies, her husband inherits her."

P. Said R. Menaḥem b. Nappaḥ, in the name of R. Eliezer Haqqappar, M'ŚH B: "R. Ṭarfon betrothed three hundred girls to permit them to eat heave-offering, for the years were years of famine."

Q. And already did Yoḥanan b. Bagbag send to R Judah b. Betera in Nisibis, saying to him, "I heard about you that you rule, 'An Israelite girl betrothed to a priest eats heave-offering.'"

R. He sent back and said to him, "I was sure that you are an expert in the inner chambers of the law. But you don't even know how to construct an argument *a fortiori*! Now if in the case of a Canaanite slave-girl, sexual relations do not constitute an act of acquisition so that she may eat heave-offering, but a money-payment does constitute an act of acquisition so that she may eat heave-offering—

S. "an Israelite girl, for whom the act of sexual relations constitutes an act of acquisition so that she may eat heave-offering—logically the transfer of a money-payment should [also] constitute an act of acquisition sufficient for her to eat heave-offering!

T. "But what shall I do! For lo, sages have said, 'An Israelite girl who is betrothed does not eat heave-offering until she enters the marriage-canopy.

U. "'If she marries, her husband [nonetheless] inherits her estate.'"

5:2 A. What is the law as to providing food for the sister-in-law awaiting levirate marriage?

B. So long as the husband is obligated [having supported her in his lifetime], the levirs are obligated.

C. [If] the husband is not obligated, the levirs are not obligated.

D. Who controls the fruit of her labor?

E. If she is supported by them, lo, they belong to them, and if not, lo, they remain her own possession.

F. What she inherits and what she finds, one way or the other, lo, they belong to her.

5:3 A. *He who sanctifies to the Temple the fruit of his wife's labor* [M. Ket. 5:4A]—

B. lo, this one provides food for her from it [the fruit of her labor].

C. But the remainder is sanctified.

5:4 A. The kinds of work which a woman does for her husband—

B. seven basic categories of labor did they enumerate.

C. And the rest did not require enumeration [M. Ket. 5:5A–B].

D. *If she brought* slaves to him, whether on his account or on her account, *she does not spin or bake or do laundry* [M. Ket. 5:5C].

E. He may not force her to work for his son, daughter, his brothers, or her brothers, or to feed his cattle.

F. In a place in which it is not customary to do any one of these [listed at M. Ket. 5:5B], he cannot force her to do them.

G. R. Judah says, "Also: He cannot force her to work in flax, for it makes the mouth swell and cuts the lips."

5:5 A. If she took a vow not to give suck to her child—

B. The House of Shammai say, "She pulls her teats from his mouth."

C. And the House of Hillel say, "He forces her to give suck to her child."

D. If she was divorced, however, they do not force her to give suck to him.

E. If her son recognized her [as his mother], they give her a wage, and she gives suck to him,

F. because of the danger [to the child's life].

G. The husband cannot force his wife to give suck to the child of his fellow.

H. And the wife cannot force her husband to permit her to give such suck to the child of her girl-friend.

5:6 A. *He who takes a vow not to have sexual relations with his wife—*

B. *the House of Shammai say, "[He may remain married] for two weeks,*

C. "equivalent to the period of uncleanness after the birth of a female."

D. *And the House of Hillel say, "One week,*

E. "equivalent to the period of uncleanness after the birth of a male,

F. "and equivalent to the menstrual period" [M. Ket. 5:6A–C].

G. [If it lasts] longer than this, he must put her away and pay off her marriage-contract.

H. *Workers [must engage in sexual relations] twice a week.*

I. If they were employed in another town, then they must have sexual relations at least once a week.

J. Ass-drivers must have sexual relations once in two weeks, *camel drivers once in thirty days, sailors once in six months* [M. Ket. 5:6F].

5:7 A. *She who rebels against her husband, etc.* [M. Ket. 5:7A]—

B. this is the first Mishnah.

C. Our rabbis ordained that a court should warn her four or five consecutive weeks, twice a week.

D. [If she persists] any longer than that, even if her marriage-contract is a hundred *maneh,* she has lost the whole thing.

E. All the same is the betrothed girl and the woman awaiting levirate marriage,

F. and even a menstruating woman, or a sick woman.

5:8 A. *He who supports his wife by means of a third party* [M. Ket. 5:8A]—

B. all of them are measured out by Italian measure.

C. Even a menstruating woman, and even a sick woman, and even a sister-in-law awaiting levirate marriage [receive the support specified at M.

Ket. 5:8].

D. He gives her a cup, a plate, a bowl, an oil-cruse, a lamp, and a wick.

E. She has no claim for wine, for the wives of the poor do not drink wine.

F. She has no claim for a pillow, for the wives of the poor do not sleep on pillows.

5:9 A. The excess of food [beyond her needs] goes back to him. The excess of worn-out clothing belongs to her.

B. If he gets rich she goes up with him, but if he becomes poor, she does not go down with him.

C. M'ŚH B: The sages awarded to the daughter of Naqdimon b. Gurion five hundred golden *denars* daily for a fund for spices, and she was only a sister-in-law awaiting levirate marriage.

D. But she cursed [them] and said, "So may you award for your own daughters!"

5:10 A. Said R. Eleazar b. R. Ṣadoq. "May I [not] see comfort, if I did not see her picking out pieces of barley from under the hoofs of horses in Akko.

B. "Concerning her I pronounced the following Scripture, *If you do not know, O most beautiful of women* (Song 1:8)."

6:1 A. *He who died and left sons and daughters—*

B. *when the property is abundant, the sons inherit and the daughters are fed and maintained* [from his estate] [M. Ket. 13:3].

C. How [do we interpret the statement,] "The sons inherit"?

D. We do not say, "If their father were alive, he would have given such-and-so to them." But we regard one as if he were the father present [for this purpose], and they give to them.

6:2 A. How [do we interpret the statement], "The daughters are fed and maintained"?

B. We do not say, "If their father were alive, he would have given such-and-so to them." But we regard how [women] who are equivalent to them in status are maintained, and we provide for them accordingly.

6:3 A. Rabbi says, "Each and every one takes a tithe of the property."

B. *R. Judah says, If a man had married off his first daughter, to the second should be given [a dowry] along the lines of that which he had given to the first"* [M. Ket. 6:6D].

C. They said to him, "There is he who marries off his daughter and takes money, and there is he who marries off his daughter and hands over money after her."

6:4 A. And so did R. Judah say, "*He who marries off his daughter without specified conditions should not assign to her less than five selas* [M. Ket. 6:5A].

B. For to begin with he would have purchased for her with that sum of money all her needs.

6:5 A. [If] she agreed to bring in to him two *selas,* they are treated as equivalent to six *denars* [M. Ket. 6:4A].

B. *What the husband agrees [to have inscribed in the marriage-contract] he agrees to, less a fifth* [M. Ket. 6:3G],

C. except with regard to the two hundred *zuz* to be paid to the virgin, and the *maneh* to be paid to the widow [which are paid in full].

D. [If] she agreed to bring in to him gold, lo, gold is equivalent to utensils [and diminished from the estimated value].

E. [If] she stipulated to bring into him golden *denars* lo, the gold is then treated as equivalent to ready money [M. Ket. 6:3A–B. 6:4A].

F. Said Rabban Simeon b. Gamaliel, "And that is the way the matter goes: In a place in which they do not customarily break down golden *denars,* they leave them as they are, and the gold is treated as equivalent to utensils" [M. Ket. 6:4C].

G. [If] she brought in to him [things of value], whether estimated in value or ready money, and he contemplated divorcing her, [right after the marriage, before the capital and goods have been utilized], she may not say to him, "Give me the estimated value [of what I brought in to you]." And he may not say to her, "Take your money."

H. But she takes everything which he has written over to her in her marriage-contract.

6:6 A. *[If] she agreed to bring in to him ready money, selas are treated as equivalent to six denars* [M. Ket. 6:4A].

B. A bridegroom takes upon himself to provide ten *denars* per *maneh* for money for cosmetics.

C. Said R. Yosé, "And so with regard to the estimated value of the goods which she brings into the marriage."

D. [If] she went to a place in which they were not accustomed to diminish the value of the estimate, or to increase the value over that of the ready money, they do not vary from the customs of the place.

E. [If] she agreed to bring in to him five hundred *denars* of estimated value [of goods], and he wrote over to her a thousand *denars* in her marriage-contract,

F. if she made her stipulation, she takes what he wrote over to her.

G. And if not, he takes off three denars for each and every *sela* [written into the contract].

H. If she agreed to bring into him five hundred *denars* in ready money [and] he wrote over to her a thousand *denars* in her marriage-contract,

I. if she made her stipulation, she takes what he wrote over to her.

J. And if not, he takes off six *denars* for each and every *sela* [written into the contract].

K. If she brought into him a thousand *denars* in her marriage-contract, and he wrote over to her a field worth twelve *manehs,*

L. if she made her stipulation, she takes what he wrote over to her.

M. And if not, he should not pay less to a virgin than two hundred *zuz* and to a widow a *maneh.*

6:7 A. He who married off his daughter and agreed with his son-in-law that she should stand naked and he, [the son-in-law] should clothe her,

B. they do not say, "Let her stand naked and have him clothe her."

C. But he covers her in a manner fitting to her.

D. *And so they who marry off an orphan-girl should not provide for her less than fifty zuz.*

E. *And if there is sufficient money in the fund, they provide her with a dowry according to the honor due her* [M. Ket. 6:5D–E].

6:8 A. *An orphan-girl whose mother or brothers married her off for whom they wrote over a hundred zuz or fifty zuz*— [M. Ket. 6:6A–B]

B. even though the husband wrote for them, "I have no judgment or claim with her,"

C. *she can, when she grows up, exact from them what should rightly have been given to her* [M. Ket. 6:6C].

D. A man makes an agreement in behalf of his daughter, but a woman does not make an agreement in behalf of her daughter.

E. An orphan-boy or an orphan-girl who seek to be supported—

F. they support the orphan-girl first, then they support the orphan-boy,

G. for the orphan-boy can go begging in any event, but the orphan-girl cannot go begging in any event.

H. An orphan-boy and an orphan-girl who seek to marry—

I. they marry off the orphan-girl first, and then they marry off the orphan-boy,

J. for the shame of a girl is greater than that of a boy.

K. An orphan-boy who seeks to marry—they rent a house for him, then they lay out a bed, and afterward they marry off a girl to him.

L. since it is said, [*But you shall open your hand to him] and lend him sufficient for his need, whatever it may be* (Deut. 15:8)—even a slave, even a horse.

M. *For him*—this refers to a wife, since it says elsewhere, *I shall make for him a help-mate* (Gen. 2:18)—

N. Just as *for him* in the other context refers to a wife, so *for him* in this context refers to a wife.

6:9 A. He who appoints a third party to oversee money for his son-in-law, to purchase with the funds a field for his daughter,

B. and she says, "Let them be given to him [my husband],"

C. "If this is at the stage of betrothal, the third party should carry out what he has been designated to do.

D. "If this is at the stage of consummation of the marriage, the power is in her hand [to instruct the appointee]," the words of R. Meir.

E. R. Yosé says, "If she was a minor, whether at the stage of betrothal or at the stage of marriage, the third party should carry out what he has been designated to do" [M. Ket. 6:7].

6:10 A. He who says, "Give over a *sheqel* from my property to my children for their maintenance for a week," but they are supposed to take a *sela*—they give over to them a *sela.*

B. But if he said, "Give them only a *sheqel,*" they give them only a *sheqel.*

C. If he said, "If they die, let others inherit me," whether he said, "Give," and whether he did not say, "Give," they give them over to them only a *sheqel.*

D. As to food for the widow and the daughters, whether he said, "Give," or said, "Do not give," they give to them a *sela.*

E. Rabban Simeon b. Gamaliel says, "Meir did say, 'He who says, 'Give a *sheqel* from my property to my children for a week,' but they are supposed to take a *sela*—they give over to them a *sheqel.* And as to the rest of their needs, they are supported from the charity-fund.'"

F. But sages say, "They continue to derive support [from his estate] until the property is all gone. Only afterward are they supported by the charity-fund."

7:1 A. "*For a period of thirty days he appoints an agent* [M. Ket. 7:1A], and in the case of a priest-girl, for three months," the words of R. Meir.

B. *R. Judah says, "In the case of an Israelite, for one month he continues in the marriage. After two he must put her away and pay off the marriage-contract. And in the case of a priest, for two months he may continue in the marriage. After three he must put her away and pay off the marriage-contract."*

7:2 A. [If] he prohibited her by vow from tasting any type [of produce whatsoever, M. Ket. 7:2A],

B. whether it is foul or delectable food,

C. even if she for her part had never tasted that sort of produce once in her entire life,

D. he must put her away and pay off her marriage-contract.

E. Said R. Judah, "Israelite girls prefer not to taste cooked dishes and produce, and not to go forth for a single day from their husbands [on this account]."

7:3 A. [If] he prohibited her by vow from adorning herself with any sort of adornment [M. Ket. 7:4A],

B. even if she is a young girl, and he prohibited her by vow from putting on the clothes of an old lady,

C. even if she is an old lady, and he prohibited her by vow from putting on the clothes of a young girl,

D. he must put her away and pay off her marriage-contract.

E. *R. Yosé says, "In the case of poor girls, [if] he has not assigned a time-limit [he must divorce her forthwith]. But in the case of rich girls, [he may persist in the marriage if he set a time limit of] thirty days"* [M. Ket. 7:3B–C].

7:4 A. [If] he prohibited her by vow from lending a sieve or a strainer, mill-stones or oven [to her girl-friend], he must put her away and pay off her marriage-contract,

B. because he gives her a bad name among her neighboring women.

C. And so she who prohibited him by vow from lending a sieve or a strainer, mill-stones or oven, must go forth without payment of her marriage-contract,

D. because she gives him a bad name in his neighborhood.

7:5 A. [If] he prohibited her by vow from going to a house of mourning or to a house of celebration, he must put her away and pay off her marriage-contract,

B. because sometime later she will be laid out [for burial] and not a single human being will come to pay respects to her.

7:6 A. Said R. Meir, "What is the meaning of the verse, [*It is better to go to the house of mourning than to go to the house of feasting; for this is the end of all men,] and the living will lay it to heart* (Qoh. 7:1)?

B. "Do [for others], that they may do for you; accompany [others to the grave], that they may accompany you; mourn [for others], that they may mourn for you; bury others, that they may bury you,

C. "as it is said, *It is better to go to the house of mourning,*" etc.

D. [If] he required her by vow to give a taste of what she was cooking to everybody [who came by],

E. or that she draw water and pour it out onto the ashheap [M. Ket 7:5D],

F. or that she tell everybody about things which are between him and her [M. Ket. 7:5D],

G. he must put her away and pay off her marriage-contract,

H. because he has not behaved with her in accord with the law of Moses and of Israel.

I. *And so she who goes out with her hair flowing loose* [M. Ket. 7:6D],

J. who goes out with her clothes in a mess,

K. who acts without shame in the presence of her boy-slaves and girl-slaves and her neighbors,

L. *who goes out and spins wool in the market-place* [M. Ket. 7:6],

M. who washes and bathes in the public bath with just anyone,

N. goes forth without payment of her marriage-contract,

O. for she has not behaved with him [her husband] in accord with the law of Moses and Israel [M. Ket. 7:6].

P. R. Meir says, "If he knows that she is subjected to a vow and does not keep it, he should not again place her under a vow."

Q. R. Judah says, "If he knows that she does not cut off the dough-offering, he must put her away and arrange matters properly [with the dough-offering] in her wake" [M. Ket. 7:6B].

7:7 A. *What is a loud-mouth? Anyone who, when she talks in her own house—her neighbors can hear her voice* [M. Ket. 7:6P].

B. All these women who have transgressed the law must have fair warning, but [if they persist after fair warning], then they go forth without receiving payment of their marriage-contract.

C. [If] one did not give them fair warning, he must put her away but pay off her marriage-contract—

D. and one need not say it is two hundred to a virgin and a *maneh* to a widow.

E. But as to more than this: Even if her marriage-contract is in the sum of a hundred *manehs,* she has lost the whole thing.

F. She takes merely the old rags which are laid out before her [and leaves].

7:8 A. *He who betrothes a woman on condition that there are no encumbering vows upon her, and it turns out that there are encumbering vows upon her—she is not betrothed* [M. Ket. 7:7A–B =M. Qid. 2:5].

B. [If] she went to a sage and he released her vow, lo, this woman is betrothed.

C. *If he married her without further specification and encumbering vows turned out to be upon her, she must go forth without payment of her marriage-*

contract [M. Ket. 7:7C].

D. [If] she went to a sage and he released her vow, lo this one confirms the marriage.

E. [*If he betrothed her] on condition that she had no blemishes on her, and blemishes turned up on her, she is not betrothed* [M. Ket. 7:7D].

F. [If] she went to a physician and he healed her, lo, this woman is betrothed.

G. *[If] he married her without further specification and blemishes turned up on her, she must go forth without payment of her marriage-contract* [M. Ket. 7:7E].

H. Even though she went to a physician and he healed her, she goes out without receiving payment of her marriage contract.

I. Of what sort of vows did they speak? For example, [if] she vowed not to eat meat, not to drink wine, or not to wear stylish clothing.

7:9 A. *All those blemishes which invalidate priests invalidate women* [M. Ket. 7:7F].

B. In addition to them in the case of the woman are bad breath, a sweaty body-odor, and a mole that has no hair on it.

7:10 A. He who says to his fellow, "Betrothe this daughter of yours to me on condition that there are no blemishes on her,"

B. [if] he [the father] said to him, "This daughter of mine is sick, is an idiot, is epileptic, is demented"—

C. [if] there was some other sort of blemish on her, and he concealed it among these blemishes [which he did specify],

D. lo, this is a purchase made in error [and null] [M. Ket. 7:7].

E. [If, however, he said], "There are these blemishes, and there is yet another [unspecified] blemish among them," this is by no means a purchase made in error.

F. Sages concede to R. Meir in the case of blemishes which are congenital, that even though she is yet in her husband's house, her father has to bring proof [that they did not occur before she was betrothed] [M. Ket. 7:8].

G. [If] he married her without specification, and blemishes and encumbering vows were found on her, lo, this one continues the marriage.

H. Rabban Simeon b. Gamaliel says, "If she was lame in one foot, blind in one eye, they are major blemishes and he must put her away and pay off her marriage-contract" [M. Ket. 7:9B–C].

7:11 A. Who is *one who collects* [M. Ket 7:10A3]? This is a tanner.

B. And some say, "This is one who collects dog-excrement."

C. *A coppersmith* [M. Ket. 7:10A4]—this is a metal-pourer.

D. R. Yosé b. R. Judah [says], "*One who has a polypus*— [M. Ket.

7:10A2]—this is one who has bad breath."

E. Under what circumstances did they rule, *He must put her away* [M. Ket. 7:10A] and pay off her marriage-contract?

F. When he wants, but she does not want, [or] she wants, but he does not want [to continue the marriage].

G. But if both want [to continue the marriage], they do continue the marriage.

H. One who is afflicted with boils—even though both of them want [to continue the marriage], they may not continue the marriage [M. Ket. 7:10D–E].

I. Said Rabban Simeon b. Gamaliel, "We found an old man afflicted with boils living near Sepphoris, who told me, 'There are twenty-four types of boils, and among all of them, there are none for which the woman is bad, except for those who suffer from *ra'atan.*'"

8:1 A. Said R. Judah, "They stated before Rabban Gamaliel, 'Since, when she is betrothed, she is his wife, and when she is married, she is [equally, but no more], his wife, just as this one [the woman at the stage of the consummated marriage] sells off her property and the transaction is null, so that one [the woman at the stage of betrothal], sells off her property and the transaction is null.'

B. *"He said to them, 'We are at a loss concerning the new[ly received property or goods]! Now will you turn attention to the old ones'?"* [M. Ket. 8:1G–H].

C. Said R. Ḥanina b. 'Aqabya, "Not in this manner did Rabban Gamaliel reply to them. But thus did he say to them:

D "'No. If you have stated the rule concerning the woman in a fully consummated marriage, in which case the husband takes possession of the things which she finds and of the fruits of her labor and has the right to abrogate her vows, will you say the same rule in the case of the betrothed woman, of the things which she finds and of the fruits of her labor he does not take possession, and the vows of whom he has no right to abrogate?'

E. "They said to him, 'Now lo, *if property fell to her before she was married and then she got married* [M. Ket. 8:1K]?'

F. "He said to them, "This too she should not sell. *[But] if she sold or gave it away, the transaction is valid* [M. Ket. 8:1L].'

G. "They said to him, 'Since this one is fully his wife and so is that one [the betrothed, the married women, respectively], just as the sale of this one is null, so the sale of that one [the betrothed woman] should be null.'

H. *"He said to them, 'We are at a loss concerning the new! Now will you turn our attention to the old*'?" [M. Ket. 8:1M–N].

I. Then our rabbis went and voted [the following rule]:

J. In the case of property which fell to her before she was married, and then she was married, if she sold or gave it away, the transaction is null.

K. *R. Simeon makes a distinction between one sort of property and another: Property about which the husband is informed, she should not sell. And if she sold it or gave it away, the transaction is null,*

L. for it was for this purpose that he married her.

M. *Property about which the husband is not informed she should not sell. But if she sold or gave it away, the transaction is valid,*

N. for it was for this purpose that he confirmed her as his wife [M. Ket. 8:2].

8:2 A. He who enters his wife's estate and contemplates divorcing her,

B. if he went ahead and plucked up produce from the ground in any measure at all,

C. lo, this one is rewarded for his promptness [M. Ket. 8:4].

8:3 A. He who enters into an expropriated estate and heard a report that they [assumed to have died and left the estate] are returning—

B. if he went ahead and plucked up produce from the ground in any measure at all,

C. lo, this one is rewarded for his promptness.

D. What is meant by the expropriated estate?

E. Any whose father or brothers or one of those who leave him an inheritance went overseas and he heard that they had died, and he entered into his inheritance.

F. What is an abandoned estate?

G. It is any estate, the death of the owner of which has not been reported, but into which one nonetheless one has entered for purpose of inheritance.

H. R. Simeon b. Gamaliel says, "I have heard that an expropriated estate is equivalent to an abandoned estate.

I. "He who takes over an abandoned estate—they retrieve it from his possession.

J "And in the case of all of them, they estimate their value [for restoring what is misappropriated] as if he is a tenant-farmer."

K. What is abandoned property?

L. Any of which the location of the owner is not known.

8:4 A. The robber or the thief who grabbed from this one and gave to the other—

B. what he has grabbed, he has grabbed, and what he has given he has given.

C. The thief who grabbed from this one and gave to that one—
what he has grabbed he has grabbed, and what he has given he has given.

D. The Jordan River which took from this one and gave to that one—
what it has taken, it has taken, and what it has given it has given.

E. If the river swept away wood, stones, and beams from this one and deposited them on the property of that one,

F. if the owner has despaired of recovering his property, lo, these belong to him [on whose property they have been swept up].

G. And if the owner pursued [his property, as it flowed down the river], or if he was in some other place [and did not know about the flood], lo, this remains in the possession of the owner.

8:5 A. "He who writes over his property to his son has to write in the document, 'From this time forth, and after death,'" the words of R. Judah.

B. R. Yosé says, "He does not have to do so, because the date of the document proves matters in any event."

C. Said to him R. Judah, "But does not the date of the document give proof only from the time that it was written?"

D. Also: He who writes over his property to his son and went and acquired other property—whatever was not included in the original gift, lo, this goes to the heirs [of the estate in general].

E. If the son sold off the property or the father died, if there is property attached to the ground, they make an estimate of its value.

8:6 A. He who acquires a field from his fellow as a share-cropper, and it is an irrigated field or an orchard,

B. if there is produce attached to the ground,

C. they make an estimate of its value.

8:7 A. He who acquires a field from his fellow as a share-cropper and the year of release came,

B. if there is produce attached to the ground,

C. they make an estimate of its value.

D. He who acquires a field from his fellow as a share-cropper, and the time came for him to quit the land [and make a final reckoning],

E. if there is produce there attached to the ground,

F. they make an estimate of its value.

G. And in the case of all of them, they make an estimate as in the case of a sharecropper.

8:(8)9 A. He who takes over ruins belonging to someone else and rebuilt it without permission,

B. [if] when he leaves them, he says, "Give me my wood and stones,"

C. they do not accept his claim.

8:10 A. He who takes over ruins belonging to someone else and rebuilt them without permission,

B. they estimate its value.

C. But his hand is on the bottom.

D. [If he did so] with permission, they estimate its value, and his hand is now on top.

E. How is it that his hand is on the bottom?

F. If the increase in value is greater than the outlay for the restoration,

G. he [who retrieves his property] pays him his expenses.

H. But if the expenses are greater than the increase in value, he pays him only the increase in value.

9:1 A. He who died and left his wife awaiting marriage with her deceased childless husband's brother,

B. even if he left an estate worth a hundred *manehs* and the charge of her marriage-contract is only a *maneh,*

C. the heirs cannot sell [his estate],

D. for all of his property is encumbered for the payment of her marriage-contract [M. Ket. 8:8a–b].

E. What should [the levir] do?

F. He should consummate the marriage, then divorce her, and she gives him a quittance for her marriage-contract.

G. [If] his brother left ready cash [M. Ket 8:7A], or the deceased childless brother's widow owed her husband money,

H. he should not say, "Since I am going to inherit it anyhow, I take possession of it."

I. But they sieze it from him,

J. and land is purchased for it, and he has the usufruct.

9:2 A. "She who wants to shelter her property from her husband writes them over to someone else in a writ of indebtedness signed on faith (PSṬYS)," the words of Rabban Simeon b. Gamaliel.

B. And sages say, "He just ridicules her [and grabs what he wants, such a writ having no weight whatsoever].

C. "But: She writes them over in a writ of donation, 'From this date to any time I want.'"

D. R. Judah says, "Under all circumstances he has the usufruct of the usufruct [M. Ket. 9:1J].

E. "How so?

F. "He sells the usufruct, then purchases real estate with the proceeds. And he has the usufruct of the produce [of that field]."

G. *Rabban Simeon b. Gamaliel* and R. Yoḥanan b. Beroqah *say, "If she died, he inherits her. For he has made a condition against what is written in the Torah. And whoever makes a condition against what is written in the Torah—his condition is null*" [M. Ket. 9:1M–N].

9:3 A. He who died and left movable property,

B. and the marriage-contract of his wife and a creditor laid claim against it—

C. whoever siezes it first has effected acquisition [of whatever he left] [M. Ket. 9:2–3].

D. And [there being nothing left for burial costs], he is buried by the philanthropic fund.

E. Who are the heirs who are her legal successors [M. Ket. 9:5C]?

F. Any to whom she sold [her property] or to whom she gave [her property] as a gift.

G. *[If] he wrote to her, "I have no claim to impose either a vow or an oath upon you"* [M. Ket. 9:5A], the heirs [also] cannot impose an oath on her [that she has not misappropriated] items of which she made use after the death of her husband.

H. Under what circumstances?

I. *When she went along from the grave of her husband to her father's house* [M. Ket. 9:6A].

J. But if she went from the grave of her husband to her father-in-law's house,

K. even if he wrote to her, "I have no claims to impose either a vow or an oath upon you,"

L. the heirs can impose an oath on her concerning items of which she made use after the death of her husband [M. Ket. 9:6D–E].

M. A husband cannot impose an oath on his wife unless he sets her up as a storekeeper or appoints her guardian [of his property] [M. Ket. 9:4A–C].

N. "As to the woman, *so long as she claims her marriage-contract, the heirs impose an oath on her. [If] she does not lay claim to her marriage-contract, the heirs do not impose an oath on her," the words of R. Simeon* [M. Ket. 9:8P–Q].

O. And sages say, "One way or the other, the heirs impose an oath on her."

P. A sharecropper—so long as he is a share-cropper, [he is subject to an oath]. When he has gone forth from his position as share-cropper, lo, he is equivalent to any other person.

Q. A partner—so long as he is a partner, [he is subject to an oath]. When he has gone forth from his partnership, lo, he is equivalent to any other person.

R. A guardian—so long as he is a guardian, [he is subject to an oath]. When he has gone forth from his guardianship, lo, he is equivalent to any other person.

S. A member of the household of whom they spoke [at M. Shabu. 7:8]—it is not this one who [merely] walks in and out, but the one who brings in produce and takes out produce, hires workers and dismisses workers.

T. [If] one borrows from him on the eve of the Seventh Year and in the Seventh Year, and, in the year after the Seventh Year, he is made a partner of his, or a share-cropper, he is exempt [from the requirement of an oath].

U. But if he is made a partner or a share-cropper on the eve of the Seventh Year and in the Seventh Year, and in the year after the Seventh Year he went and borrowed from him, they obligate him for [an oath covering] all.

9:4 A. She who claims less than the full value of her marriage-contract collects it without an oath.

B. How so?

C. [If] her marriage-contract had a value of a thousand *zuz*, and he said to her, "You have collected your marriage-contract," and she says, "I have not collected it, but it is of a value of only a *maneh*," she collects that amount without an oath [M. Ket. 9:7A, 9:8A–C].

D. As to [collecting what is owed to her by seizing] mortgaged property [M. Ket. 9:7C2], it is not necessary to say after her husband's death, but even while her husband is yet alive [does she collect only through an oath].

E. As to the property belonging to the orphans, it is not necessary to say, that of the adults [minors], but even that of the minors [adults] [does she collect only through an oath].

9:5 A. [If] she produced a writ of divorce, and a marriage-contract is not attached to it [M. Ket. 9:9A]—

B. a virgin collects two hundred *zuz*, and a widow, a *maneh*.

C. *[If she produced] a marriage-contract, and a writ of divorce is not attached to it* [M. Ket. 9:9B],

D. she collects nothing,

E. because if *she says, "My writ of divorce got lost," then he counters, "My quittance got lost"* [M. Ket. 9:9C–D].

9:6 A. "At the outset they used to rule, 'She who produces a marriage-contract must also produce with it a writ of divorce,'' the words of R. Meir.

B. And sages say, "From the time of the danger and thereafter, they ordained that she should tear it up in court when she collected by means of [that document]" [M. Ket. 9:9G–I].

C. Two marriage-contracts, a writ of divorce, and a [certificate of] death—she collects two marriage-contracts.

D. *A writ of divorce, marriage-contract, and a [certificate of] death* [M. Ket. 9:9L]—

E. if the date of the marriage-contract is prior to that on the writ of divorce, *she collects only one marriage-contract.*

F. *For he who divorces his wife and remarries her—on the strength of the first marriage-contract does he remarry her* [M. Ket. 9:9N–O].

9:7 A. [If] she gave him a quittance while she is subject to his authority, then he divorced her and remarried her and died, (and) she collects a *maneh* as her marriage-contract.

B. But if he made a new document, she collects what he has made afresh.

C. *A minor-boy whose father married him off—the [wife's] marriage-contract is confirmed [as valid after he reaches maturity]. For on the strength of that document he confirmed the marriage* [M. Ket. 9:9Q–R].

D. And if he made a new document, she collects what he has made afresh.

E. And so: *A proselyte who converted, and his wife alongside [did the same]—her [original] marriage-contract is valid, For on the strength of that document he [the husband] confirmed the marriage* [after conversion] [M. Ket. 9:9S–U].

F. And if he made a new document, she collects what he made afresh.

10:1 A. *He who was married to two wives and died—the first [wife] takes precedence over the second, and the heirs of the first take precedence over the heirs of the second* [M. Ket. 10:1A–C].

B. [If] he divorced the first and remarried her, and made a new marriage-contract for her,

C. the first marriage-contract of the first wife takes precedence over the second and her heirs, then the second [wife] and her heirs take precedence over the second marriage-contract of the first wife.

D. Under what circumstances?

E. In the case of [the collection of] the marriage-contract.

F. But as to maintenance, both of them are equal [and neither claims priority].

G. The wife and daughters—both of them enjoy equal claim.

H. *[If] he married the first and she died, then he married the second and he died* [M. Ket. 10:1D],

I. and there was there [the value of both marriage-contracts], plus one *denar,*

J. then these collect the marriage-contract of their mother, and those collect the marriage-contract of their mother.

K. And the rest do they divide [as an estate].

L. But if there is not there [the value of both marriage-contracts], plus one *denar,*

M. the second wife or her heirs collect the marriage-contract of their mother, and the rest divide equally [the residuary estate].

10:2 A. [If] he promised in writing to support the daughter of his wife and the son of his wife, lo, they are deemed equivalent to creditors and take precedence over all claimants.

B. He may not say to them, "Go and do work, and I will support you."

C. But they remain at home, and he provides food for them.

D. [If] he promised in writing to support the daughter of his wife, and she [the wife] gave him a quittance—

E. she has not the power to do so.

F. For they provide an advantage to a minor, but they do not impose a disadvantage upon him [or her].

10:3 A. A woman who said, "My husband has died," either derives maintenance or collects her marriage contract.

B. [If she said], "My husband has divorced me," she is supported to the extent of her marriage-contract.

C. What is the difference between [the severance of the marriage through] death and [the severance of the marriage through] divorce?

D. In the case of death, she cannot deny [the facts].

E. But in the case of divorce, she can deny the facts of the matter.

F. And she indeed may say right to his face, "You did divorce me" [*cf.* M. Ket. 2:5].

10:4 A. Three who put their money into one purse, which was stolen from them

B. bring what is left to the middle [=divided equally] and divide it up.

C. Two who put their money into one purse—

D. this one puts in a *maneh* and this one put in two hundred *zuz,*

E. and they did business—

F. the profits are in the middle [divided equally].

G. [If] this one then took part of his, and that one took part of his, and they entered into partnership,

H. this one then takes in accord with what he has put in.

I. [If] three bills of debt went forth against him simultaneously,

J. the first takes an oath to the second, and the second takes an oath to the third.

K. [If] the second did not want to impose an oath on the first, the third can prevent him from [refraining from doing so].

L. [If] one borrowed from one person and sold his field to two others,

M. and the creditor wrote to the second, "I have no case or claim against you,"

N. he [the creditor] cannot collect what is owing to him,

O. because he has left himself no place from which to make a collection.

P. A proselyte who died and whose property Israelites took over,

Q. and the wife's marriage-contract and a debt were brought for collection to his property—

R. they collect from the last who had taken over his property.

S. [If] that one does not have enough, they collect from the one before him, and so they continue.

11:1 A. A widow who lays claim on her marriage-contract,

B. and the heirs say to her, "You have received your marriage-contract"—

C. [if] this is before she was married, they have to bring proof that her marriage-contract has been received [paid off].

D. [If] this is after she was married, she has to bring proof that her marriage-contract has not been received.

E. [If] she sold off her marriage-contract, [or] pledged her marriage-contract, [or] set up her marriage-contract as a mortgage,

F. she has lost her claim for support [from the estate of her husband].

G. R. Simeon says, "Even if she sold off part of it,

"even if she pledged part of it,

"even if she set up part of her marriage-contract as a mortgage,

H. "she has lost her claim for support."

I. One need not say that this is the rule [if she did so] after the death of her husband.

J. But it is even the rule [if she did so] while her husband is yet alive.

K. "And she writes, 'These did I sell for my marriage-contract,' and, 'Those did I sell for my claim of support,'" the words of R. Judah [M. Ket. 11:3F].

L. R. Yosé says, "She sells and writes without specification.

M. "Therefore her claim is strong."

N. Just as a widow sells without court permission, so the heirs [or] those who are her lawful successors sell without court permission.

O. R. Simeon says, "A widow sells without court permission. But her heirs [or] those who come as her lawful successors do not sell without court permission."

P. Said R. Simeon, "On what account did they say, 'the widow sells without court permission?'

2 Q. "To improve the claim of the orphans, that she should not disperse their property."

R. [If] she went down into a field which had been set up as a mortgage and consumed the crop, and she laid out money for the expenses of the upkeep of the field,

S. they make an estimate of the value of the usufruct which she has enjoyed, and they make an estimate of what she has laid out for the tending of the field.

T. If this estimate has been made for her in court, what they have estimated is valid.

11:2 A. Three who went down to estimate the value of a field—

B. one says, "It is worth a *maneh,"*

C. and two say, "It is worth two hundred *zuz*"—

D. one says, "It is worth two hundred,"

E. and two say, "It is worth a *maneh"*—

F. the minority view is null.

G. [If] one says, "It is worth a *maneh* [100 *zuz*],"

H. and one says, "It is worth twenty [*selas,* 80 *zuz*],"

I. and one says, "It is worth thirty [*selas,* 120 *zuz*],"

J. they estimate its value at a *maneh.*

K. R. Eleazar b. R. Ṣadoq says, "They estimate its value at ninety *denars.*"

L. Others say, "They add up the difference among themselves and divide it by three [= 93 1/3 *zuz*]."

11:3 A. What is a deed of inspection [M. Ket. 11:5D]?

B. The time alloted for the estimate of the value of property accruing to orphans is thirty days.

C. And the time alloted for the estimate of the value of property accruing to the sanctuary is sixty days.

D. [If] they sold something worth a *maneh* for two hundred *zuz,* or something worth two hundred *zuz* for a *maneh,*

E. the sale is confirmed.

F. Rabban Simeon b. Gamaliel says, "If the estimate of the value made by judges was a sixth too little or a sixth too much, their sale is valid" [*vs.* M. Ket. 11:5A].

G. She who sold what was worth a *maneh* and a *denar* for a *maneh,*

H. *even if she says, "I shall return the denar to the purchaser's heirs"—*

I. *her sale is null.*

J. *Rabban Simeon b. Gamaliel says, "Under all circumstances is her sale valid* [M. Ket. 11:4F], and she returns the *denar* to the heirs.

L. "But this is on condition that she [not] leave over a [usable] portion."

M. Therefore [G–I], if she estimated it at too little or estimated it at too much, she claims only in accord with the price at which she sold the property.

11:4 A. R. Eliezer says, "An orphan-girl [whose mother has married her off and who exercises the right of refusal] has a claim on indemnity for used clothes."

B. R. Judah says in the name of R. Eliezer, "An orphan-girl [as above] has a claim on the increase" [of *melog*—property] [*vs.* M. Ket. 11:6A–B].

C. A son whose father died, [and] whose mother says, "Let him grow up with me,"

D. and the heirs say, "Let him grow up with us"—

E. they do not allow him to grow up living with someone who is suitable to serve as his heir.

F. There was a case of this sort, and they slaughtered him on the evening of Passover.

11:5 A. A woman whose husband had died dwells in her house just as she did when her husband was alive.

B. She makes use of the man-slaves and women-slaves, silver utensils and golden utensils, just as she made use of them when her husband was alive.

C. For thus does he write for her, "You will dwell in my house and enjoy support from my property so long as you spend your widowhood in my house."

11:6 A. He who says, "Give over a house of widowhood to my daughter," "Give a house to So-and-so for a dwelling,"

B. and the house fell down—

C. the heirs are liable to [pay to] rebuild it.

D. He who says, "This house is a house for the widowhood of my daughter," "This house is for So-and-so for a dwelling"—

E. then the heirs are not liable to rebuild it [if it fell down].

11:7 A. He who says, "Give a house of widowhood for my daughter"—

B. they give it over to her only if she took upon herself to live in it.

C. The heirs can prevent her should she rent it to someone else.

D. Therefore when she dies, they inherit the house.

11:8 A. He who lends money to his fellow relying on a pledge, and the pledge is lost, collects the debt from other property [belonging to the debtor].

B. If he [the borrower] said to him, "On condition that you may make your collection only from this object,"

C. then he does not collect the debt from any other property belonging to the debtor.

D. He who sets up his field as a mortgage for the marriage-contract of his wifc, and the river washed it out—

E. she collects from other property belonging to him.

F. If he said to her, "On condition that you may make your collection only from this field,"

G. then she does not collect the debt from any other property belonging to her husband.

12:1 A. In earlier times, when [property set aside for payment of] her marriage-contract was in her father's hands, it was a light thing in his [the husband's] view to divorce her.

B. Simeon b. Shataḥ therefore ordained that [that property to cover] her marriage-contract should be with her husband [who might do business with it, signing it over for a mortgage and the like].

C. And he therefore writes for her, "*All* property which I have is liable and obligated for the payment of your marriage-contract."

12:2 A. They do not set aside movable property for the payment of the marriage-contract of a woman,

B. for the sake of good order.

C. Said R. Yosé, "And what good order is involved in this ruling? But [the reason is] that there is no limit to the matter."

D. On what account did they rule, "For the compensation for damages, they make an estimate based on the value of the finest property?"

E. On account of thugs and grabbers.

F. So that [such felons] might say, "Why should I rob? Why should I grab? Tomorrow, lo, the court is going to estimate the value of my best field [and seize it from me]."

G. They found support for this policy from the following Scripture: *He shall make restitution from the best in his own field and in his own vineyard* (Ex. 22:4).

H. On what account did they rule that a creditor is repaid from a field of a middling sort?

I. On account of deceitful people.

J. So that such people might not set their gaze on the finest field of their fellow or on his finest courtyard, then lend him money on the strength of that field or courtyard, then jump and grab the field or the courtyard.

K. But if that is the main consideration, then should the compensation not be assessed in the poorest-quality-property?

L. But that is not the case, so as not to fence off the path before those who need to borrow money,

M. so that someone should not seek a loan and find no one to lend him what he needs.

12:3 A. "The marriage-contract of a woman is collected from land of the poorest quality," the words of Rabbi.

B. R. Judah says in the name of R. Simeon, "On what account did they rule, 'The marriage-contract of a woman is collected from land of the poorest quality'?

C. "Because, more than a man wants to marry, a woman wants to get married.

D. "And, further, because the shame of a woman [at not being married] is greater than the shame of a man.

E. "If so, should there be no marriage-contract at all? But if that were the case, then a woman would go forth both when she wants and when she does not want to do so. But a man would put her forth only when he wants to do so."

F. If there is available only real property of the best quality, all of them [who are owed damages, debts, or marriage-contracts] collect what is due them from property of the best quality.

G. [If there is available only] property of middling quality, all of them collect what is due them from property of middling quality.

H. [If there is available only] property of poor quality, all of them collect what is due them from property of poor quality.

I. [If there is] property of the best and of middling quality, then compensation for damages is collected from property of the best quality, and compensation for a debt and for the marriage-contract is collected from property of middling quality.

J. [If there is] property of the best and of the poorest quality, then compensation for damages is collected from property of the best quality, and compensation for a debt and for the marriage-contract is collected from property of the poorest quality.

K. [If there is available only] property of middling and of poorest quality, then compensation for damages and for debts is collected from property of middling quality, and compensation for the marriage-contract is collected from property of poor quality.

L. [If the party who owes these monies] sold them [his properties] off to one person, or simultaneously three together, and they took over the property in place of the owner—

M. then compensation for damages is collected from property of the best quality, for a creditor from property of middling quality, and for payment of the wife's marriage-contract from property of the poorest quality.

N. [If] he sold them off to three people, one after the other in sequence,

O. even compensation for damages, from property of the poorest quality, or payment for the wife's marriage-contract, from property of the finest quality, do they collect from the [land bought by] the last —f the three purchasers.

P. [If] he does not have [enough], they collect from the one before him. [If] he does not have enough, they collect from the one before him.

Q. Rabban Simeon b. Gamaliel says, "He who makes his field over as a mortgage for the marriage-contract of his bride—her hand is uppermost.

R. "[If] she wants, she collects it from him, and [if] she wants, she collects her marriage-contract from other property."

S. *A widow who said, "I don't want to move from my husband's house"* [M. Ket. 12:3A]—

T. the heirs cannot stop her.

U. For this is honor paid to her [deceased] husband.

V. [If] she said, "I don't want to move from my father's house,"

W. the heirs can stop her.

X. For the blessing of a house [is proportionate to its] size [the larger the household, the lower the individual's cost of living].

Y. "*So long as she is in her father's house, she may collect her marriage-contract at any time. So long as she is in her husband's house, she collects her marriage-contract within twenty-five years, for in twenty-five years she may do good [for friends] lorresponding to the value of her marriage-contract," the words of R. Meir, which he said in the name of Rabban Simeon b. Gamaliel* [M. Ket. 12:4A–D].

Z. R. Ishmael says, "Thirty years."

AA. *And sages say, "So long as she is in her husband's house, she collects her marriage-contract at any time. So long as she is in her father's house,* she calls attention [to her uncollected] *marriage-contract for twenty-five years"* [M. Ket. 12:4E–F].

BB. Just as she calls attention to her uncollected marriage-contract for a period of twenty-five years, so her heirs and her legal successors call attention to her uncollected marriage-contract for a period of twenty-five years [M. Ket. 12:4G].

CC. But a creditor collects at any time [without limit],

DD. even though he has not [before] called attention [to the uncollected debt].

12:4 A. He who went overseas and came back,

B. and his wife claims support—

C. if he said, "Pay out her wages in exchange for her support,"

D. he has the right to do so.

E. But if a court had directed that support be provided for her, what [the court] has directed, it has directed [and he has no such claim].

F. Said R. Yosé b. R. Judah, "Admon and sages did not differ concerning a case in which her father made the arrangement in her behalf [M. Ket. 13:5D].

G. "[For in such a case she can claim], 'Father made the agreement for me. What can I do about it? Either marry me or let me go!'

H. "Concerning what case did they differ?

I. "Concerning a case in which she herself made the agreement.

J. "Admon says, She can claim, 'I thought that father indeed would give me [what I promised to my betrothed]. But now that father does not provide for me [what I need to pay off my agreement with you], either marry me or let me go.'"

K. *Said Rabban Gamaliel, "I prefer the opinion of Admon"* [M. Ket. 13:5D].

L. He who makes an agreement to provide funds for his minor daughter and then showed the leg [defaulted]—

M. they force him to provide [what he has promised].

N. For they impute an advantage to a minor, but they do not put him at a disadvantage.

12:5 A. *There are three provinces in what concerns marriage:* [1] *Judah,* [2] *Transjordan, and* [3] *Galilee* [M. Ket. 13:10A]:

B. Under what circumstances [does M's rule apply that women may be removed from one town to another, [M. 13:10C]?

C. When the groom was from Judah and betrothed a girl from Judah, or was from Galilee and betrothed a girl from Galilee.

D. But if he was from Judah and betrothed a girl from Galilee, or from Galilee and betrothed a girl from Judah, they force her to go away [M. Ket. 13:10B],

E. for it was on this assumption that she married him.

F. If, however, he said, "I, So-and-so from Judah, have married a girl from Galilee," they do not force her to go away.

G. But [if he writes, "I married a girl] in Galilee," they force her to go away.

H. They remove a wife from a town which has a gentile majority to a town which has an Israelite majority, but they do not remove a wife from a town which has an Israelite majority to a town which has a gentile majority.

I. [If] he wants to come to the Land of Israel, and she does not want to come, they force her to come.

J. [If] she wants to come, and he does not want to come, they force him to come.

K. [If] he wants to leave the Land of Israel, and she does not want to leave, they do not force her to leave.

L. [If] she wants to leave, and he does not want to leave, they force her not to leave.

12:6 A. He who produces a writ [of indebtedness] in Babylonia collects on the strength of it in Babylonian coinage.

B. [If he does so] in the Land of Israel, he collects on the strength of it in the coinage of the Land of Israel.

C. [If] it was written without specification—

D. [if] he produces it in Babylonia, he collects on the strength of it in Babylonian coinage.

E. [If he produces it] in the Land of Israel, he collects on the strength of it in the coinage of the Land of Israel.

F. [If] it was written on coinage without specification, lo, this one collects [in the coinage of] any place which he wants,

G. which is not the case for the marriage-contract of a woman [paid only in Palestinian coinage under this circumstance].

H. *[If] he married a girl in the Land of Israel and divorced her in the Land of Israel, he pays her off in the coinage of the Land of Israel* [M. Ket. 13:11D].

I. [If he married her] in the Land of Israel and divorced her in Babylonia, he pays her off in the coinage of the Land of Israel.

J. [If he married her] in Babylonia and divorced her in the Land of Israel, he pays her off in the coinage of the Land of Israel.

K. Rabban Simeon b. Gamaliel says, "[Coinage for payment of] the marriage-contract of a woman and for a creditor [follow the coinage] of the place of the marriage [or the place in which the writ of indebtedness is written, in the case of payment of a debt]."

L. The five *selas* for redemption of the first born, the thirty for a slave, the fifty paid by the one who rapes or seduces a girl, the hundred paid by one who spreads malicious rumors about a girl—all of them, even though they are in Babylonia, collect on their account in the coinage of the Land of Israel.

M. The coinage concerning which the Torah speaks at every point, this is the coinage of Tyre.

N. Tyrian coinage—this is the coinage of Jerusalem.

NEDARIM

1:1 A. [He who says,] "By the right hand,"—lo, this is an oath.

B. "By the left hand"—lo, this is an oath.

C. "By the Name"—lo, this is an oath.

D. "For the Name"—lo, this is a *qorban.*

E. [If he said:] "Like the freewill-offering of evil folk"—he has said nothing,

F. for evil people do not bring freewill-offerings.

G. "Like the freewill-offering of suitable folk"—

H. R. Judah says, "This is a valid vow in the case of a Nazirite-vow [M. Ned. 1:1H–I].

I. "For the pious men of old used to make freewill-offerings of Nazirite-vows.

J. "For there is not sufficient place [on the altar] for the bringing of offerings in expiation for inadvertent sins in their behalf.

K. "So they would offer Nazirite-vows as freewill-offerings,

L. "so that they might bring an offering."

M. Rabban Simeon b. Gamaliel says, "[He who says,] 'Like the freewill offering of suitable folk,' has not made a valid vow in the case of a Nazir,

N. "for the pious men of old did not make freewill-offerings of Nazirite-vows.

O. "For [in any case] if one wanted to bring a whole-offering, he might bring it. [If he wanted to bring] peace-offerings, he might bring them. [If he wanted to bring] a thank-offering and the four kinds of bread which go with it, he might bring [them].

P. "They did not volunteer freewill-offerings of Nazirite-vows, because they require atonement, since it says, *And he shall make atonement for him, because he sinned against the soul* [Num. 6:11]."

1:2 A. He who says, "I do not vow,"—lo, this one is permitted.

B. [He who says], "I already should have vowed"—lo, this one is prohibited.

C. "It is [not] *qorban* if I taste it"—he is permitted.

D. "It is not *qorban,* and I shall not taste it"—he is prohibited.

E. Rabban Simeon b. Gamaliel says, "He who says, '[By] Mohi [Moses = by Him who sent Moses],' and 'As Mohi says'—lo, these are substitutes for an oath."

F. And so did Rabban Simeon b. Gamaliel say, "Two who were taking vows, one against the other—

G. "one of them said to his fellow, 'This loaf is *qorban* if I taste it,'

H. "his fellow said to him, 'It is not *qorban* if you taste it,'

I. "'Lo, I shall be a Nazir if I eat this bread,'

J. "his fellow said to him, 'I am not a Nazir if I eat it'—

K. "whichever one's words are null is prohibited."

L. *R. Judah says, "He who says, 'Jerusalem,' has said nothing* [M. Ned. 1:3G], unless he so intends as to vow [by the offerings] of Jerusalem."

M. Sages concur with R. Judah in the case of him *who says, "Qorban . . .," "A whole-offering . . .," "A meal-offering . . .," "A sin-offering . . .," "A thank-offering . . .," "Peace-offerings . . .," "If I eat with you—"*

"that he is permitted" [M. Ned. 1:4A–B],

N. for he has intended only to vow [by the life of] a sacrifice [*qorban]* itself.

1:3 A. [He who says,] "Jerusalem," "To Jerusalem," "In Jerusalem,"

"*Hekhal,*" "To the *Hekhal,*" "In the *Hekhal,*"

"Altar," "To the altar," "In the altar,"

"Lamb," "To the lamb," "In the lamb,"

"Sheds," "To the sheds," "In the sheds,"

"Wood," "To the wood," "In the wood,"

"Fires," "To the fires," "On the fires,"

"Dishes [of frankincense]," "To the dishes," "On the dishes"—

B. any one of these—"if I eat with you"

C. is prohibited [M. Ned. 1:3C–F].

D. [He who says,] "That I shall not eat with you [any of these]" is permitted.

E. [He who says,] "Unconsecrated food," "For unconsecrated food," "With unconsecrated food,"

F. whether he said, "That I shall eat with you," or whether he said, "That I shall not eat with you,"

G. is permitted.

H. [He who says,] "Not-unconsecrated-food if I shall eat with you," is prohibited.

I. [He who says,] "Unconsecrated food if I shall eat with you," "If I shall not eat with you," is permitted.

J. [If he said,] "If I shall not eat with you," he is permitted.

K. "Not-a-whole-offering shall I not eat with you"—

L. R. Jacob prohibits.

M. And sages permit.

N. He who says, "Lo, it is unto me," even if he did not mention the word *qorban,* lo, this is a vow.

O. "It is *qorban* like my mother's flesh," "Like my sister's flesh," "Like a foreskin," "Like mixed seeds in a vineyard,"

P. he is permitted.

Q. For he has not declared anything to be sanctified [which actually is subject to sanctification].

1:4 A. He who vows "by the Torah"—lo, this is not binding.

B. He who vows "by what is written in the Torah"—lo this is binding.

C. He who vows " by what is in the Torah and by what is written in it"—it is binding [*cf.* M. Ned. 2:1].

D. What is a vow which prohibits [that which is written] in the Torah? [Num. 30:3].

E. He who says, "Lo, I take upon myself that I shall not eat meat, " and "that I shall not drink wine," "as on the day on which I saw Jerusalem in ruins," or "as on the day on which So-and-so was slain"—

F. it is binding.

1:5 A. A more strict rule applies to vows than to oaths, and to oaths than to vows [M. Ned. 2:1–2].

B. For vows apply to matters which are a matter of choice as well as to those which are subject to commandment,

C. which is not the case with oaths [M. Ned. 2:2H–K].

D. A more strict rule applies to oaths.

E. For oaths apply to something which is of substance and to something which is not of substance,

F. which is not the case of vows.

G. In the case of vows, how so [A–C]?

H. *[If] one said, "Qonam is the Sukkah which I am making," "the lulab which I am taking," "the tefillin which I am putting on"—*

I. *it is binding in the case of vows and not binding in the case of oaths* [M. Ned. 2:2H–I].

J. How so [D–F]?

K. *If he said, "Qonam if I sleep," "if I speak," "if I walk,"* [M. Ned. 2:1F],

L. it is binding in the case of oaths and not binding in the case of vows [M. Ned. 2:1I–J].

M. "*Qonam* is my mouth if it speaks with you," "my hands if they work with you," "my feet if they walk with you"—

N. it is binding in the case of vows and binding in the case of oaths [M. Ned. 1:4J–K].

1:6 A. *Vows which are not spelled out are subject to a more stringent rule* [M. Ned. 2:4A]:

B. "Why did you take an oath?"

C. If he said, "I do not know. But I saw my buddies taking oaths that way"—

D. it is binding.

E. "[If] one vowed [to be a Nazirite] and violated his vow,

F. "they do not accept an inquiry from him [about releasing the vow]

G. "until he will act as if he is bound by the vow for at least as many days as he acted as if he was not bound by it," the words of R. Meir.

H. Said R. Yosé, "Under what circumstances?

I. "When it is a vow lasting for a long time.

J. "But if it was a vow which was to last for a short time, it is sufficient for him to observe it for thirty days."

K. *R. Judah says, "A statement referring to heave-offering not bearing further specification made in Judah is binding"* [M. Ned. 2:4T].

L. R. Eleazar b. R Ṣadoq says, "Statements that something is devoted, without further specification, are not binding in Judah and are binding in Galilee" [M. Ned. 2:4V].

2:1 A. *R. Eliezer b. Jacob says, "He who wants to force his fellow by a vow to eat with him* [M. Ned. 3:1E],

B. "and this one vowed that he would not eat with him,

C. "even though both take oaths against one another,

D. "lo, these are deemed vows of incitement."

E. [If one said], "*Qonam* if I was not counted for a Passover whose fat-tail weighed ten *litrim,*"

F. "If I did not drink wine worth golden *denar* for a *log,*"

G. "*if I did not see a snake as big as the beam of an olive-press*" [M. Ned. 3:2C]—

H. just as vows of exaggeration are not binding, so oaths of exaggeration are not binding.

2:2 A. They attribute [produce subject to seizure] by assessors and tax-collectors to heave-offering, or to gentile ownership, or to the ownership of the government [M. Ned. 3:4A–C].

B. But they do not attribute ownership to another Israelite.

2:3 A. [He who says], "*Lo, these plants are qorban until they are cut down,*" "*This cloak is qorban until it is burned,*" [M. Ned. 3:5D–E]

B. "This cow is *qorban,* until it is slaughtered,"

C. once they have been cut down, burned, or slaughtered, they have gone forth to the status of unconsecrated objects.

2:4 A. He who vows not to derive benefit from Israelites is prohibited from deriving benefit from proselytes.

B. He who vows not to derive benefit from proselytes is permitted to derive benefit from Israelites.

C. He who vows not to derive benefit from Israelites is prohibited from deriving benefit from priests or Levites.

D. He who vows not to derive benefit from priests and Levites is permitted to derive benefit from Israelites.

E. He who vows not to derive benefit from priests is permitted to derive benefits from Levites.

F. He who vows not to derive benefit from Levites is permitted to derive benefit from priests.

G. He who vows not to derive benefit from garlic-eaters—

H. R. Judah prohibits [him from deriving benefit] also from Samaritans [M. Ned. 3:10B].

I. He who vows that Israelites will not derive benefit from him buys for less and sells for more [M. Ned. 3:11D].

J. R. Yosé says, "They do not pay attention to him" [M. Ned. 3:11E].

K. It does not say, *For you are going to take a wife from the Philistines* (Judges 14:3) who are idolators, who have sexual relations with women prohibited to them, who are murderers, but *who are uncircumcised.*

L. And so we observe that the judgment of the nations of the world is sealed only on account of uncircumcision, since it says, *And all of them who are uncircumcised fall by the sword* (Ez. 32:23–25).

2:5 A. *Rabbi says, "Great is circumcision, for, despite all the commandments which Abraham our father carried out, he was called complete and whole only when he had circumcised himself, as it is said, Walk before me and be perfect"* (Gen. 17:1).

2:6 A. Another matter: Great is circumcision, for it is deemed equivalent to all the other commandments in the Torah put together,

B. since it says, "*Lo, the blood of the covenant which the Lord made* (Ex. 24:8)."

2:7 A. Another matter: Great is circumcision, for if it were not for that, the heaven and the earth could not endure, since it says, *Thus says the Lord: But for my covenant day and night, I should not have set forth the ordinances of heaven and eath* (Jer. 33:25).

B. *There is no difference between him who is forbidden by vow from enjoying any benefit from his fellow* without specification, *and him who is forbidden by vow from deriving food from him, except for setting foot in his house and us-*

ing utensils with which food is not prepared [M. Ned. 4:1A–B].

C. He who is forbidden by vow from deriving benefit from his fellow and who died—

D. he [the fellow] brings a coffin and shrouds for him, wailing pipes and wailing women,

E. for the dead get no benefit [from these things].

F. He gives testimony in his behalf in property cases and in criminal cases.

G. If he fell ill, he [the fellow] goes into visit him [M. Ned. 4:4A].

H. But if [the one who took the vow] has someone ill [in his house], [the fellow] does not go in to visit him or inquire after his welfare.

I. [If] he [the fellow] was a priest, he tosses the blood of his [the one subject to the vow] sin-offering in his behalf, and the blood of his guilt-offering,

J. for the sake of peace [M. Ned. 4:3B].

K. He washes with him in the same bath tub *and sleeps with him in the same bed* [M. Ned. 4:4D–E].

L. R. Judah says, "He sleeps with him in a small bed in the sunny season and in a large bed in the rainy season [M. Ned. 4:4F].

M. "He washes with him in a large tub and sweats with him in a small steam-bath" [M. Ned. 4:4D].

2:8 A. *He who is forbidden by vow from enjoying benefit from his fellow*

B. *before the Seventh Year does not go down into his field and may not eat what is planted there* [M. Ned. 4:5A–B].

C. In the Seventh year, he does go down into his field and eats what is planted there.

2:9 A. "[He who says] 'This loaf of bread is sanctified,'

B. "and either he or his fellow ate it,

C. "lo, this one has committed an act of sacrilege.

D. "Therefore it is subject to redemption.

E. "If he said, 'Lo, it is [incumbent] on me,' and he ate it,

F. "he has transgressed by committing sacrilege to the extent of his thanks for enjoying the loaf of bread.

G. "[If] someone else ate it, lo, that one has not committed sacrilege.

H. "Therefore it is not subject to redemption," the words of R. Meir.

I. R. Simeon says, "Neither this one nor that one has committed sacrilege."

J. *And that one takes it and eats it* [M. Ned. 4:8D].

K. *R. Yosé prohibits* because his vow has come before his act of declaring the food to be ownerless property [M. Ned. 4:8E].

L. Just as both of them [the two men who have prohibited themselves by a vow from deriving benefit from one another] are prohibited from dwelling in the same courtyard [M. Ned. 5:1A], so they are prohibited from living in the same alleyway.

M. Just as both of them are prohibited from raising chickens [M. Ned. 5:1C], so both of them are prohibited from raising small cattle [in the common courtyard].

N. [If] one of them was accustomed to prohibiting others by vow from deriving benefit from his share, they force the one who is accustomed to do so to sell his share [M. Ned. 5:1F].

O. A public square through which the public way passes, lo, this belongs to the immigrants from Babylonia.

P. [But if] the public way does not pass through, lo, it belongs to the men of that town [M. Ned. 5:5].

2:10 A. He who is prohibited by vow from deriving benefit from his town or from the people of his town,

B. and someone came from the outside and lived there for thirty days—

C. he [who took the vow] is permitted to derive benefit from him.

D. [But if he was prohibited by vow from deriving benefit] from those who dwell in his town, and someone came from the outside and lived there for thirty days, he is prohibited [from deriving benefit from him] [M. Ned. 5:4–5].

E. He who is prohibited by vow from deriving benefit from his fellow [in a vow made] in his presence—

F. they accept inquiry [for absolution from the vow] from him only in his presence.

G. But if he vowed not to derive benefit from his fellow not in his presence,

H. they accept inquiry from him either in his presence or not in his presence.

3:1 A. He who vows not to eat what is cooked is prohibited from eating what is roasted and what is seethed and what is boiled [M. Ned. 6:1B].

B. And he is prohibited from eating soft bisquits, because sick people eat their bread with them.

C. He who vows not to eat what goes down into a pot is prohibited from eating what goes down into a pan.

D. [He who vows not to eat] what goes down into a pan is permitted to eat what goes down into a pot.

3:2 A. [He who vows not to eat] what is prepared in a pot is permitted [to eat] what is prepared in a pan.

B. [He who vows not to eat] what is prepared in a pan is permitted [to eat] what is prepared in a pot.

C. [He who vows not to eat what] goes down into an oven is prohibited [from eating] only bread alone.

D. [He who vows not to eat] what is prepared in an oven is prohibited [from eating] anything which is prepared in an oven.

E. He who vows [not to eat] what is curdled is permitted to eat cheese.

F. He who vows [not to eat] cheese is prohibited from eating what is curdled [M. Ned. 6:5].

G. He who vows not to eat the meat sediment is permitted to eat the broth. He who vows not to eat the broth is permitted to eat the sediment.

H. R. Judah says, "If he said, '*Qonam* if I eat meat,' he is prohibited to eat it, its broth, and its meat-sediment" [M. Ned. 6:6].

3:3 A. [*He who takes a vow not to eat] oil is permitted to eat sesame-oil* [M. Ned. 6:9B].

B. But in a place in which they make use of sesame-oil as a staple he is prohibited even from using sesame-oil.

C. *R. Judah b. Betera says, "Anything which is called after the name of that which is made from it, and one takes a vow not to have it—he is prohibited also from eating that which comes from it*" [M. Ned. 6:8C].

D. R. Simeon b. Eleazar says, "If something is usually eaten and what exudes from it is usually eaten, and one has vowed not to eat it, he is prohibited also from eating what exudes from it.

E. "If he takes a vow not to eat what exudes from it, he is prohibited from eating it as well.

F. "What is usually eaten, but that which exudes from it is not usually eaten, and one has taken a vow not to eat it—he is permitted to eat what exudes from it.

G. "[If he took a vow not to eat] what exudes from it, he is permitted to eat it.

H. "What is not usually eaten and what exudes from it is usually eaten and one has taken a vow not to eat it,—this one has intended his vow to cover only what exudes from it."

3:4 A. He who takes a vow not [to wear anything made of] wool is permitted [to wear something made of] flax. [If he took a vow not to wear anything made of] flax, he is permitted [to wear something made of] wool [M. Ned. 7:3].

B. R. Simeon b. Eleazar says, "As to that which is usually used for clothing and that which comes from it is usually used for clothing, and one has taken a vow not to make use of it—he is prohibited also from making use of what comes from it.

C. "If he took a vow not to use what comes from it, he is prohibited from making use of it.

D. "As to something usually used for clothing, but what comes from it is not usually used for clothing, and one has taken a vow not to use it—he is permitted to make use of what comes from it.

E. "If he took a vow not to use what comes from it, he is permitted to make use of it.

F. "As to something which is not usually used for clothing but what comes from it is usually used for wearing, and one has taken a vow not to make use of it,

G. "this one has intended only to refrain from using what comes from it."

3:5 A. He who takes a vow not to eat meat is prohibited from eating every kind of meat.

B. He [also] is prohibited from eating the head, feet, and windpipe, and fowl.

C. But he is permitted to eat the flesh of fish and locusts.

D. Rabban Simeon b. Gamaliel says, "He who vows not to eat meat is prohibited from eating all kinds of meat.

"But he is permitted to eat the head, feet, windpipe, and fowl, fish, and locusts."

E. And so did Rabban Simeon b. Gamaliel say, "The innards are not the meat, and people who eat them are not men."

F. R. Simeon b. Eliezer says, "If he said, '*Qonam* if I eat fish,' he is prohibited from eating big fish but permitted to eat little ones.

G. "If he said, '*Qonam* if I eat little fish,' he is prohibited from eating little ones but permitted to eat big ones.

H. "[If he said,] '*Qonam* I eat fish,' he is prohibited from eating big fish and prohibited from eating little fish."

3:6 A. He who in the Seventh Year takes a vow not to eat vegetables is prohibited from eating wild vegetables.

B. [If he vowed not to eat] gourds, he is prohibited only from eating Greek gourds alone.

C. *If he vowed not to eat cabbage, he is prohibited from eating asparagus. If he vowed not to eat asparagus, he is permitted to eat cabbage* [M. Ned. 6:10A–B].

D. If he vowed not to eat leeks, in a place in which they call shallots leeks, he is prohibited to eat shallots.

E. [If he vowed not] to eat shallots, he is permitted to eat leeks [M. Ned. 6:9E.]

F. [If he vowed not to eat] onions, he is prohibited from eating scallions.

G. And R. Yosé permits it.

H. If he vowed not to eat scallions, he is permitted to eat onions.

I. *If he vowed not to eat lentils, he is prohibited from eating lentil-cakes.*

J. And R. Yosé permits it [M. Ned. 6:10I–J].

K. [If he vowed not to eat] grits-porrage, he is permitted to eat garlic [M. Ned. 6:10:F–G].

3:7 A. R. Judah says, "If he said, '*Qonam* if I eat a grit,' he is permitted to eat it raw but prohibited from eating it cooked.

B. "If he said, '*Qonam* if I eat grits,' he is prohibited from eating them raw but permitted to eat them cooked.

C. "If he said, '*Qonam* if I eat a grain of wheat,' he is permitted to chew it but prohibited from baking it.

D. "If he said, '*Qonam* if I eat wheat,' he is prohibited from chewing it and prohibited from baking it" [M. Ned. 6–10 L–N].

4:1 A. He who vows not to eat the produce of a given year is prohibited from eating all the produce of that year.

B. But he is permitted to eat [meat of the] calves, lambs and sheep, and milk, and pigeons [produced that year].

C. If he said, "[*Qonam* if I taste what is] produced in this year," he is prohibited from eating all of them.

D. He who vows not to eat summer fruit is prohibited only from eating figs alone.

4:2 A. Rabban Simeon b. Gamaliel says, "Grapes also fall into the category of summer fruit."

4:3 A. He who vows not to eat *pe'ah* is prohibited from eating cucumbers, gourds, and chate-melons, but permitted to eat fruit which grows on trees.

B. He who vows not to drink fruit-juice is prohibited from drinking all kinds of sweet juice, but permitted to drink wine.

C. He who vows not to use spices is prohibited from using raw spices but permitted to eat cooked spices.

D. If he said, "Lo, they are prohibited to my mouth," "Lo, they are incumbent on me," he then is prohibited from eating them whether they are raw or cooked.

E. He who vows not to eat bread is prohibited only from eating bread which comes from the five varieties [of grain of the Land] [M. Ned. 7:2B].

F. He who vows not to eat grain is *prohibited from eating Egyptian beans when they are fresh but permitted to eat them when they are dried* [M. Ned. 7:1F].

G. And he is permitted to eat rice, split grain, groats of wheat, and barley-groats.

H. He who vows not to wear clothing is prohibited from putting on a belt or a *fascia*.

I. But he is permitted to put on a leather coat, a spread, shoes, pants, and a hat.

4:4 A. Under what circumstances did *R. Judah say, "All depends upon the one who makes a vow"* [M. Ned. 7:3D]?

B. [If] he was bearing a burden of wool and was suffering on its account and said, "*Qonam* if wool touches me again," he is prohibited from carrying it but permitted to wear it.

C. [If] he was wearing wool and was suffering on its account and said, "*Qonam* be wool if it touches me," he is prohibited from wearing it but permitted to carry it in a bundle.

4:5 A. He who says, "*Qonam* be this loaf of bread which I am tasting if I go to such and such a place tomorrow"—

B. if he ate it, lo, he is subject to *not* going to that place.

C. And if he went to that place, he is subject to [violation of] the rule, *He shall not profane his word* (Num. 30:2).

4:6 A. Even though there are vows which we have said are not binding, how do we know that one should not make such a vow with the plan of annulling it?

B. Scripture says, *He shall not profane his word* (Num. 30:2).

C. That is to say, he should not treat his words as profane [and unconsecrated].

D. Another matter: *He should not profane his word*—

E. even a sage does not annul his vow for himself.

F. [If] he said to him, "Lend me your spade," [and the other said, "*Qonam* be this spade] if it is mine," "*Qonam* be these things to me if I have a spade [at all],"

G. one may be sure that [now] he has no spade at all.

4:7 A. He who makes a vow up until the summer [in the mountains of Galilee] and went down into the valleys, even though the summer came in the valleys, he is prohibited until the summer comes to Galilee [M. Ned. 8:4D–F].

B. Said R. Yosé, "At first they ruled, 'He who is prohibited by vow from deriving benefit from his fellow without further specification until Passover is prohibited until the moment at which the Passover-lamb is slaughtered.'

C. "After the Temple was destroyed, the vow remained in effect for the entire day" [M. Ned. 8:5H–I].

D. This is the general principle: As to any occasion whose time is fixed, and he said, ". . . until it," he is prohibited until "before it" [M. Ned. 8:2C]—

E. *R. Meir says, "He is prohibited until it comes."*

F. *R. Yose says, "He is prohibited until it passes"* [M. Ned. 8:2].

G. [If he said], "Until the rains end," he is prohibited until the first night of Passover [M. Ned. 8:5C–D].

H. [If he said], "Until the *Sukkot* are torn down," he is prohibited until the last night of the Festival [of *Sukkot*].

I. [If he said], "Until Adar," it means, the first.

J. And if the year was intercalated with the addition of a second Adar, he is prohibited until the second Adar [M. Ned. 8:5F–G].

4:8 A. *He who says to his fellow, "Qonam if I derive any benefit whatsoever from you, if you do not come and collect for your child a kor of wheat and two jugs of wine,"* [M. Ned. 8:7A]—

B. and [between times] an occasion of mourning befell him, or he was prevented by constraint, or he had an occasion for a banquet, or there were rains—

C. he is permitted [the vow is not binding].

D. "But under all circumstances he is prohibited [from deeming the vow null] until he will find absolution for his vow through the ruling of a sage," the words of R. Meir.

E. And sages say, "Also: *This one can annul his vow without consultation with a sage.*

"He may say to him, 'Did you not speak only to do me honor? But this [not taking your wheat and wine for my children] is what I deem to be honorable!'" [M. Ned. 8:7B–C].

F. *And so: He who says to his fellow, "Qonam if you derive benefit from me, if you do not come and give my son a kor of wheat and two jugs of wine"* [M. Ned. 8:7D].

G. *[If] one was nagging his fellow to eat with him* during a banquet *[and] said, "Qonam be your house if I enter it"* [M. Ned. 8:7L]—

H. during the banquet, he is prohibited from going in there.

I. After the banquet, he is permitted to go in there.

J. R. Judah says, "If one was nagging his fellow during the festival to eat with him and said to him, '*Qonam* be your house, if I enter it.'

"during the festival he is prohibited from entering it.

"After the festival he is permitted to enter it."

4:9 A. *[If] one was nagging his fellow to eat with him* during a banquet *and*

said to him, "Qonam be your house if I enter it,"
during the banquet, he is prohibited from going in there.
After the banquet he is permitted to go in there.

B. *[If] he said, "Qonam be your house if I enter it," "If I drink a single drop of cold water of yours,"* [M. Ned. 8:7L],

C. *he is permitted to enter his house* [M. Ned. 8:7L],

D. and to wash with him in cold water.

E. But he is prohibited from eating or drinking with him.

5:1 A. He who prohibits himself by a vow from deriving benefit from a house [and] an upper room,

B. and finds out that, before his vow, they had fallen to him by inheritance or had been given to him as a gift,

C. [and said], "If I had known that that was the case, I should never have taken such a vow,"—lo, this [vow] is not binding.

D. M'ŚH B: A certain man prohibited his wife by vow from going up to Jerusalem.

E. And she went and treated his vow as not binding.

F. And he turned to R. Yosé.

G. He [Yosé] said to him, "Now if you had known that she would treat your words as null not in your presence, would you have imposed a vow on her?"

H. He said to him, "Never!"

I. And R. Yosé declared the vow not binding.

J. R. Ishmael b. R. Yosé says, "They say to him, 'If someone had appeased you, would you have taken such a vow?'

K. "If he says, 'No,'

L. "then lo, this [vow] is not binding."

M. R. Judah b. Betera says, "They say to him, 'If you [then] had this [present] attitude, would you have taken such a vow?'

N. "if he says, 'No,'

O. "then, lo, this [vow] is not binding."

P. R. Nathan says, "There is a sort of vow, part of which is not binding and part of which is binding [*vs.* M. Ned. 9:6C].

Q. "How so?

R. "[If] he took a vow not to eat fruit in a basket in which were *shuah*-figs, [and then] he said, 'Had I known that there were *shuah*-figs in it, I would have taken a vow only in regard to the rest of what is in the basket,' he is permitted to eat the *shuah*-figs in the basket but prohibited from eating any of the other fruit in the basket.

S. "[If] he took a vow not to eat onions, [and then] he said, 'Now If I had known that Cyprus-onions are good for the heart, I would have taken a vow only not to eat other kinds of onions,' he is permitted to eat Cyprus-onions but prohibited from eating all other kinds of figs."

T. [Now this was the case] *until R. 'Aqiba came along and taught that an oath, part of which is unloosed is wholly unloosed* [M. Ned. 9:C].

U. *How so?*

V. *[If] he says, "Qonam be what I enjoy from any one of you," and [if] his vow with respect to one of them is declared not binding, then the vow with reference to all of them is declared not binding* [M. Ned. 9:7A–C].

W. *[If he said], "Qonam be what I enjoy from this one and from that one,* and from the other one," *and the vow pertaining to the one in the middle was declared not binding, then from him and onward, it is not binding, but from him and backward, it is binding* [M. Ned. 9:7G].

X. [If he said,] "*Qonam* be what I enjoy from So-and-so," and then he hesitated for a time sufficient to say something and went and said, "Also for So-and-so," he is prohibited in the case of the first, but permitted in the case of the second.

Y. How much is an interval sufficient to say something?

Z. Time enough for a master to ask after the welfare of his disciple.

AA. [If he said,] "*Qonam* be what I enjoy from Mr. So-and-so, and further, from Mr. Such-and-such,"

BB. [or if he said], "For Mr. So-and-so and Mr. Such-and-such, *Qonam* be what I derive benefit," lo, these are deemed to be two separate and distinct vows.

CC. [If] the first is declared not binding, then the second is not binding.

DD. [If] the second is not binding, the first has not been declared not-binding [and has to be unloosed on its own] [M. Ned. 9:7E, F].

5:2 A. [If he said,] "*Qonam* be benefit I derive from So-and-so and from anyone from whom I may obtain absolution for him"—

B. they go and obtain obsolution in respect to the first and then go and gain absolution in respect to the second.

5:3 A. [If] he intended to take a vow by a whole-offering and took a vow as a Nazirite,

B. by an offering, and took a vow by an oath,

C. it is not binding.

D. [If] he intended to take a vow by a whole-offering and took a vow by an offering,

E. by a *herem* and took a vow by that which is sanctified [to the Temple],

F. it is binding.

5:4 A. [If] he took a vow as a Nazir, by an offering, and by an oath, they unloose his vow by a single pretext covering all of them.

B. If he said, "I have taken a vow but I do not know by which of these two I have taken a vow," they unloose his vow through a single pretext covering all of them.

5:5 A. He who takes a vow not to derive benefit from a town (and) seeks absolution from a sage in that town,

B. and one does not scruple that he grants absolution for his own interest.

C. [If he takes a vow not to derive benefit] from an Israelite, he seeks absolution from a sage who is an Israelite,

D. and one does not scruple that he grants absolution in his own interest.

5:6 A. R. Judah b. Betera says, "*They unloose a vow for a man by reference to his own honor and by reference to the honor of his children*" [M. Ned. 9:9A].

B. R. Ishmael said to him, "You have acquired possession of her and of her clothing on her back" [M. Ned. 9:10J].

C. When he died, what did they say before his bier?

D. "*Israelite girls,* weep over R. Ishmael, *who clothed you in scarlet delicately, who put ornaments of gold upon your apparel*" (II Samuel 1:24) [M. Ned. 9:10L–M].

6:1 A. R. Yosé b. R. Judah and R. Eleazar b. R. Simeon say, "The annulment of vows is done over a twenty-four hour period [after the wife has taken her vow]" [*cf.* M. Ned. 10:8A].

B. How [do they annul vows]?

C. [If] his wife was subject to five vows, or he had five wives and each had taken a vow,

D. and he said, "It is annulled,"

E. all of them are annulled.

F. [If] he said, "It is annulled for you," he has annulled the vow only pertaining to her.

G. [If he said] "This vow [is annulled]," he has annulled only that particular vow.

H. [If he said] "Now why did you take a vow? "I don't what you to take a vow," "This is not a vow," he has said nothing whatsoever.

I. [If he said] "This is annulled, "This is cancelled," lo, this is cancelled.

J. [If he said,] "It is confirmed for you," "You did very nicely," "So may I be like you," "If you had not vowed as you did, I should have imposed a vow upon you,"

K. he has no power to annul that vow.

6:2 A. Under what circumstances did they rule that *if the husband died, his power passes to the father* [M. Ned. 10:2B]?

B. When he [the husband] did not hear [the vow], and annulled it, and died on that very day.

C. But if he [the husband] heard the vow and remained silent, [or] heard it and confirmed it, and died on the next day, he [the father] has not got the power to annul it.

D. [If] the husband heard the vow and did not annul it, and the father did not suffice to hear the vow before the husband died,

E. this [too] is the case concerning which they ruled, *If the husband died, his power [to annul the vow] passes to the father.*

6:3 A. [If] her father heard the vow before the father died,

B. this is the sort of case concerning which they ruled, *[If] the father died, the right to annul her vows does not pass to the husband* [M. Ned. 10:2A].

C. [If] her husband heard the vow and annulled it, but the father did not suffice to hear the vow before he died, lo, this is a case in which annulment is prohibited.

D. For the husband has the power to annul the vow only in conjunction with the father [M. Ned. 10:2C].

E. [If] her father heard the vow and annulled it for her, but the husband did not suffice to hear the vow before he died, let the father go back and annul the share of the husband.

F. Said R. Nathan, "This indeed represents the opinion of the House of Shammai.

G. "The House of Hillel say, 'He has not got the power to annul the vow.'"

6:4 A. A betrothed girl—*her father and her last husband annul her vows* [M. Ned. 10:3].

B. [If] the father heard the vow and annulled it for her, but the husband did not suffice to hear the vow before he died,

C. and she then was betrothed, even to ten [further] men—

D. this is the case concerning which they ruled, *Her father and her last husband annul her vows.*

E. [If] her father heard the vow and annulled it, but the husband did not suffice to hear the vow before he died,

F. and she was betrothed to another,

G. let her second husband go and annul the share [in the vow] of the first husband.

H. Said R. Nathan, "This indeed is the opinion of the House of Shammai.

I. "The House of Hillel say, 'He has not got the power to annul the vow.'"

J. Under what circumstances?

K. When he divorced her that day and remarried her that day [M. Ned. 10:3C], or he divorced her that day, and she was betrothed to someone else.

L. But if she reached maturity and was married,

M. or if she awaited consummation of the marriage or twelve months [and was not then married],

N. He [the father] has not got the power to annul her vows any longer.

6:5 A. *A deceased childless brother's widow awaiting levirate marriage, whether with a single levir or with two levirs—*

B. *R. Eliezer says, "He annuls her vows."*

C. *R. Joshua says, "That is the case with one, but not with two."*

D. *R. 'Aqiba says, "That is the case neither with one nor with two"* [M. Ned. 10:6A–D].

E. Said R. Eliezer, "Now in the case of a woman in whom I have no part before she enters my domain, once she enters my domain, she is wholly in my power [so that I may annul her vows], in the case of a woman in whom I have some part before she comes into my domain [in that the woman cannot marry anyone other than the levir in the event that her childless husband dies], once she enters my domain, is it not logical that she should be wholly in my power [so that I may annul her vows]?"

F. Said to him R. 'Aqiba, "No. If you have so stated matters in the case of a woman in whom I have no part before she comes into my domain, while once she enters my domain, she is wholly within my power, the fact is that, just as I have no part in her, so others have no part in her.

G. "But will you say the same of a woman in whom I have a part before she enters into my domain, and who, once she enters my domain, is wholly within my power? For just as I have a part in her, so others [=other Levirs at that point] have a part in her."

H. *Said to him R. Joshua, "'Aqiba, your argument applies to a case of two levirs. What will you reply in the case of one levir"* [M. Ned. 10:6G]?

I. He said to him, "Just as you have not made a distinction for us between a case in which there is a single levir and one in which there are two levirs,

J. "or in a case in which he bespoke the widow and one in which he did not bespeak the widow,

K. "so in the case of vows and oaths you should make no distinction."

L. He said to him, "It would have been too bad for you had you been around in the time of R. Eleazar b. 'Arakh and given an answer of this sort!"

M. He said to R. Eliezer [in reference to M. Ned. 10:7], "The case of an immersion pool will prove the matter as I see it. It raises things which have become unclean from their status of uncleanness, but it does not rescue things which are clean from becoming unclean."

N. R. Eliezer went and offered a different mode of argument, which is as follows: "No. If in a situation in which he cannot annul his own vows once he has made them, lo, he has the power to annul his own vows before he has made them [by declaring them null in advance,] in a situation in which he may annul the vows of his wife once she has made them, is it not logical that he should be able to annul the vows of his wife before she makes them?"

O. They said to him, "Now if he is able to annul his own vows before he makes them, it is also true that if he wanted to confirm his vows [by actually making] them, he also does confirm them.

"But may he annul the vows of his wife before she actually vows? For if he wanted to confirm them [before she makes them], he has not got the power to do so" [M. Ned. 10:7A].

6:6 A. "Another matter: *Her husband will confirm it and her husband will annul it* (Num. 30:14)—

B. "*A vow which enters the category of confirmation enters the category of annulment. A vow which does not enter into the category of confirmation does not enter into the category of annulment*" [M. Ned. 10:7F–G].

6:7 A. [If one said], "This ox will be sanctified once I have purchased it,"

"This house will be sanctified once I have purchased it,"

"This ox will be sold to you, once I have purchased it,"

"This house is sold to you, once I have purchased it,"

"Give this divorce to my wife, once I have betrothed her,"

B. he has said nothing.

C. [If he said], "The ox which I shall inherit from father is sold to you,"

"What will come up in my trap is sold to you,"

D. he has said nothing.

E. [If he said,] "What I shall inherit from father *today* is sold to you," "What will come up in my trap *this day* is sold to you," his statements are confirmed [and put into force] [*cf.* M. Ned. 10:8A].

7:1 A. Any matter in which there is inflicting of self-punishment [M. Ned. 11:1B],

B. whether it involves something between him and her,

C. or between her and other people,

D. he annuls.

E. But a matter in which there is no inflicting of self-punishment,

F. [if it is] between him and her, he annuls it.

G. [If it is] between her and other people, he does not annul it.

H. How so?

I. *[If] she said, "Qonam if I work for father," ". . . for your father," ". . . for my brother," ". . . for your brother"* [M. Ned. 11:4A],

J. "if I feed your cattle,"

K. he has not got the power to annul [such vows], because these are between her and other people.

L. [If she said, "*Qonam*] if I put on eye-shadow," " . . . if I put on rouge," ". . . if I adorn myself," " . . . if I have sexual relations with you,"

M. lo, this one annuls such vows as these, because they relate to matters which are between him and her.

N. [If she said, "*Qonam*] if I lay out the bed," ". . . if I wash your feet," ". . . if I mix the cup for you,"

O. he does not have to annul [such a vow] but forces her to do these services against her will.

P. Rabban Gamaliel says, "He annuls [even] such vows as these, since it is said, *He shall not profane his word* (Num. 30:2)."

7:2 A. [If] she vowed not to taste a particular sort of produce,

B. whether it be inedible or edible,

C. even if she had never in her life tasted that sort of produce [which she had vowed not to taste],

D. he annuls the vow.

E. [If] she said, "*Qonam* be pepper which I taste," ". . . be white bread which I taste,"

F. even if she had never had that sort of thing in her entire life,

G. he annuls that vow,

7:3 A. [If] she said, "*Qonam* be the produce of the Land of Israel for me,"

B. if he has a share in them, he annuls that vow.

C. But if not, let him provide produce for her from other countries.

D. [If she said,] "*Qonam* be the produce of this hyparchy for me,"

E. if he has a share in them, he annuls that vow.

F. But if not, let him provide produce for her from some other province.

G. [If] she said, "*Qonam* be the produce of this stall for me,"

H. if there is there another stall, he does not annul that vow, but if not, he does annul that vow.

I. R. Yosé says, "Even if there were there a hundred other stalls, if he derived provisions only from that stall, lo, this one annuls that vow,

J. "since this is a vow which affects the relationship between him and her" [M. Ned. 11:2B–E].

7:4 A. *[If she said,] "Qonam if I derive benefit from anybody," he has not got the power to annul that vow. But she can derive benefit from Gleanings, the Forgotten Sheaf, and the Corner of the Field* [M. Ned. 11:3A–B],

B. and from the tithe set aside for the poor.

C. *If his wife took a vow,* and he annulled it for her, *and he thought that his daughter had taken a vow,*

D. *or if his daughter took a vow,* and he annulled it for her, *and he thought that his wife had taken the vow* [M. Ned. 11:5A, B],

E. lo, this one may confirm the vow.

F. But if he wanted to annul it, he annuls it.

G. [If] his wife took a vow, and he confirmed it for her and he thought that his daughter had taken the vow,

H. [if] his daughter took a vow, and he confirmed it for her, and he thought that his wife had taken the vow,

I. lo, this one annuls the vow.

J. But if he wanted to confirm it, he confirms it.

K. [If] she vowed not to eat figs and grapes [and] he annulled the vow confirming figs but did not annul the vow concerning grapes,

L. she is prohibited from eating figs and grapes [M. Ned. 11:6C].

M. [If] he annulled the vow not to eat grapes but did not annul the vow not to eat figs, she is prohibited from eating grapes and figs [M. Ned. 11:6C].

N. [If] he annulled the vow concerning the figs and it got dark, she is prohibited from eating figs and grapes [cf. M. Ned. 10:8A].

O. [If] he annulled the vow concerning grapes and it got dark, she is prohibited from eating grapes and figs.

P. *If she said, "Qonam be a fig which I eat, and furthermore [qonam be] grapes which I eat," lo, these are deemed two distinct vows* [M. Ned. 11:6D].

Q. He annuls whichever one he wants and confirms whichever one he wants,

R. since it is said, *Her husband will confirm it* [regarding this one], *and her husband will annul it* [regarding the other one].

7:5 A. A more strict rule applies to confirming vows than applies to annulling vows, and a more strict rule applies to annulling vows than applies to confirming vows.

B. For silence [on the part of the husband who hears a vow] is tantamount to confirmation, but it is not tantamount to annulment.

C. The husband may confirm a vow in his heart, but he may not annul the vow in his heart [but must say so explicitly].

D. And there is a rule governing confirmation of vows which does not apply to annuling them, and there is a rule applying to annulling vows which does not apply to confirming vows.

E. Once the husband has confirmed a vow, he cannot annul it.

F. Once he has annulled a vow, he has not got the power to confirm it.

7:6 A. A married woman who said, "Lo, I am a Nazirite when I shall have been divorced"—

B. R. Ishmael says, "He does not annul such a vow."

C. R. 'Aqiba says, "He annuls such a vow."

D. A widow who said, "Lo, I am a Nazirite when I shall have been married"—

E. R. Ishmael says, "He annuls such a vow."

F. R. 'Aqiba says, "He does not annul such a vow."

G. For R. Ishmael says, "*But any vow of a widow or of a divorcee, anything by which she has bound herself, shall stand against her* (Num. 30:9)—so long as it be a prohibition which takes place at the moment at which she is a widow or a divorcee."

H. R. 'Aqiba says, "*By which she has bound herself shall stand against her*—so long as it be a prohibition binding at the moment at which she binds herself" [M. Ned. 11:9].

7:7 A. [If she said,] "*Qonam* if I do any work for you, which benefits father"—

B. R. Nathan says, "He annuls such a vow."

C. And sages say, "He does not annul such a vow" [M. Ned. 11:11].

7:8 A. [She who says], "*I am removed from the Jews* if I serve you"—

B. *let him annul his share in the vow so that she may serve him* [M. Ned. 11:12H].

C. R. Nathan says, "He does not annul such a vow."

D. And sages say, "He annuls such a vow."

NEZIRUT

1:1 A. The House of Shammai say, "Euphemisms for euphemisms are binding."

B. And the House of Hillel say, "Euphemisms for euphemisms are not binding" [M. Naz. 1:1A].

C. The House of Shammai say, "They do not give testimony [that a woman's husband has died] on the basis of what is heard merely through an echo."

D. And the House of Hillel say, "They give testimony on the basis of what is heard merely through an echo" [Cf. M. Yeb. 16:6].

1:2 A. He who says, "Nazirite-vows"—

B. Rabban Simeon b. Gamaliel says, "Lo, this one is a Nazir for two spells."

C. [If he said,] "Lo, I am a Nazir and one," lo, this one is a Nazir for two spells [M. Naz. 1:3D].

D. [If he said,] ". . . and more," lo, he is a Nazir for three spells.

E. [If he said,] ". . . one and more and again," lo, this one is a Nazir for four spells.

F. Sumkhos says, "[If he said,] 'Lo, I am a Nazir *tetragon,*' lo, this one is a Nazir for four spells; '. . . *digon,*' lo, three Nazirite-spells [are incumbent on him]; '. . . *drigon,*' lo, two Nazirite-spells [are incumbent on him]."

1:3 A. [He once said,] "Lo, I am a Nazir, if I do not [reveal] the families [which are impure]," let him be a Nazir and let him not reveal the families [which are impure].

B. "Lo, I am a Nazir in accord with the hours of the day," ". . . in accord with the months of the year," lo, this one is a Nazir for twelve spells.

C. ". . . in accord with the days of the week," ". . . in accord with the years of the septennate," ". . . in accord with the years of release of a Jubilee," lo, this one is a Nazir for seven spells.

D. "Lo, I am a Nazir in accord with the days of the solar year," he is a Nazir for three hundred sixty-five spells of Naziriteship, in accord with the number of days of the solar year.

E. ". . . in accord with the days of the moon," ". . . in accord with the number of the days of the moon,"—he is a Nazir for three hundred fifty-four spells of Naziriteship, in accord with the number of the days of the lunar year.

F. Rabbi says, "[This is valid] only if he will say, 'Lo, I am a Nazir for the number of Nazirite spells equivalent to the days of the solar year,' '. . . equivalent to the number of days of the solar year,' '. . . equivalent to the days of the lunar year,' '... equivalent to the number of days of the lunar year.'"

G. R. Judah says, "[If] he said, 'Lo, I am a Nazir in accord with the sheaves of the summer harvest,' or, '... the paths of the year of release,' lo, this one is a lifetime Nazir.

H. "And he shaves once in thirty days."

I. [If he said, "Lo, I am a Nazir] ... a jarful," or "... a *basketful*" [M. Naz. 1:5A], lo, this one is a lifetime Nazir.

J. And he shaves once in thirty days.

K. [This is so] unless he says to them, "It was not to that purpose [that I intended in taking a vow]."

1:4 A. *[If he said], "Lo, I am a Nazir like the hairs of my head," "... like the dust of the earth," "... like the sand of the sea," lo, this one is a lifelong Nazir.*

B. *And he cuts his hair once in thirty days.*

C. *Rabbi says, "This one does not shave once in thirty days* [M. Naz. 1:4A–C].

D. "For this is not a lifelong Nazir."

E. [If he said,] "Lo, I am a Nazir from now until the border," "... from the earth to the firmament," lo, this one is a lifelong Nazir.

F. [If he said,] "Lo, I am a Nazir all my days," "Lo, I am a lifelong Nazir," lo, this one is a lifelong Nazir.

G. [If he said, "Lo, I am a Nazir] for a hundred years," or "... for two hundred years," this one is not a lifelong Nazir.

1:5 A. Just as euphemisms for Nazirite-vows are equivalent to Nazirite-vows, so euphemisms for Samson-vows are equivalent to Samson-vows [M. Naz. 1:2C].

B. R. Judah says, "A Nazir in the status of Samson is permitted to become unclean with corpse-uncleanness.

C. "For Samson himself became unclean with corpse-uncleanness" [M. Naz. 1:2H].

D. R. Simeon says, "He who says, 'Lo, I am like Samson,' has said nothing.

E. "For the language of Naziriteship has not gone forth from his lips [to encumber] him" [*vs.* M. Naz. 1:2C].

F. Naziriteship applies in the Land and abroad,

G. whether the man has hair or does not have hair.

H. Even though it is said, *[And the Nazirite shall shave his consecrated head at the door of the tent of meeting] and shall take the hair from his consecrated head [and put it on the fire]* (Num. 6:18).

I. And it applies whether or not he has hands,

J. even though it is said, *[And the priest shall take the shoulder of the ram . . . and one unleavened cake out of the basket, and one unleavened wafer,] and shall put them upon the hands of the Nazirite* [Num. 6:19].

1:6 A. A totally hairless Nazir—

B. the House of Shammai say, "He has to pass a razor across his whole body."

C. And the House of Hillel say, "He does not have to do so."

D. And so is the dispute concerning the *meṣora'*, and so is the dispute concerning Levites.

E. A more strict rule applies to the Nazir than applies to the *meṣora'*, and to the *meṣora'* that does not apply to the Nazirite.

F. A Nazirite, if he shaved on the day of completion of his vow, incurs forty stripes, which is not the case with the *meṣora'*.

G. A *meṣora'* shaves his head, his beard, and his eyebrows, which is not the case with the Nazirite.

1:7 A. A more strict rule applies to Nazirite-vows than applies to oaths, and to oaths than to Nazirite-vows.

B. For a Nazirite-vow may be found within another such vow, but an oath is not contained within another oath [M. Ned. 2:3].

C. A more strict rule applies to oaths, for an oath made inadvertently is binding, but a Nazirite-vow made inadvertently is not binding.

2:1 A. The House of Shammai say, "Euphemisms for euphemisms are binding."

B. How so?

C. *[If] he said, "Lo, I am a Nazir from dried figs and from fig-cake,"*

D. the House of Shammai say, "He is a Nazir" [M. Naz. 2:1].

2:2 A. *[If he said], "Lo, I am a Nazirite on condition that I shall be drinking wine and making myself unclean with corpse-uncleanness"*

B. *lo, this one is a Nazir* [M. Naz. 2:4A–B].

C. But his prior stipulation is null.

D. For he has made a condition contrary to what is written in the Torah, and whoever makes a condition contrary to what is written in the Torah—his condition is null.

2:3 A. *"I recognize that there are Nazirs, but I do not recognize that Nazirs are prohibited from drinking wine"* [M. Naz. 2:4D]

B. "that it is prohibited to drink wine and to become unclean with corpse-uncleanness"—.

C. R. Simeon says, "You have no greater pretext than such a statement [for annulling the vow]" [M. Naz. 2:4F].

2:4 A. *"Lo, I pledge myself to offer half of a Nazir's hair-offering,"*

"lo, this one offers the whole of a Nazir's offering," the words of R. Meir [M. Naz. 2:6A, B].

B. R. Simeon declares him exempt.

C. For he has not volunteered to do so in the normal way in which people make such voluntary pledges.

2:5 A. [If one said,] *"Lo I am a Nazir, and it is incumbent upon me to offer the hair-offering of a[nother] Nazir"* [M. Naz. 2:5A],

B. and if he [first] offered his own hair-offering, he has not fulfilled the terms of his pledge.

2:6 A. "Lo, I pledge myself to offer half of the hair-offering of a Nazir," and he further said, "Lo, I am a Nazir,"

B. if he [first] offered his own hair-offering, he has not fulfilled the terms of his pledge.

C. [If he said], "These are the offerings an account of which I shall separate [myself as a Nazir],"

D. he has said nothing,

E. since it says, *His offering for the Lord on account of his Nazirite-vow* (Num. 6:21), and not his Nazirite-vow on account of his offering.

2:7 A. "Lo, I pledge myself to offer the sin-offering or the guilt-offering owed by Mr. So-and-so"—

B. if he said so with the other's knowledge, the other has fulfilled his obligation.

C. [If he said so] not with the other's knowledge, he has not fulfilled his obligation.

D. "Lo, this is the sin-offering or the guilt-offering owed by Mr. So-and-so"—

E. and the other went and brought offerings in his own behalf—

F. lo, these [brought by the first party] are in the status of a sin-offering or a guilt-offering, the owner of which has effected atonement [through some other animal].

2:8 A. *"Lo, I am a Nazir if I have a son," and a son was born to him* [M. Naz. 2:7A]—

B. it is a matter of doubt whether or not the foetus is viable—.

C. R. Judah declares him exempt.

D. For in Nazirite-vows a vow subject to doubt is not binding.

E. R. Simeon declares him liable.

F. For in Nazirite-vows a vow subject to doubt is binding.

G. *He therefore should say, "If it was viable, lo, I am a Nazir out of obliga-*

tion. And if not, lo, I am a Nazirite out of free will" [M. Nazir 2:8B].

2:9 A. "Lo, I am a Nazir, on condition that in this pile of wheat there should be a hundred *kor,*"

B. and he went and found it had been stolen or had gotten lost—

C. it is a matter of doubt whether or not there was that volume of wheat in the mound—.

D. R. Judah declares him exempt.

E. For in Nazirite-vows a vow subject to doubt is not binding.

F. R. Simeon declares him liable.

G. For in Nazirite-vows, a vow subject to doubt is binding.

H. He therefore should say, "If matters were as I said, lo, I am a Nazir out of obligation. And if not, lo, I am a Nazir out of free will."

2:10 A. "Lo, I am a Nazir after twenty days, a Nazir from now for a hundred days,"

B. he counts twenty, and afterward he counts thirty,

C. and he counts eighty to complete his first Nazirite-vow [*cf.* M. Naz. 2:10].

D. R. Simeon b. Eleazar says, "The House of Shammai and the House of Hillel did not differ concerning one who vowed to be a Nazir for thirty days,

E. "that, if he cut his hair on the thirtieth day, he has not fulfilled his obligation [M. Naz. 3:1C–D].

F. "Concerning what did they dispute?

G. "Concerning a case in which one vowed without further specification.

H. "For: The House of Shammai say, 'If he cut his hair on the thirtieth day, he has not fulfilled his obligation.'

I. "And the House of Hillel say, 'If he cut his hair on the thirtieth day, he has fulfilled his obligation'" [M. Naz. 3:1A–B].

2:11 A. He who took two successive vows to be a Nazir, the first a vow to be a Nazir without specification [as to length], and the second a vow to be a Nazir for thirty days,

cuts his hair for the first oath on the thirty-first day and for the second on the sixty-first day [M. Naz. 3:2A].

B. *But if he cut his hair for the first on the thirtieth day, he cuts his hair for the second on the sixtieth day* [M. Naz. 3:2B],

C. [and] he has fulfilled his obligation.

D. [If the time specified for] for the first Nazirite-vow was thirty days and for the second vow was not specified,

E. he cuts his hair for the first vow on the thirty-first day and for the second on the sixty-first day.

F. And if he cut his hair on the sixtieth day, he has not fulfilled his obligation.

2:12 A. *He who said, "Lo, I am a Nazir," and was made unclean on the thirtieth day loses the whole [thirty days which he already has counted in accord with the rules of being a Nazir].*

B. R. Judah says in the name of *R. Eliezer, "He has lost only seven days."*

C. *[If he said], "Lo, I am a Nazir for thirty days," and was made unclean on the thirtieth day, he loses the whole [thirty days already observed].*

2:13 A. *"Lo, I am a Nazir for a hundred days," and he was made unclean on the hundredth day, he loses the whole [period already observed].*

B. R. Judah says in the name of *R. Eliezer, "He has lost only thirty days."*

C. *[If] he was made unclean on the hundred and first day, he loses thirty days.*

D. R. Judah says in the name of *R. Eliezer, "He has lost only seven"* [M. Naz. 3:3–4].

E. This is the general principle which R. Judah said in the name of R. Eliezer, "Whoever was made unclean on the day on which it is [not] suitable to bring his offering and who has to count [more days of Naziriteship loses all. If he does not have to count], he loses thirty days.

F. "And whoever was made unclean on a day on which it is (not) suitable to bring his offering and who does not have to count [more days of his Naziriteship] has lost only seven days [reading: *TK*, pp. 523–24],

G. "exclusive of the days on which he is unclean only."

2:14 A. He who was unclean and took an oath as a Nazir is prohibited from cutting his hair and from drinking wine and from contracting corpse-uncleanness.

B. And if he cut his hair, drank wine, or contracted corpse-uncleanness, he receives forty stripes.

C. He is sprinkled and repeats the process [on the third and seventh days of becoming unclean with corpse-uncleanness].

D. The days on which he is unclean do not count toward the fulfillment of his vow.

E. But also: the seventh day does count toward the fulfillment of his vow.

F. All cases concerning which they have said, "He does not begin to count [the clean days for the purposes of his Nazirite-vow] until he becomes clean"—the seventh day does not count toward the fulfillment of the vow.

G. All cases concerning which they have said, "He begins to count [the clean days for the purposes of his Nazirite-vow] forthwith"—the seventh day does count toward the fulfillment of his vow [*cf.* M. Naz. 7:2].

H. [If] he counted out the days in fulfillment of his Nazirite-vow but did not bring his offerings, he is prohibited from cutting his hair, from drinking wine, and from contracting corpse-uncleanness.

I. And if he cut his hair, drank wine, or contracted corpse-uncleanness, lo, this one receives forty stripes.

J. R. Simeon says, "Once the blood of one of his sacrifices has been tossed in his behalf, he is released from his vow as a Nazir and may drink wine or contract corpse-uncleanness" [M. Naz. 6:9].

2:15 A. He who took two vows as a Nazir, counted out the first but did not bring his offerings, and afterward sought absolution for the first from a sage to declare it not binding for him—

B. the second vow to be a Nazir goes forth with the loosening of the first.

C. [If] he counted out the days required for both of them, and brought the offerings for both of them at one time,

D. he gets credit only for one of them.

E. [If] he set aside the offerings for one of them by itself and the offering for the other by itself and went and offered this one in place of that one, he has not fulfilled his obligation.

3:1 A. Said R. Ishmael b. R. Yoḥanan b. Beroqah, "The House of Shammai and the House of Hillel did not differ concerning a case in which there were two sets of witnesses, in which there were two sets of witnesses giving testimony concerning him, that he is a Nazir for the shortest period [specified in their joint testimony].

B. "Concerning what sort of case did they differ?

C. "Concerning a case in which there were two individual witnesses giving testimony concerning him.

D. "For: *The House of Shammai say, 'The testimony is divided, so that there is no obligation to be a Nazir here at all.'*

E. *"And the House of Hillel say, 'In the sum of five are two spells. So let him serve out two spells of Naziriteship'"* [M. Naz. 3:7].

3:2 A. *He who said, "Lo, I am a Nazir,"* and then hesitated for a time sufficient for a break in conversation,

B. *and his friend heard and said, "And me too"* [M. Naz. 4:1A–B]—

C. he is bound [by the oath], but his friend is not bound by it.

D. And how long is a time sufficient for a break in conversation?

E. Sufficient time to ask after someone's welfare.

3:3 A. *"Lo, I am a Nazir,"*

B. *and his friend heard and said, "Let my mouth be like his mouth, and my hair like his hair," lo, this one also is a Nazir* [M. Naz. 4:1E].

C. [If he said], "Let my hand be like his hand." "My foot like his foot," lo, this one is a Nazir.

D. [If he said], "My hand is a Nazir," "My foot is a Nazir," he is not a Nazir.

E. "My head is a Nazir," "My liver is a Nazir,"—lo, this one is a Nazir.

F. This is the general principle: [If he spoke of] something upon which life depends, he is a Nazir. [If he spoke of] something on which life does not depend, he is not a Nazir.

3:4(5) A. He who says to his wife, "Lo, I am a Nazir, and you?"

B. If she said, "Yes," both of them are bound by his oath.

C. If he wanted to annul her vow, he annuls her vow, because [his] vow came before [her acceptance and his] confirmation [M. Naz. 4:2].

D. If not, [B] he is bound by his vow, and she is not bound by his vow.

E. He who says to his wife, "Lo, I am a Nazir, and [if] you [are]?"

F. If she said, "Yes," both of them are bound by his oath.

G. And if not, both of them are not bound,

H. because he makes his vow contingent upon her vow.

3:6 A. [If] his wife said to him, "Lo, I am a Nazir, and you?"

B. [If] he said, "Yes," both of them are bound by her oath.

C. If he wanted to annul her vow, he cannot annul it,

D. because his confirmation [of her vow] came before his vow.

E. If not, she is bound and he is permitted.

3:7 A. [If] his wife said to him, "Lo, I am a Nazir, [if] you are?"

B. If he said, "Yes," both of them are bound by her vow.

C. If not, both of them are not bound,

D. because she made her vow contingent upon his vow.

3:8 A. He who said to his friend, "Lo, I am a Nazir, and you?"

B. If he said, "Yes," both of them are bound.

C. If not, he is bound, and his friend is not bound.

3:9 A. He who says to his friend, "Lo, I am a Nazir, and [if] you [are]?"

B. If he said, "Yes," both of them are bound.

C. And if not, both of them are not bound,

D. because he made his vow contingent upon the vow of his [friend].

E. [If] his friend said to him, "Lo, are you a Nazir?"

F. [If] he said to him, "Are you?"

G. If he said to him, "Yes," he is bound, and his friend is not bound.

H. [If] his friend said to him, "Lo, are you Nazir?"

I. If he said to him, "And you?"

J. If he said to him, "Yes," then both of them are bound.

K. And if not, both of them are not bound,

L. because he made his vow continent upon the vow of his [friend].

3:10 A. The woman who took a vow and her girl-friend heard and said, "And me too," and afterward the husband of this one [who originally took the vow] came and annulled it for her—

B. she is not bound by her vow, but her girl-friend is bound by it.

C. R. Simeon says, "If she [the girl-friend] has said, 'Also I intended only to be like her,' then both of them are not bound by the vow."

3:11 A. [If she said], "By an oath that I not enter this house,"

B. and she made a mistake and went into it—

C. she is not bound as to the past but is bound as to the future.

3:12 A. A woman who took an oath to be a Nazir, and her husband heard and did not annul the vow for her—

B. R. Meir and R. Judah say, "He has put his finger between her teeth.

C. "If he wanted to annul the vow, he may do so.

D. "And if he said, 'I do not want a wife who is a Nazir,' he puts her away and pays off her marriage-contract."

3:13 A. R. Yosé and R. Simeon say, "She has put her finger between her teeth.

B. "For if the husband wanted to annul the vow, he cannot do so.

C. "And if he said, 'I do not want a wife who is a Nazir,' she goes forth without receiving payment of her marriage-contract."

3:14 A. *The woman who took a vow to be a Nazir—*

B. *her husband annulled the vow for her, but she did not know that her husband had annulled the vow,*

C. *she went around drinking wine and contracting corpse-uncleanness* [M. Naz. 4:3A–C]—

D. lo, this one receives forty stripes [*vs.* M. Naz. 4:3D].

E. And when R. 'Aqiba would reach this matter, he would cry, saying, "Now if someone who intended to take up in his hand pig-meat and took up in his hand lamb-meat and who ate it has to effect atonement, he who intends to take up in his hand pig-meat and who actually does take up in his hand pig-meat—how much the more so that he requires atonement and forgiveness!"

F. *Under what circumstances?*

G. *In the case of the hair-offering in a state of cleanness.*

H. *But in the case of the hair-offering in a state of uncleanness, he may annul the vow.*

I. For he is as if he annuls the vow for the future.

J. *For he has to the power to say, "I do not want a wife who is disgraceful."*

K. *Rabbi says, "Also in the case of cutting the hair in a state of cleanness, any time before she has cut her hair, he may annul the vow.*

L. "For he has the power to say, 'I do not want a wife who has shaved her head'" [M. Naz. 4:5].

3:15 A. He who took a vow to be a Nazir but went around drinking wine and contracting corpse-uncleanness,

B. and afterward sought absolution from a sage, and the sage absolved him of the vow,

C. does not receive forty stripes.

D. Said R. Judah, "If he does not receive forty stripes, he receives stripes for rebellion against the law."

3:16 A. [If] he sets aside coins for the purchase of offerings for his Naziriteship,

B. they are not available for benefit but are not subject to the laws of sacrilege,

C. for all of them [the coins which have been set aside] are suitable to serve for bringing peace-offerings.

D. [If] he died, coins which have not been designated for the purchase of a particular sacrifice fall for the purchase of a freewill-offering [M. Naz. 4:4F].

E. Coins which have been designated [for the purchase of a particular sacrifice are dealt with as follows]:

F. *Those which have been set aside for the purchase of a sin-offering go off to the Salt Sea. They are not available for benefit but are not subject to the laws of sacrilege.*

G. *Those which have been set aside for the purchase of a burnt-offering are used for the bringing of a burnt-offering. And they are subject to the laws of sacrilege.*

H. *Those which are set aside for the purchase of a peace-offering are used for the offering of a peace-offering, which is eaten for one day and which does not require a bread-offering* [M. Naz. 4:4A–M].

I. [If he said,] "These are for my burnt-offering, and the rest of the money is for the purchase of the rest of the offerings for my Naziriteship," and then he died,

J. with the money set aside for the purpose of a burnt-offering, let [the executor] bring a burnt-offering. And the rest of the money falls for the purchase of a freewill-offering.

K. [If he said that] these are for his peace-offering, and the rest is for the remainder of the offerings for his Naziriteship, and then died,

L. with the money set aside for the purchase of a peace-offering, let one bring a peace-offering. And the rest of the money falls for the purchase of a freewill-offering.

M. [If he said,] "These [coins] are for the purchase of my burnt-offering, and these for the purchase of my sin-offering, and the rest are for the purchase of the rest of the offerings for my Naziriteship," and then he died,

N. the money set aside for the sin-offering goes off to the Salt Sea. It is not available for benefit but is not subject to the laws of sacrilege.

O. [If he said,] "These are for my sin-offering, and these are for my burnt-offering, and these are for my peace-offering," and the coins got mixed up together,

P. lo, this one should purchase with them three beasts, whether from one part [of the mixture] or from three distinct [parts of the mixture of coins].

Q. He renders the coins set aside for the purchase of a sin-offering unconsecrated on account of the animal to be used for the sin-offering [which he now has purchased], and the coins set aside for the purchase of a burnt-offering [are rendered] unconsecrated on account of the burnt-offering, and the coins set aside for the purchase of a peace-offering [are rendered] unconsecrated on account of the peace-offering.

R. And he pays the coins over to the owners of the several animals.

S. He should not pay out the money to the owners until he renders the coins unconsecrated by means of each of the animals [which he is purchasing].

3:17 A. The House of Shammai say, "A man does not impose a Nazirite-vow upon his son."

B. And the House of Hillel say, *"He does impose a Nazirite-vow on his son"* [M. Naz. 4:6A].

C. [If] he imposed such a vow on him while he was a minor,

D. [if] he then shaved,

E. or produced two pubic hairs,

F. the Nazirite vow imposed on him by his father is null.

3:18 A. Under what circumstances did they rule, *A man brings a hair-offering [with the offerings 'et aside] for the Nazirite-vow of his father?*

B. "When he took a Nazirite-vow in the lifetime of the father.

C. "But if he took a vow to be a Nazir after the death of his father,

D. "he does not bring a hair-offering [with an offering set aside] for the Nazirite-vow of his father," the words of R. Yosé, R. Eleazar, and R. Simeon [M. Naz. 4:7E–I].

E. R. Meir and R. Judah say, "One way or the other, one does not bring a hair-offering [with offerings set aside] for the Nazirite-vow of his father.

F. "And under what circumstances did they rule, *A man brings a hair-offering [with offerings set aside] for the Nazirite-vow of his father?*

G. "When his father left him money which had not been designated [for particular animals in fulfillment] of his Naziriteship, and [then his father] died.

H. "But if his father left money which had been designated, or a cow [designated in fulfillment of his Nazirite-vow], then he does not bring a hair-offering [with offerings set aside] for the Nazirite-vow of his father."

3:19 A. He who vowed to be a Nazir and sought absolution from a sage, who declared his vow to be binding—

B. the House of Shammai say, "He counts out the days from the moment at which he made inquiry."

C. And the House of Hillel say, "He counts out the days from the moment at which he treated the vow as not binding."

D. [If] he sought absolution from a sage, who declared his vow to be not binding, these and those concur that *if he had a beast set aside [for his offerings], it should go forth and pasture in the herd* [M. Naz. 5:2D–E].

E. *This error did Nahum the Mede make* [M. Naz. 5:4D] when he declared a vow to be released.

F. *[If people] were walking on the way and some one was coming toward them,*

G. *one of them said, "Lo, I am a Nazir, if this is So-and-so,"*

H. *and one of them said, "Lo, I am a Nazir if it is not So-and-so,"*

I. *"Lo, I am a Nazir if one of you is a Nazir,"*

J. *and one of them says, "Lo, I am a Nazir if one of you is not a Nazir,"*

K. *"Lo, I am a Nazir if both of you are Nazirs,"*

L. *and one of them says, "Lo, I am a Nazir if all of you are Nazirs,"*

M. *the House of Shammai say, "All of them are Nazirs."*

N. *And the House of Hillel say, "A Nazir is only one whose statement was not confirmed."*

O. And they bring an offering in partnership.

P. R. Judah says in the name of *R. Tarfon, "Not a single one of them [is a Nazir]* [M. Naz. 5:5], because a Nazirite-vow applies only when it is clearly and unambiguously expressed beyond a shadow of a doubt."

Q. Said R. Yosé, "The House of Shammai did say in the case of one who says, 'Lo I am a Nazir if this is Joseph,' and it turned out to be Joseph, '. . . if this is Simeon,' and it turned out to be Simeon, that he is a Nazir."

R. [If] one saw a person with both male and female sexual traits and said, "Lo, I am a Nazir if this is a man,"

S. and one says, "Lo, I am a Nazir if this is not a man,"

T. "Lo, I am a Nazir if this is a woman,"

U. and one of them says, "Lo, I am a Nazir if this is not a woman,"

V. "Lo, I am a Nazir if this is both a man and a woman,"

W. and one of them says, "Lo, I am a Nazir if this is neither a man nor a woman,"

X. "Lo, I am a Nazir if one of you is a Nazir,"

Y. "Lo, I am a Nazir if none of you is a Nazir,"

Z. "Lo, I am a Nazir if both of you are Nazirs,"

AA. "Lo, I am a Nazir if all of you are Nazirs,"

BB. all of them are Nazirs [*cf.* M. Naz. 5:7].

CC. And all of them count out nine vows of Naziriteship.

4:1 A. A Nazir who ate anything which is prohibited to him or drank anything which is prohibited to him,

B. [if he was subject] to a single admonition not to do so, he is liable on only one count.

C. [But if] people admonished him and he nonetheless ate, people admonished him and he nonetheless drank, he is liable for each and every count [*cf.* M. Naz. 6:4].

D. And what is the measure [to impose liability] for them?

E. In the volume of an olive's bulk [M. Naz. 6:1C].

F. And all of them join together to form the requisite volume of an olive's bulk [M. Naz. 6:1B].

G. Wine and vinegar follow suit.

H. "What does he do [to reckon the liquid-volume of an olive]? He brings a cup filled with wine, and he brings a summer olive, and he puts it into the cup and lets it spill over.

I. "If he drank as much as spills out of the cup, he is liable, and if not, he is exempt," the words of R. 'Aqiba.

J. R. Eleazar b. 'Azariah declares him exempt unless he drinks a quarter-*log* of wine [M. Naz. 6:1D]—

K. whether he mixed it and drank it or whether he drank it straight.

4:2 A. R. Eleazar says, "A Nazir who put his mouth over the mouth of a jug of wine and drank the whole thing up under a single admonition not to do so is liable only on one count.

"But if they were admonishing him not to do so and he nonetheless drank, admonishing him not to do so and he nonetheless drank, he is liable for each count."

B. And so did R. Eleazar rule, "[If] he took a single grape-cluster and ate it while subject to a single admonition, he is liable only on one count.

C. "But if people were admonishing him and he ate, admonishing him and he ate, he is liable for each and every count."

D. If he ate from it [a grape-cluster] fresh grapes and dried ones, ate from it two grape-pits and a single grape-skin, or squeezed from it an olive's bulk of wine and drank it [*cf.* M. Naz. 4:1],

E. he is liable for each and every thing [he ate].

4:3 A. A Nazir who shaved or who rubbed his head or who pulled out a hair with a scissors in any amount at all, lo, this one is liable.

B. But he loses [the days he already has observed] only if he does so with a razor to the greater part of his head.

C. R. Simeon b. Judah says in the name of R. Simeon, "Just as to two hairs [if left] prevent him [from completing his Nazirite vow when he shaves on the thirtieth day], so two hairs cause him to lose the days he already has observed" [*cf.* M. Naz. 6:3B].

4:4 A. A more strict rule applies to the cutting of the hair.

B. For the cutting of the hair is subject to no limit.

C. And [the law] treats the one who cuts the hair as equivalent to the one whose hair is cut,

D. which is not the case for the other two things [M. Naz. 6:5].

E. How is it so that *for that which goes forth from the vine there is no exception* [M. Naz. 6:5E]?

F. A Nazir who drank wine in the status of heave-offering –r in the status of second tithe—

G. one who said, "By an oath! I shall not drink wine," but drank it—

H. such as these are liable for each and every such action.

I. How is it so that *cutting of the hair is allowed an exception in the case of a religious duty* [M. Naz. 6:5F]?

J. A man who had been certified as a *meṣora'*, lo, this one cuts his hair. One need not say that he cuts his hair in connection with his *ṣara'at,* but he even does so also to allow for the inspection-sign of his boil—to see whether or not it spread.

K. Whether he was made unclean or others made him unclean, whether inadvertently or deliberately, whether under constraint or willingly, *he loses all the days already observed, and is liable for an offering* [M. Naz. 6:5H].

L. Whether he cut his own hair or others cut his hair, whether inadvertently or deliberately, whether under constraint or willingly, *he loses only thirty days* [M. Naz. 6:5H].

4:5 A. Under what circumstances did they rule, *Cutting the hair causes the loss of thirty days [already observed]* [M. Naz. 6:5I]?

B. When he had no more days to count.

C. But if he had yet more days to count, lo, this one does not lose any days.

D. [If] he cut his hair on account of a sacrifice, and it turned out to be invalid,

E. he loses thirty days.

4:6 A. *All cast hair under the cauldron, except for someone who cut his hair in the provinces on account of uncleanness* [so Meir, M. Naz. 6:8H],

B. because his hair is to be buried.

C. "He who was made unclean [and who cuts his hair] in the sanctuary casts his hair under the cauldron of the sin-offering or of the guilt-offering," the words of R. Meir.

D. R. Judah says, "The one who cuts his hair in a state of uncleanness here and there does not toss his hair under the cauldron.

E. "The one who cuts his hair in a state of uncleanness here and there does cast his hair under the cauldron."

F. And sages say, "The one who cuts his hair by reason of uncleanness here and there, and the one who cuts his hair in a state of uncleanness in the provinces do not cast their hair under the cauldron.

G. "You have only a Nazir who cuts his hair in a state of cleanness and who does so at the door of the Tent of meeting who casts his hair under the cauldron, since it is said, *And the Nazir will cut his hair at the door of the tent of meeting"* (Num. 6:18) [*cf.* M. Naz. 6:8F–G].

H. R. Simeon Shezuri says, "A man casts his hair under the cauldron, but a woman does not cast her hair under the cauldron,

I. "on account of the young priests."

J. How does one cast it under the cauldron?

K. One puts some broth on it and casts it under the cauldron of the peace-offering.

L. But if one cast it under the cauldron of the sin-offering or of the guilt-offering, he has fulfilled his obligation.

4:7 A. Said Simeon the Righteous, "In my entire life I ate a guilt-offering of a Nazir only one time.

B. M'SH B: "A man came to me from the south, and I saw that he had beautiful eyes, a handsome face, and curly locks. I said to him, 'My son, on what account did you destroy this lovely hair?'

C. "He said to me, 'I was a shepherd in my village, and I came to draw water from the river, and I looked at my reflection, and my bad impulse took hold of me and sought to drive me from the world.

D. "'I said to him, 'Evil one! You should not have taken pride in something which does not belong to you, in something which is going to turn into dust, worms, and corruption. Lo, I take upon myself to shave you off for the sake of Heaven.'

E. "I patted his head and kissed him and said to him, 'My son, may people like you become many, people who do the will of the Omnipresent in Israel. Through you is fulfilled this Scripture, as it is said, *A man or a woman, when he will express a vow to be a Nazir, to abstain for the sake of the Lord*' " (Num. 6:2).

4:8 A. A Nazir who was made unclean and again was made unclean and again was made unclean brings a single offering for the whole spell of uncleanness.

B. "[If] he was made unclean on his seventh day and again was made unclean on his eighth day [thereafter], he brings an offering for each one of the times he was made unclean," the words of R. Eliezer.

C. R. Simeon says, "A single offering for all the times he was unclean, until he brings his guilt-offering.

D. "[If] he brought his guilt-offering and was made unclean, brought his guilt-offering and again was made unclean, he is liable for an offering for each and every time he was made unclean."

E. And sages say, "He brings a single offering for all such incidents until he brings his sin-offering.

F. "[If] he brought his sin-offering and was made unclean, again brought his sin-offering and was made unclean, he is liable to bring an offering for each and every incident of uncleanness.

G. "And he does not begin to count clean days until he brings his sin-offering.

H. "[If] he brought his sin-offering but did not bring his guilt-offering, he nonetheless begins to count the days of his vow."

I. R. Ishmael b. R. Yoḥanan b. Beroqah says, "Just as his sin-offering stands in his way, so his guilt-offering stands in his way [= C]."

J. R. Simeon concedes that if he cut his hair after his sin-offering was made under an improper designation, and afterward brought the rest of his offerings under their proper designation, [that] his cutting of the hair is invalid, and his sacrifices have not gone to his credit.

4:9 A. That which is appropriate to be brought at the age of one year which he brought at the age of two years,

B. at the age of two years which he brought at the age of one year,

C. or if one of the animals which he brought had committed bestiality with a human being, or had suffered bestiality with a human being, or had been set aside for idolatrous worship, or had actually been worshipped, or was the fee paid to a harlot or the price paid for a dog, or had one hip larger than the other, or had uncloven hoofs—

D. his cutting of the hair is invalid, and his sacrifices have not gone to his credit [M. Naz. 6:10A].

E. And as to the remainder of the peace-offering of a Nazir which he brought not in accord with its requirement, it is eaten for one day and the following night, and it does not require either a bread offering or the giving of the shoulder to the priest.

F. *He in whose behalf one of the drops of blood was properly tossed and who was made unclean—*

G. *R. Eliezer says, "He loses all [the offerings he already had made in a state of cleanness]."*

H. *And sages say, "He brings the rest of his offerings when he is clean* [M. Naz. 6:11A–C].

I. "because the hair already has been sanctified by the blood."

4:10 A. M'ŚH B: *One of the drops of blood had been properly tossed for Miriam of Tadmor, and then they came and told her that her daughter was dying.*

B. *She went and found her daughter dead,* and she was made unclean on her account.

C. *Sages said, "Let her bring the rest of her offering when she is clean* [M. Naz. 6:11D–E],

D. "because the hair already has been sanctified in the blood."

4:11 A. He who took two vows of Naziriteship, counted out the first but did not bring his offerings, is prohibited from cutting his hair and from drinking wine and from contracting corpse-uncleanness.

B. [If] he was made unclean before he cut his hair,

C. R. Eleazar says, "He has to bring an offering on account of his having suffered uncleanness [while a Nazir]."

D. R. Yosé says, "He who does not have to do so,

E. "because he has gone forth from the category of the first vow but has not yet entered into the category of the second vow."

5:1 A. All those concerning whom they have ruled, *"He does not begin to count [the days of his Nazirite-vow] until he becomes clean"* [M. Naz. 7:2J]—

B. if he becomes unclean, he does not bring an offering on account of his uncleanness.

C. All those concerning whom they have ruled, *"He begins to count and counts [his Nazirite days] forthwith,"* [M. Naz. 7:3E], if he is made unclean, he does bring an offering on account of uncleanness.

D. A bit of corpse-uncleanness which is located above the wall, even half on one side and half on the other—

E. and so too: living rows of cattle, wild beasts, or fowl, which were walking one after the other, even if the head of one is between the hind-legs of the other—

a Nazir does not cut his hair on account of [their having overshadowed both him and a bit of corpse-matter].

F. And people [affected by their overshadowing] who enter the Temple or touch its Holy Things] are not liable for contaminating the Temple and its Holy Things [M. Naz. 7:4A–C].

G. R. Eliezer says, "At the outset the elders were divided.

H. "Some of them say, 'A quarter-*log* of blood and a quarter-*qab* of bones,' and some of them say, 'A half-*qab* of bones and a half-*log* of blood' [impart corpse-uncleanness so that the Nazir has to cut his hair].

I. "The court which followed them ruled, 'A quarter-*log* of blood and a quarter-*qab* of bones as regards [burning] heave-offering and Holy Things [made unclean on their account].

J. "'A half-*qab* of bones and a half-*log* of blood as regards [rendering unclean] the Nazir and the sanctuary'" [*cf.* M. Naz. 7:2–3].

K. Said R. Leazar, "When I went to 'Ardasqim, I came upon R. Meir and R. Judah b. Petera, the Chief, who were in session and reasoning about matters of law.

L. "R. Judah b. Paterah said, 'On account of a quarter-*log* of blood a Nazir does not cut his hair, and people are not liable who come into the sanctuary or touch its Holy Things.'

M. "Said to him R. Meir, 'Now *why should this be less stringent than a dead creeping thing* [M. Naz. 7:4C].

N. "'Now if on account of a dead creeping thing, which is of lesser weight, a Nazir cuts his hair, and they are liable for entering the sanctuary and touching its Holy Things, on account of a quarter-*log* of blood, which is more stringent, is it not logical that a Nazir should cut his hair and that people should be liable for entering the sanctuary and touching its Holy Things?'

O. "R. Judah b. Peterah remained silent before him.

P. "I said to him, 'Meir, don't disgrace him. He was an expert in your behalf in the matter of Joshua b. Mamal.'

Q. "He said to me, 'Indeed so, and he was a true master of laws.'

R. "I stated to him [a rule] in the following language: 'He said to me in the name of R. Joshua:

S. "'*On account of any form of corpse-uncleanness on account of which the Nazir cuts his hair are they liable for entering the sanctuary, and on account of any form of corpse-uncleanness because of which a Nazir does not cut his hair, they are not liable or entering the sanctuary*' [M. Naz. 7:4A].

T. "And I recognize the correctness of his opinion."

5:2 A. They said to R. Simeon b. Yohai, "Lo, if one was [simultaneously] a Nazir and a *meṣora'*—

B. "what is the law as to [the Nazir's] cutting his hair one time and receiving credit on that account for his Nazirite-vow and for his *ṣara'at*-purification-rites [both of which require it]?"

C. He said to them, "He does not cut his hair [one time for both purposes of purification]."

D. They said to him, "Why not?"

E. He said to them, "Now if this one were cutting his hair merely to remove the hair and that one were cutting his hair merely to remove the hair, you would have ruled quite well.

F. "But the Nazir cuts his hair to remove the hair, and the *meṣora'* cuts his hair in order thereafter to grow hair."

G. They said to him, "But we too state the rule only so that it should not count for him for the days of the certification of his uncleanness. But let it [the single hair-cutting] count for him toward the days of his counting."

H. He said to them, "If this one cut his hair after entering water, and that one cut his hair after entering water, you should have ruled quite well.

I. "But while a Nazir cuts his hair after entering water, a *meṣora'* cuts his hair before entering water."

J. They said to him, "But we too do not state the rule so that the hair-cutting should go to his credit in a state of uncleanness. But let it go to his credit if he brings his offerings on account of uncleanness."

K. He said to them, "If this one cut his hair after the tossing of blood, and that one cut his hair after the tossing of blood, you should have ruled quite well.

L. "But a Nazir cuts his hair after the tossing of blood, while a *meṣora'* cuts his hair before the tossing of blood."

M. They said to him, "The correct view of the matter: Let it not go to his credit in the days of the completion of his certification for uncleanness, but let it go to his credit for the days of counting.

N. "Let it not go to his credit in a case of cleanness, but let it go to his credit in a case of uncleanness:

O. "A Nazir who was afflicted by *ṣara'at* and a *meṣora'* who took a vow as a Nazir will then cut the hair one time for both requirements."

5:3 A. *Two Nazirs, to whom someone said, "I saw one of you made unclean, but I do not know which one of you it was"—*

B. *they count out thirty days and bring an offering for uncleanness and an offering for cleanness.*

C. *And they say, "If I was the unclean one, then the offering for uncleanness is mine and the offering for cleanness is yours, and if I am the clean one, then the offering for cleanness is mine, and the offering for uncleanness is yours."*

D. *And they count out thirty days more and bring an offering for cleanness.*

E. *And one says, "If I am the unclean one, then this offering for uncleanness was mine and the offering for cleanness is yours, and this is the offering for my state of cleanness. But if I was the clean one, then the offering for cleanness was mine, and the offering for uncleanness was yours, and this offering is for your state of cleanness"* [M. Naz. 8:1A–E].

5:4 A. *If one of them died,*

B. *said R. Joshua, "Let the other seek out someone from the market to take a vow as a Nazir as his counterpart, and let him say,*

C. *"'If I was unclean, lo, you are a Nazir forthwith. And if I was clean, you will be a Nazir after thirty days.' Then they count thirty days and bring an offering because of uncleanness and an offering because of cleanness.*

D. *"And he says, 'If I was the one who was unclean, the offering because of uncleanness is mine, and the offering because of cleanness is yours, and if I was the clean one, then the offering because of cleanness was mine, and the offering because of uncleanness of yours is subject to doubt.'*

E. *"And they count out another thirty days and bring an offering because of cleanness.*

F. *"And he says, 'If I was the one who was unclean, then the offering because of uncleanness was mine, and the offering because of cleanness was yours, [and this is the offering because of my being clean]. If I was clean, the offering because of cleanness was mine, and the offering because of uncleanness was yours, and this is the offering because of your being clean'"* [M. Naz. 8:1F–J].

G. During the first thirty days and the second thirty days he [the new Nazir] is prohibited from cutting his hair and from drinking wine and from contracting corpse-uncleanness.

H. And if he cut his hair, drank wine, or contracted corpse-uncleanness, he incurs forty stripes.

I. He [the survivor of the first pair] himself is liable for the first days but exempt for the second days.

6:1 A. [If] it is a matter of doubt whether a Nazir was unclean or clean, but it is certain that he was a Nazir,

B. if it is a matter of doubt whether a *meṣora'* was unclean or clean, but it is certain that he was a *meṣora'*,

C. *he eats Holy Things after sixty days,*

D. *drinks wine and contracts corpse-uncleanness after one hundred and twenty days* [M. Naz. 8:2A–C].

E. How so?

F. [If] they said to him, "You are an unclean Nazir, and an unclean Nazir cuts his hair only after seven days, so go and count out seven days," and he was sprinkled and the sprinkling-process was repeated, and he cut his hair and brought an offering,

G. [if] he counted out seven days and sought to cut his hair, and they said to him, "You are a clean Nazir, and a clean Nazir cuts his hair only after thirty days, go and count out twenty-three more days to complete the required thirty days,"

H. he cut his hair and brought his offering,

I. [if] he counted out thirty days and sought to cut his hair and they said to him, "You are a clean Nazir, and a clean Nazir cuts his hair only after the blood has been tossed,"

J. what should he then do?

K. He brings a burnt-offering in the form of a beast and makes the following stipulation concerning it, saying,

L. "Now if I am clean, lo, this is brought in fulfillment of my obligation, and if not, lo, this is a freewill-offering."

3 M. How should it be done for him to impose the more stringent ruling upon him [as a possibly-confirmed *meṣora'*]?

N. He brings a new clay jug and puts into it a quarter-*log* of spring water and brings two wild birds and slaughters one of them over the earthenware utensil into the spring water.

O. He digs a hole and buries it in his presence, and it is prohibited for the benefit [of anybody].

P. Then he brings a sin-offering in the form of a bird and makes the following stipulation concerning it, saying,

Q. "Now if I am unclean, the sin-offering is in fulfillment of my obligation, and the burnt-offering is a freewill-offering.

R. "But if I am clean, then the burnt-offering is in fulfillment of my obligation and the sin-offering is subject to doubt."

S. And he cuts the hair on his head, beard, and eyebrows, just as *meṣora's* cut their hair, and he brings the burnt-offering of a beast and makes the following condition concerning it, saying,

T. "Now if I was unclean, the first burnt-offering was a freewill offering, and this one is in fulfillment of my obligation. And the sin-offering in the form of fowl is on account of my obligation.

U. "But if I am clean, then the first burnt-offering was a fulfillment of my obligation. And this one is a freewill-offering. And the sin-offering in the form of a bird is subject to doubt."

V. And he cuts off the hair of his head, beard, and eyebrows, just as the *meṣora's* cut off their hair.

W. R. Simeon says, "On the morrow he brings his guilt-offering and its *log* of oil with it and sets them up at the Nicanor gate and makes the following condition concerning them, saying:

X. "'If I am a *meṣora'*, lo, this is his [my] guilt-offering, and if not, lo, this is a peace-offering given as a freewill-offering.'"

Y. This guilt-offering then is slaughtered on the north side of the altar. And its blood has to be placed on the thumbs and big toes of the man, and it requires laying on of hands, and drink-offerings, and the waving of the breast and thigh, and it is eaten by the male priests.

Z. But sages did not concur with R. Simeon,

AA. for the man thus brings Holy Things to the house invalidly.

BB. To offer a sin-offering of a beast is something he cannot do,

CC. because a sin-offering in the form of a beast is not offered in a case of doubt.

DD. To offer a sin-offering in the form of a bird is something he cannot do.

EE. For *a rich man who brouoht the offering of a poor man has not fulfilled his obligation* [M. Neg. 14:12].

FF. So what should he do?

GG. Let him write over his property to someone else and then bring the offering of a poor man.

HH. It turns out that the poor man brings a sin-offering in the form of a bird, and makes the following condition concerning it, saying,

II. "If I was a *Mesora'*, lo, this is in fulfillment of my obligation. And if not, lo, this is given because of the doubt concerning me."

JJ. And he is permitted to eat Holy Things forthwith.

KK. But as to drinking wine and contracting corpse-uncleanness, these are things he has not got the power to do.

LL. For the days of his Nazirite-vow are not credited on account of the days in which he is subject to *ṣara'at*.

MMm How should he do things in accord with the opinion of Ben Zoma [M. Naz. 8:1]?

NN. Let him count out thirty days and bring a burnt-offering in the form of a beast and cut his hair, and bring a sin-offering in the form of a bird and make the following condition concerning it, saying:

OO. "If I was unclean, this sin-offering is in fulfillment of my obligation, and the burnt-offering is a freewill-offering. If I am clean, the burnt-offering is in fulfillment of my obligation, and the sin-offering is subject to doubt."

PP. Then he counts out thirty days and brings the whole of his offerings.

QQ. And he brings a burnt-offering in the form of a beast and makes the following condition concerning it, saying:

RR. "If I was unclean, the first burnt-offering was in fulfillment of my obligation, and this one is a freewill-offering.

SS. "And the sin-offering in the form of a bird is on account of his obligation.

TT. "If I am clean, the first burnt-offering was a freewill-offering, and this one is brought in fulfillment of my obligation. And the sin-offering in the form of a bird is on account of the doubt which concerns me."

UU. Then he drinks wine and contracts corpse-uncleanness forthw/th.

VV. Under what circumstances?

WW. When he took the vow of a Nazir for thirty days.

XX. But if he took the vow as a Nazir for twelve months, he eats Holy Things only after two years have passed.

YY. And he drinks wine and contracts corpse-uncleanness after four years have passed.

ZZ. If one was in doubt as to being unclean but certainly shut up as a *meṣora'*, he eats Holy Things after eight days.

AAA. He drinks wine and contracts corpse-uncleanness after sixty-seven days.

BBB. If he was certainly unclean but subject to doubt as to whether he was a *meṣora'*,

CCC. he eats Holy Things after thirty-seven days,

DDD. he drinks wine and contracts corpse-uncleanness after seventy-four days.

EEE. If he was unclean of a certainty and determined to be a *meṣora'* of a certainty,

FFF. he eats Holy Things after eight days.

GGG. And he drinks wine and contracts corpse-uncleanness after forty-four days.

6:2 A. For all offerings of the community and the individual, the priestly frontlet effects expiation for uncleanness of the blood and for uncleanness of the body [of the owner],

B. except for the case of the Nazir and the one who prepares the Passover.

C. For in these cases the priestly frontlet effects expiation for uncleanness of the blood, but it does not effect expiation for uncleanness of the body.

D. But if he is made unclean by reason of uncleanness of the nethermost depths, lo, it does effect uncleanness in his behalf.

E. How so?

F. [If] he was going along to slaughter his Passover or to circumcise his son, and they said to him, "There was a corpse with you in that house which you entered," or ". . . under the stone on which you were sitting,"

G. and if he was informed of this fact, whether he had already prepared his Passover or whether he had not already prepared his Passover,

H. he has to prepare a second Passover.

I. But [if] they told to him, "There was a grave in the nethermost depths with you in that house into which you entered," or ". . . under that stone on which you were sitting,"

J. if he was so informed of that fact before he had prepared his Passover, then he has to prepare a second Passover [in a state of cleanness].

K. But if he was so informed after he had prepared his Passover, he does not have to prepare a second Passover.

6:3 A. And so is the rule in the case of a Nazir who went to offer his offerings, and they said to him, "There was a corpse with you in that house which you entered," or ". . . under the stone on which you were sitting,"

B. and he was so informed, whether this was before or after he brought his offerings,

C. he has to bring an offering on account of uncleanness.

D. But [if] they told him, "There was a grave in the nethermost depths with you in that house which you entered," or ". . . under that stone on which you were sitting,"

E. and he was so informed before he had brought his offerings,

F. he has to bring an offering on account of uncleanness.

G. But if this was told to him after he had brought his offerings, he does not have to bring an offering on account of uncleanness [*cf.* M. Naz. 9:2A–E].

6:4 A. A more strict rule applies to a man's wife and his daughter which does not apply to his boy-servant or his girl-servant,

B. [and a strict rule applies] to his boy-servant and girl-servant which does not apply to his wife and his daughter.

C. For as to his wife and his daughter, he annuls their vows.

D. And he cannot force them to drink wine or to contract corpse-uncleanness [M. Naz. 9:1D].

E. But as to his boy-servant or his girl-servant, he does not annul their vows.

F. But he does force them to drink wine or to contract corpse-uncleanness [M. Naz. 9:1F].

G. And they drink wine only when in his presence, and they contract corpse-uncleanness only in his presence [M. Naz. 9:1L].

6:5 A. R. Yosé says, "A slave whose master said to him, 'Drink wine for two years,' or 'Contract corpse-uncleanness for two years,' drinks wine in his presence and not in his presence, and contracts corpse-uncleanness in his presence and not in his presence" [M. Naz. 9:1M].

6:6 A. Why does his master force him in the case of a Nazir but not in the case of vows or oaths [to violate his Nazirite-vow]?

B. A slave who took a Nazirite-vow and [made his offerings and] cut his hair and then went forth to freedom has fulfilled the terms of his Nazirite vow.

C. [If] he took a Nazirite-vow and did not cut his hair [completing his vow] and went forth to freedom, he has not fulfilled the terms of his Nazirite vow.

D. [If] he was made unclean and then went forth to freedom, he counts the days of his Nazirite-vow from the time at which he had become unclean.

SOTAH

1:1 A. R. Yosé b. R. Judah says in the name of R. Eliezer, "He expresses jealousy before a single witness or even on his own evidence, and he imposes on her the requirement of drinking the bitter water before two witnesses" [*vs*. M. Sot. 1:1B].

B. They replied to the opinion of R. Yosé b. R. Judah, "The matter has no limit."

1:2 A. What is the character of the first testimony [M. Sot. 1:2]?

B. This is the testimony concerning her going off alone [with such and such a person].

C. The second [testimony]?

D. This is testimony concerning her having been made unclean.

E. And how long is the time required for becoming unclean?

F. Sufficient time to have sexual relations.

G. And how much is sufficient time for having sexual relations?

H. Sufficient time for sexual contact.

I. And how much is sufficient time for sexual contact?

J. R. Eliezer says, "Sufficient to walk around the date-palm."

K. R. Joshua says, "Sufficient to mix the cup."

L. Ben 'Azzai says, "Sufficient to mix the cup for drinking."

M. R. 'Aqiba says, "Sufficient to roast an egg."

N. R. Judah b. Paterah says, "Sufficient to swallow three eggs in succession."

O. R. Eleazar b. Jeremiah says, "Sufficient for a weaver to tie a knot."

P. Ḥanan b. Pinḥas says, "Sufficient for her to put her finger into her mouth."

Q. Pelimo says, "Sufficient to put out her hand and take a loaf of bread from a basket."

R. Even though there is no clear proof for the proposition, there is at least a hint as to the proposition, since it says, *For on account of a harlot, to a loaf of bread* [Prov. 6:26].

S. *R. Judah says, "Her husband is trustworthy in regard to her [not to have sexual relations in this circumstance],* [M. Sot. 1:3G],

T. "on the basis of an argument *a fortiori:*

U. "Now if in the case of a menstruating woman, on account of sexual relations with whom one incurs the penalty of extirpation, her husband is trustworthy in regard to her, in the case of an accused wife, on account of which the husband does *not* incur the penalty of extirpation, is it not logical that her husband should be deemed trustworthy in regard to her?"

V. They said to him, "Now all the more so: Since one does not incur the penalty of extirpation for having sexual relations with her, her husband really should not be deemed trustworthy in regard to her.

W. "Another matter [*re* U]: No. If you have said the rule in the case of the menstruating woman, who becomes permitted after she is prohibited, will you state the same rule in regard to the accused wife, who will never be permitted once she is prohibited?

X. "And so Scripture says, *Stolen water is sweeter* (Prov. 9:17)."

1:3 A. R. Yosé says, "Scripture has expressed its trust in him with regard to her,

B. "since it says, *And the husband shall bring his wife to the priest* (Num. 5:15)."

1:4 A. *They bring her up to the eastern gate, which is at the entrance of Nicanor's Gate. There it is that they force accused wives to drink the bitter water and purify women after childbirth and purify lepers* [M. Sot. 1:5B–D],

B. since it is said, *If a man sins against his neighbor and is made to take an oath and comes and swears his oath before thine altar in this house, then hear thou in heaven and act and judge thy servants, condemning the guilty by bringing his conduct upon his own head* (I Kings 8:31–32)—.

C. *And her body shall swell, and her thigh shall fall away* (Num. 5:27).

D. *And vindicating the righteous by rewarding him according to his righteousness* (I Kings 8:32)—.

E. *But if the woman has not defiled herself and is clean, then she shall be free and shall conceive children* (Num. 5:28).

1:5 A. She stands inside and the priest stands outside, since it says, *And the priest shall set the woman before the Lord* (Num. 5:18)—

B. *the woman before the Lord,* not the priest before the Lord.

1:6 A. And just as the court admonishes her to repent [M. Sot. 1:4], so they admonish her not to repent.

B. Therefore they say to her, "Now my daughter, if it is perfectly clear to you that you are clean, stand your ground and drink.

C. "For these waters are only like a dry salve which is put on living flesh and does no harm.

D. "If there is a wound, it penetrates and goes through [the skin, and if there is no wound, it has no effect].

E. Two accused wives are not made to drink simultaneously,

F. so that one not be shameless before the other.

G. R. Judah says, "That is not the reason, but because it is said, *And the priest will draw her near* (Num. 5:16)—

H. "and he does not draw two women near [at the same time]."

1:7 A. Priests cast lots among themselves.

B. Whoever won the lottery, even a high priest, goes out and stands next to the accused wife.

C. *And he grabs her clothes. If they tear, they tear, and if they are ripped up, they are ripped up, until he bares her breast. And he tears her hair apart.*

D. *R. Judah says, "If her heart is pretty, he did not let it show, and if she had pretty hair, he did not pull it apart* [M. Sot. 1:5E–G],

E. "on account of the young priests."

1:8 A. Three things must be visible on the water: the dust of the red cow, the dust of the accused wife, and the blood of the bird [used to purify a *meṣora'* (Lev. 14:6)].

B. The dust of the red cow—sufficient to be visible on the surface of the water.

C. The dust of the accused wife—*sufficient to be visible on the surface of the water* [M. Sot. 2:2G].

D. The blood of the bird of a *meṣora'*—sufficient to be visible on the surface of the water.

E. The spit of a deceased childless brother's wife—sufficient to be visible to the sight of the elders.

1:9 A. Priests are permitted to put wine, oil, and honey into the residue of meal-offerings,

B. but they are prohibited from allowing them to leaven.

1:10 A. All meal-offerings which are specified in the Torah require oil and frankincense, except for the meal-offering of a sinner and the meal-offering of jealousy,

B. since it is said, *He will not pour oil into it,and he will not put frankincense in it* (Num. 5:15).

C. R. Simeon says, "All sin-offerings which are specified in the Torah do not require drink-offerings, except for the sin-offering and guilt-offering of the *meṣora'*,

D. "so that the offering of a sinner will not be made splendid."

E. R. Ṭarfon says, "Every point at which *remembrance* is mentioned in the Torah, the intention is favorable, except for this one,

F. "since it is said, *'It is a meal-offering of remembrance, calling transgression to mind* (Num. 5:15).'"

G. R. 'Aqiba says, "Also this one is favorable,

H. "since it is said, *And if the woman has not been made unclean and she is clean, then she will be guiltless and will conceive a child* (Num. 5:28)."

2:1 A. He would take her scroll and bring it into the *ulam*.

B. Now there was a gold flagstone set up there by the wall of the *hekhal*.

C. And it was visible from the *ulam.*

D. At that point he sees it, and he writes, neither leaving out anything nor adding anything.

E. He goes out and stands by the accused wife.

F. He reads it aloud and explains it and spells out every detail of the pericope.

G. And he says it to her in whatever language she understands, so that she will know for what she is drinking the bitter water and for what incident she is drinking it, on what account she is accused of being unclean, and under what circumstances she is accused of being unclean.

H. And he says to her, "I invoke an oath upon you— And may it come upon you."

I. "And may they come upon you"—this is the curse.

J. "I invoke an oath upon you"—this is an oath.

2:2 A. *R. Meir says, "[She says,] 'Amen, that I have not been made unclean.' 'Amen, that I shall not become unclean in the future'"* [M. Sot. 2:5E].

B. For it is not that the water tests her forthwith.

C. But even if she should go astray after ten years, the water will bring complaint against her,

D. since it is said, *An offering of remembrance, calling transgression to mind* [Num. 5:15].

E. He goes in and writes the scroll, comes out and blots it out.

F. *If before the scroll is blotted out, she says, "I am not going to drink it"* [M. Sot. 3:3A],

. or if she said, "I am unclean,"

H. or if witnesses came and testified that she is unclean,

I. the water is poured out.

J. And no sanctity adheres to it.

K. *And the scroll* written for her *is hidden* under the *hekhal, and her meal offering is scattered* [M. Sot. 3:3A].

2:3 A. *[If] the scroll is blotted out and she said, "I am unclean,"*

B. *the water is poured out, and her meal-offering is scattered on the ashes.*

C. *And her scroll is not valid for the water-ordeal of another accused wife* [M. Sot. 3:3C, B].

D. *If her scroll is blotted out and then she said, "I am not going to drink it," they force her and make her drink it against her will* [M. Sot. 3:3D].

E. R. Judah says, "With iron tongs they force her mouth open, and they force her and make her drink it against her will."

F. Said R. 'Aqiba, "And why do we have to test her any further? Is it not to test her? And lo, she is now tested and proved to be degraded [by her refusal to drink]!

G. "But under all circumstances she has the power to repent for her behavior, until her meal-offering has been offered.

H. "Once her meal-offering has been offered, if she said, 'I am not going to drink,' they force her and make her drink it against her will."

I. R. Eleazar says, "Two times is *jealousy* stated in the pericope (Num. 5:14).

J. *"He is jealous of her . . . he is jealous of her . . .* —

K. "Once, that she causes the husband to be jealous, and once, that she causes the Omnipresent to be jealous."

L. R. Simeon b. Eleazar says in the name of R. Meir, "What is the meaning of Scripture, *And the wife will say, Amen, Amen?*

M. "This woman was such that much worse torments were going to afflict her than these.

N. "For she has brought herself into a state of doubt.

O. "But her degradation is held to a limit,

P. "since it is said, *And she will go free* (Num. 5:28)—.

Q. "She will go free from all the torments which were coming to her."

R. R. Judah b. Petera said in the name of Eleazar b. Matya, "What is the meaning of the Scripture, *Now if the woman has not been made unclean* (Num. 5:28)?

S. "If she used to give birth with pain, now she will give birth in comfort. If she used to produce females, now she will produce males. If she used to produce ugly children, now she will produce pretty babies. If she used to produce dark ones, now she will produce light ones. If she used to produce short ones, now she will produce tall ones. If she used to produce one by one, now she will produce two by two."

T. A child who is precocious, lo, this one tires out the world.

2:4 A. For every act of sexual relations which her husband had with her, lo, he is liable on her account.

B. *If her meal-offering was made unclean before it was sanctified in a utensil, lo, it is in the status of all other such meal-offerings.*

C. *It is redeemed* [M. Sot. 3:6A–B] and eaten.

D. *[If her meal-offering was made unclean] after it was sanctified in a utensil* [M. Sot. 3:6C–D],

E. its appearance is allowed to rot, and it goes out to the place of burning.

2:5 A. [If] the meal-offering was offered, but there was not time to offer up the handful before her husband died,

B. or if she died,

C. the residue is prohibited.

D. [If] the handful was offered,

E. and afterward she died, or the husband died,

F. the residue is permitted.

G. For to begin with it was brought in a case of doubt.

H. Her doubt has been atoned for and gone its way.

2:6 A. [If] witnesses came against her to testify that she was unclean,

B. one way or the other the meal-offering is prohibited.

C. [If] they turned out to be conspiring witnesses, one way or the other her meal-offering is treated as unconsecrated.

D. In the case of any woman married to a priest, whether she is a priest-girl, or a Levite-girl, or an Israelite-girl, her meal-offering is not eaten,

E. for he has a share in it.

F. But the offering is not wholly consumed in the fire, because she has a share in it.

G. What should he do?

H. The handful is offered by itself, and the residue is offered by itself.

I. R. Eleazar b. R. Simeon says, "The handful is offered by itself, and the residue is scattered."

J. A priest stands and makes offerings at the altar, which is not the case of a priest-girl [*cf.* M. Sot. 3:7].

2:7 A. *A man has control over his daughter and has power to betrothe her through money, a writ, or an act of sexual relations, and he controls what she finds, the produce of her labor, and the abrogation of her vows* [M. Ket. 4:4],

B. which is not the case of a woman [*cf.* M. Sot. 3:8].

2:8 A. *A man is subject to [punishment for] the transgression of a commandment which has to be performed at a particular time* [M. Qid. 1:7], which is not the case with a woman.

B. A man is subject to the transgression of the commandment not to trim the beard and not to remove the beard and [in the case of a priest] not to contract corpse-uncleanness [M. Sot. 3:7F], which is not the case with a woman.

C. A man is subject to the trial as a rebellious son, but a woman is not subject to trial as a rebellious daughter [M. San. 8:1].

2:9 A. A man wraps himself in a cloak [if he is a *meṣora*‘] and he proclaims, ["Unclean, unclean,"], but a woman does not wrap herself in a cloak and so proclaim [*cf.* M. Sot. 3:8B].

B. A man may be sold repeatedly, but a woman may not be sold repeatedly.

C. A man is sold as a Hebrew slave, but a woman is not sold as a Hebrew slave.

D. A man is subjected to the ceremony of the awl [having his ear pierced to the door if he refuses to go free], but a woman is not subject to the ceremony of the awl.

E. A man acquires a Hebrew slave, and a woman does not acquire a Hebrew slave.

3:1 A. R. Meir did say, "On what basis do you rule that *by that same measure by which a man metes out, they mete out to him* [M. Sot. 1:7A]?

B. "Since it is said, *By measure in sending her away thou doest contend with her* (Is. 27:8)—I know only that he measured out with a *seah*. How do I know that if he measured out with a *qab*, a half-*qab*, a third-*qab*, a half-third-*qab*, [the same rule applies]?

C. "Since it says, *For all the armor of the armed man in the tumult* (Is. 9:4), lo, you have here many measures.

D. "I know only that this applies to something which comes by measure.

E. "How do I know that *perutot* add up to a large sum?

F. Since it is said, *Laying one thing to another to find out the account* [Qoh. 7:27]."

3:2 A. And so you find that with regard to the accused wife:

With the measure with which she measured out, with that measure do they mete out to her.

B. She stood before him so as to be pretty before him, therefore a priest stands her up in front of everybody to display her shame, as it is said, *And the priest will set the woman before the Lord* (Num. 5:18).

3:3 A. She wrapped a beautiful scarf for him, therefore a priest takes her cap from her head and puts it under foot.

B. She braided her hair for him, therefore a priest loosens it.

C. She painted her face for him, therefore her face is made to turn yellow.

D. She put blue on her eyes for him, therefore her eyes bulge out.

3:4 A. She signalled to him with her finger, therefore her fingernails fall off.

B. She showed him her flesh, therefore a priest tears her cloak and shows her shame in public.

C. She tied on a belt for him, therefore *a priest brings a rope of twigs and ties it above her breasts, and whoever wants to stare comes and stares at her* [M. Sot. 1:6C–D].

D. She pushed her thigh at him, therefore her thigh falls.

E. She took him on her belly, therefore her belly swells.

F. She fed him goodies, therefore her meal-offering is fit for a cow.

G. She gave him the best wines to drink in elegant goblets, therefore the priest gives her the bitter water to drink in a clay pot.

3:5 A. She acted in secret, as it is said, *The eye also of the adulterer waiteth for the twilight, saying, No eye shall see me* (Job 24:15).

B. And she does not know that He who is enthroned in the secret place of the world directed his face against her, since it is said, *And he disguises his face* (Job 25:14).

C. This teaches that the Omnipresent brings her secret out into the open, since it is said, *Though his hatred cover [itself with guile, his wickedness shall be openly showed before the congregation]* (Prov. 26:26).

3:6 A. The generation of the Flood acted arrogantly before the Omnipresent only on account of the good which he lavished on them, since it is said, *Their houses are safe from fear, neither is the rod of God upon them* (Job 21:9). *Their bull genders and fails not, their cow calves and casts not her calf* (Job 21:10). *They send forth their little ones like a flock, and their children dance* (Job 21:11). *They spend their days in prosperity and their years in pleasures* (Job 36:11).

3:7 A. That is what caused them to say to God, *Depart from us, for we do not desire knowledge of thy ways. What is the Almighty, that we should serve Him, and what profit should we have, if we pray to him* (Job 21:14).

B. They said, "Do we need Him for anything except a few drops of rain? But look, we have rivers and wells which are more than enough for us in the sunny season and in the rainy season, since it is said, *And a mist rose from the earth* (Gen. 2:6)."

3:8 A. The Omnipresent then said to them, "By the goodness which I lavished on them they take pride before me? By that same good I shall exact punishment from them!"

B. What does it say? *And I, behold, I bring a flood of water upon the earth* (Gen. 6:17).

3:9 A. R. Yosé b. Durmasqit says, "The men of the Flood took pride only on account of [the covetousness of] the eyeball, which is like water, as it is said, *The sons of God saw that the daughter of men were fair, and they took them wives from all which they chose* (Gen. 6:2).

B. "Also the Omnipresent exacted punishment from them only through water, which is like the eyeball, as it is written, *All the fountains of the great deep were broken up, and the windows of heaven were opened* (Gen. 7:11)."

3:10 A. The men of the Tower acted arrogantly before the Omnipresent only on account of the good which he lavished on them, since it is said, *Now the whole earth had one language and few words. And as men migrated from* *the east, they found a plain in the land of Shinar and settled there* (Gen. 11:1–2).

B. And *settling* refers only to eating and drinking, since it is said, *And the people settled down to eat and drink and rose up to play* (Ex. 32:6).

C. That is what caused them to say, *Come, let us build ourselves a city, and a tower with its top in the heavens* (Gen. 11:4).

D. And what does Scripture say thereafter? *From there the Lord scattered them abroad over the face of the earth* (Gen. 11:8).

3:11 A. The men of Sodom acted arrogantly before the Omnipresent only on account of the good which he lavished on them, since it is said, *As for the land, out of it comes bread . . . Its stones are the place of sapphires, and it has dust of gold . . . That path, no bird of prey knows . . . The proud beasts have not trodden it* (Job 28:5–8).

3:12 A. Said the men of Sodom, "Since bread comes forth from our land, and silver and gold come forth from our land, and precious stones and pearls come forth from our land, we do not need people to come to us.

B. "They come to us only to take things away from us. Let us go and forget how things are usually done among us."

C. The Omnipresent said to them, "Because of the goodness which I have lavished upon you, you deliberately forget how things are usually done among you. I shall make you be forgotten from the world."

D. What does it say? *They open shafts in a valley away from where men live. They are forgotten by travelers. They hang afar from men, they swing to and fro* (Job 28:4). *In the thought of one who is at ease there is contempt for misfortune; it is ready for those whose feet slip. The tents of robbers are at peace, and those who provoke God are secure, who bring their god in their hand* (Job 12:5–6).

E. And so it says, *As I live, says the Lord God, your sister Sodom and her daughters have not done as you and your daughters have done. Behold, this was the guilt of your sister Sodom: she and her daughters had pride, surfeit of food, and prosperous ease, but did not aid the poor and needy. They were haughty and did abominable things before me. Therefore I removed them when I saw it* (Ez. 16:48–50).

3:13 A. The Egyptians took pride before the Omnipresent, blessed be He, only on account of water, as it is said, *Then Pharaoh commanded all his people, "Every son that is born to the Hebrews you shall cast into the Nile"* (Ex. 1:22).

B. So the Omnipresent, blessed be He, exacted punishment from them only by water, as it is said, *Pharaoh's chariots and his host he cast into the sea.*

3:14 A. Sisera took pride before the Omnipresent, blessed be He, only on account of [his volunteer] legions which do not receive a reward [for their service to him], since it is said, *The kings came, they fought; then fought the kings of Canaan* (Judges 5:19).

B. So the Omnipresent, blessed be He, exacted punishment from them only by [volunteer] legions which do not receive a reward, as it is said, *From heaven fought the stars, from their courses they fought against Sisera* (Judges 5:20).

C. And in the end they did not pay him honor or take heed of him because [he ran away by foot] like an ordinary foot-soldier.

3:15 A. Samson rebelled by using his eyes, as it is said, *Then Samson said to his father, I saw one of the daughters of the Philistines at Timnah; now get her for me as my wife* (Judges 14:3).

B. So he was smitten through his eyes, as it is said, *And the Philistines seized him and put out his eyes* (Judges 16:21).

C. Rabbi says, "The beginning of his corruption took place in Gaza, so his punishment took place only in Gaza."

3:16 A. Absalom rebelled through his hair, as it is said, *Now in all Israel there was no one so much to be praised for his beauty as Absalom; from the sole of his foot to the crown of his head there was no blemish in him. And when he cut the hair of his head (for at the end of every year he used to cut it; when it was heavy on him, he cut it), he weighed the hair of his head, two hundred shekels by the king's weight* (II Sam. 4:25–26).

B. Therefore he was smitten through his hair.

C. R. Judah the Patriarch says, "Absalom was a lifelong Nazir, and he cut his hair once in twelve months, as it is said *And at the end of four years Absalom said to the king, 'Pray let me go and pay my vow, which I have vowed to the Lord, in Hebron. For your servant vowed a vow while I dwelt at Geshur in Aram, saying, If the Lord will indeed bring me back to Jerusalem, then I will offer worship to the Lord'*" (II Sam. 15:7–8).

D. R. Nehorai says, "He cut his hair once in thirty days, as it is said, *For at the end of every year*" (II Sam. 14:26).

E. R. Yosé says, "He cut it every Friday, for so it is the custom of kings, to cut their hair every Friday, as it is said with regard to priests, *They shall not shave their heads or let their locks grow long; they shall only trim the hair of their heads*" (Ez. 44:20).

F. *He weighed the hair of his head, two hundred shekels by the king's weight* (II Sam. 14:26)—which the men of Tiberias and the men of Sepphoris do not do [cutting their hair on Fridays].

G. *Because he had sexual relations with ten concubines of his father, therefore they thrust ten spear-heads into his body, as it is said, And ten young men that carried Joab's armor surrounded and smote Absalom and killed him* (II Sam. 18:15) [M. Sot. 1:7C].

3:17 A. *And since he stole three hearts—the heart of his father, and the heart of the court, and the heart of all Israel—*

B. *therefore three darts were thrust into him, since it is said, And he took three darts in his hand and thrust them through the heart of Absalom* (II Sam. 18:14) [M. Sot. 1:8D].

3:18 A. Sennacherib took pride before the Omnipresent only through an agent, as it is said, *By your messengers you have mocked the Lord and you have said, "With my many chariots I have gone up the heights of the mountains . . . I dug wells and drank foreign waters, and I dried up with the sole of my foot all the streams of Egypt"* (II Kings 19:23–24).

B. So the Omnipresent, blessed be He, exacted punishment from him only through an agent, as it is said, *And that night the messenger of the Lord went forth and slew a hundred and eighty-five thousand in the camp of the Assyrians* (II Kings 19:35).

C. And all of them were kings, with their crowns bound to their heads.

3:19 A. Nebuchadnezzar said, "The denizens of this earth are not worthy for me to dwell among them. I shall make for myself a little cloud and dwell in it," as it is said, *"I will ascend above the heights of the clouds, I will make myself like the Most High"* (Is. 14:14).

B. Said to him the Omnipresent, blessed be He, *You said in your heart, I will ascend to heaven; above the stars of God I will set my throne on high—I shall bring you down to the depths of the pit* (Is. 14:13, 15).

C. What does it say? *But you are brought down to Sheol, to the depths of the pit* (Is. 14:15).

D. Were you the one who said, "The denizens of this earth are not worthy for me to dwell among them"?

E. The king said, *Is not this great Babylon, which I have built by my mighty power as a royal residence and for the glory of my majesty? While the words were still in the king's mouth, there fell a voice from heaven, O King Nebuchadnezzar, to you it is spoken; The kingdom has departed from you, and you shall be driven from among men, and your dwelling shall be with the beasts of the field, and you shall be made to eat grass like an ox* (Dan. 4:29–32).

F. *All this came upon King Nebuchadnezzar at the end of twelve months* (Dan. 4:28–29).

4:1 A. I know only with regard to the measure of retribution that *by that same measure by which a man metes out, they mete out to him* [M. Sot. 1:7A]. How do I know that the same is so with the measure of goodness [M. Sot. 1:9A]?

B. Thus do you say:[1]

C. The measure of goodness is five hundred times greater than the measure of retribution.

D. With regard to the measure of retribution it is written, *Visiting the sin of the fathers on the sons and on the grandsons to the third and fourth generation* (Ex. 20:5).

E. And with regard to the measure of goodness it is written, *And doing mercy for thousands* (Ex. 20:6).

F. You must therefore conclude that the measure of goodness is five hundred times greater than the measure of retribution.

G. And so you find in the case of Abraham that *by that same measure by which a man metes out, they mete out to him.*

H. He ran before the ministering angels three times, as it is said, *When he saw them, he ran to meet them* (Gen. 18:2), *And Abraham hastened to the tent* (Gen. 18:6), *And Abraham ran to the herd* (Gen. 18:7).

I. So did the Omnipresent, blessed be He, run before his children three times, as it is said, *The Lord came from Sinai, and dawned from Seir upon us; he shone forth from Mount Paran* (Deut. 33:2).

4:2 A. Of Abraham it is said, *He bowed himself to the earth* (Gen. 18:2).

B. So will the Omnipresent, blessed be He, respond graciously to his children in time to come, *Kings will be your foster fathers, and their queens your nursing mothers. With their faces to the ground they shall bow down to you and lick the dust of your feet* (Is. 49:23).

C. Of Abraham it is said, *Let a little water be brought* (Gen. 18:4).

D. So did the Omnipresent, blessed be He, respond graciously and give to his children a well in the wilderness, which gushed through the whole camp of Israel, as it is said, *The well which the princes dug, which the nobles of the people delved* (Num. 21:18) teaching that it went over the whole south and watered the entire desert, *which looks down upon the desert* (Num. 21:20).

E. Of Abraham it is said, *And rest yourselved under the tree* (Gen. 18:4).

F. So the Omnipresent gave his children seven glorious clouds in the wilderness, one on their right, one on their left, one before them, one behind them, one above their heads, and one as the Presence among them.

G. And the pillar of cloud [the seventh] which went before them would kill snakes and scorpions and burn off thorns, brambles, and prickly bushes and level down high places and raise up low places for them, so making

1. Erfurt: *Is the measure of goodness greater, or is the measure of retribution greater?* The measure of goodness is greater than the measure of retribution by five hundred times.

them a straight path, a path flowing and moving along, as it is said, *And the ark of the covenant of the Lord went before them* (Num. 11:33).

H. They made use of it all of the forty years during which they were in the wilderness, as it is said, *And the cloud of the Lord was over them by day* (Num. 11:34).

I. What is the meaning of the Scripture, *The pillar of cloud by day and the pillar of fire by night did not depart from before the people* (Ex. 13:22)?

J. It teaches that the one which served by day completed the work of the one which served by night, and the one which served by night completed the work of the one which served by day.

4:3 A. Of Abraham it is said, *While I fetch a morsel of bread that you may refresh yourselves* (Gen. 18:5).

B. So did the Omnipresent, blessed be He, give them manna in the wilderness, as it is said, *The people went about and gathered it . . . and made cakes of it; and the taste of it was like the taste of cakes baked with oil* (Num. 11:8).

C. It was an oil similar to that which comes forth from the breast: Just as this breast is really for the suckling, and everything else is second to him, so manna was really for Israel, and everyone else is second to them.

D. Another matter: Just as in the case of a breast, if a suckling sucks from it all day long, he does no harm to it, so the manna was made that even if Israelites ate it all day long, it did them no harm.

E. So it was made for someone who was not reckoned with it. But for someone who was reckoned with it, it turned in his mouth into any sort of good-tasting thing which he wanted, as it is said, *He gave them what they asked* (Ps. 106:15). *And they ate and were well filled, for he gave them what they craved* (Ps. 78:29).

F. And not only so, but enough food for them to last for two thousand years came down for them on a single day.

4:4 A. Of Abraham it is said, *And Abraham ran to the herd and took a calf, tender and good* (Gen. 18:7).

B. So the Omnipresent, blessed be He, rained down quail from the sea for his children, as it is said, *And there went forth a wind from the Lord, and it brought quails from the sea, and let them fall beside the camp* (Num. 11:31).

C. "*It rose two amahs from the ground* (Num. 11:31)," the words of R. ʿAqiba.

D. R. Eleazar b. R. Yosé the Galilean says, "*And let them fall beside the camp, about a day's journey on this side, and a day's journey on the other side, round about the camp* (Num. 11:31)—thus, and that is all."

E. Why does Scripture say again, *And a day's journey on the other side?*

F. It teaches that it went up from the firmament and from the earth and covered the orb of the sun, and afterward it came down to earth.

G. *And about two amahs above the earth*—It was removed by two *amahs* from the earth, so that whoever came to take them would not be injured in bending over (to lift them up).

4:5 A. Of Abraham what does it say? *And Abraham stood over them* (Gen. 18:8).

B. So the Omnipresent, blessed be He, watched over his children in Egypt, as it is said, *And the Lord passed over the door* (Ex. 12:23).

4:6 A. Of Abraham what does it say? *And Abraham went with them to set them on their way* (Gen. 18:16).

B. So the Omnipresent, blessed be He, accompanied his children for forty years, as it is said, *These forty years the Lord your God has been with you* (Deut. 2:7).

4:7 A. Joseph had the merit of (burying) his father, so it was only Moses who took the trouble to care for his bones, as it is said. *And Moses took the bones of Joseph with him* (Ex. 13:19) [M. Sot. 1:9C–E].

B. This teaches that all of the people were occupied with plunder, but he was busy with the doing of a commandment, as it is said, *The wise of heart will heed commandments* (Prov. 10:8).

C. But if Moses had not taken care of him, would the Israelites not have taken care of [Joseph]?

D. [Yet] Scripture says, *And the bones of Joseph which the children of Israel brought up out of Egypt they buried in Shechem* (Joshua 24:32).

E. But since the Israelites saw Moses taking care of him, they said, "Leave him be. His [Joseph's] honor will be greater when his rites will be performed by great men rather than by unimportant ones."

F. Now if Moses and the Israelites had not taken care of [Joseph], would not his own children have taken care of him?

G. Scripture says, *And they became the inheritance of the children of Joseph* (Joshua 24:32).

H. But when his children saw Moses and the Israelites taking care of [Joseph], they said, "Leave him be. His [Joseph's] honor will be greater when his rites will be performed by many rather than by few."

I. How did Moses know where Joseph had been buried?

J. They tell:

Seraḥ daughter of Asher was [a survivor] of the generation [of Joseph], and she went and said to Moses, "In the River Nile Joseph is buried. And the Egyptians made for him metal spits and affixed them with pitch (to keep him down)." Moses went and stood at the Nile River and said, "Joseph, the time has come for the Holy One, blessed be He, to redeem Israel.

"Lo, the Presence is held up for you, and the Israelites are held up for you, and the clouds of glory are held up for you. If you show yourself, well and good, and if not, we are free of the oath which you have imposed upon our fathers."

K. Then the coffin of Joseph floated to the surface and Moses took it and went his way.

L. And do not be surprised (that metal should float), for lo, Scripture says, *As one was felling a beam, the axe-head fell into the water . . . Alas, my master, for it was borrowed. The man of God said, Where did it fall? And he showed him the place. And he cut down a stick and cast it in, and made the iron to float* (II Kings 6:5–6).

M. Now is it not a matter of an argument *a fortiori:*

N. Now if Elisha, disciple of Elijah, disciple of Moses, could do things in such a way, Moses, master of Elijah, master of Elisha, all the more so [should be able to do such things].

O. And some say that Joseph was buried in the royal cemetery, and Moses went and stood at the graves of the kings and said, "Joseph, Joseph!

"The time has come for the Holy One, blessed be He, to redeem Israel. Lo, the Presence is held up for you, and the Israelites are held up for you, and the clouds of glory are held up for you. If you show yourself, well and good, and if not, we are free of the oath which you have imposed upon our fathers."

P. At that moment the coffin of Joseph shook, and Moses took it and went along.

Q. Now there were two coffins traveling with them, one the holy ark, one the ark of the corpse. And everyone who passed by would remark, "What in fact is the character of these two arks?"

They would then reply to them, "One is the holy ark, and one is the ark of the corpse."

They would say to them, "But is it possible that the holy ark should go along with the ark of a corpse?"

They replied, "The corpse which is kept in this ark carried out what is written in that which is lying in the other ark."

4:8 A. Moses acquired merit [through burying] the bones of Joseph, so only the Omnipresent, blessed be He, took care of him, since it is said, *And he buried him in the valley* (Deut. 34:6) [M. Sot. 1:9E–F].

B. This teaches that Moses was laid upon the wings of the Presence for four *mils,* from the portion of Reuben to the portion of Gad.

C. For he died in the field of a portion of Reuben, but he was buried in a field in the portion of Gad.

D. Now how do we know that he died in the midst of a field of the portion of Reuben? Since it is said, *Ascend this mountain of the Abarim, Mount Nebo* (Deut. 32:49). And Nebo belongs only in the portion of Reuben, as it is said, *And the sons of Reuben built Heshbon, Elealeh, Kiriathaim, Nebo, and Baal-meon* (Num. 33:37–38).

E. Now how do we know that he was buried in a field in the portion of Gad? Since it is said, *And of Gad he said, Blessed be he who enlarges Gad! Gad couches like a lion, he tears the arm, and the crown of the head. He chose the best of the land for himself, for there a commander's portion was reserved* (Deut. 33:20–21).

4:9 A. And the ministering angels mourn and say before him, *With Israel he executed the commands and just decrees of the Lord* (Deut. 33:21).

4:10 A. And so it says in the case of the accused wife:

B. *And the water that brings the curse shall enter into her and cause bitter pain, and her body shall swell, and her thigh shall fall away* (Num. 5:28).

C. *Her thigh*—the place at which she first began to sin, from there the retribution begins to overtake her.

D. *With the thigh did she begin to sin first, and afterward the belly, therefore the thigh is smitten first and afterward the belly* [M. Sot. 1:7D], since it says, *And when he has made her to drink* . . . (Num. 5:27).

4:11 A. And so you find in the case of men of the generation of the Flood: man began to sin first, as it is said, *And the Lord saw that the wilderness of man was great in the earth* (Gen. 6:5).

B. So he was smitten first. But the rest did not escape, as it is said, *He blotted out every living thing that was upon the face of the ground, man and animals* (Gen. 7:23).

4:12 A. The young men of Sodom began to sin first, as it is said, *Before they lay down, the men of the city, the men of Sodom, both young and old* (Gen. 19:4).

B. So they too were smitten first. But the rest did not escape, as it is said, *And they struck with blindness the men who were at the door of the house, both small and great* (Gen. 19:11).

C. Pharaoh began to sin first, as it is said, *And a new king arose over Egypt* (Ex. 1:8).

D. He was smitten first. But the rest did not escape, as it is said, *[The Nile shall swarm with frogs which shall come up into your house and into your bedchamber and on your bed and into the houses of your servants . . .] the frogs shall come up on you and on your people* (Ex. 7:29/8:4).

4:13 A. The spies began to sin first, as it is said, *So they brought back to the people of Israel an evil report of the land* (Num. 13:32).

B. Therefore they were smitten first. But the rest did not escape, as it is said, *The men who brought up an evil report of the land died by plague before the Lord* (Num. 14:37). And the rest did not escape, as it is said, *I the Lord have spoken; surely this will I do to all this wicked congregation . . . in this wilderness they shall come to a full end, and there they shall die* (Num. 14:35).

4:14 A. The neighbors of the Land of Israel began to sin first, as it is said, *Thus says the Lord concerning all my evil neighbors who touch the heritage which I have given my people Israel to inherit* (Jer. 12:14).

B. So they were punished first. But the rest did not escape, as it is said, *Behold, I will pluck them up from their land, and I will pluck up the house of Judah from among them* (Jer. 12:14).

4:15 A. The prophets of Jerusalem began to sin first, as it is said, *For from the prophets of Jerusalem ungodliness has gone forth into all the land* (Jer. 23:15).

B. So they were punished first. But the rest did not escape, as it is said, *Because of them this curse shall be used by all the exiles from Judah in Babylonia: The Lord make you like Zedekiah and Ahab* (Jer. 29:22).

4:16 A. *Just as she is prohibited to her husband, so she is prohibited to her lover* [M. Sot. 5:1].

B. You turn out to rule in the case of an accused wife who set her eyes on someone who was not available to her:

C. What she wanted is not given to her, and what she had in hand is taken away from her.

4:17 A. And so you find in the case of the snake of olden times, who was smarter than all the cattle and wild beasts of the field, as it is said, *Now the serpent was smarter than any other wild creature that the Lord God had made* (Gen. 3:1).

B. He wanted to slay Adam and to marry Eve.

C. The Omnipresent said to him, "I said that you should be king over all beasts and wild animals. Now that you did not want things that way, *You are more cursed than all the beasts and wild animals of the field* (Gen. 3:14).

D. "I said that you should walk straight-up like man. Now that you did not want things that way, *Upon your belly you shall go* (Gen. 3:14).

E. "I said that you should eat human food and drink human drink. Now: *And dust you shall eat all the days of your life* (Gen. 3:14).

4:18 A. "You wanted to kill Adam and marry Eve? *And I will put enmity between you and the woman* (Gen. 3:15)."

B. You turn out to rule, What he wanted was not given to him, and what he had in hand was taken away from him.

4:19 A. And so you find in the case of Cain, Korah, Balaam, Doeg, Ahitophel, Gahazi, Absalom, Adonijah, Uzziah, and Haman, all of whom set their eyes on what they did not have coming to them.

B. What they wanted was not given to them, and what they had in hand was taken away from them.

5:1 A. He who expresses a warning of jealousy to his betrothed or to his deceased childless brother's widow awaiting Levirate marriage with him [cf. M. Sot. 4:1A] —

B. if after she entered into marriage with him, she went in secret [with the man against whom the prospective husband had warned her not to go],

C. she either undergoes the ordeal of drinking the water or does not receive her marriage-contract.

5:2 A. A young man who married a barren woman or a woman past menopause, and who has another wife and children—

B. she either undergoes the ordeal of drinking the bitter water or does not receive her marriage-contract [*cf.* M. Sot. 4:3].

5:3 A. A woman made pregnant by the husband himself or who gives suck to the child of the husband himself either undergoes the ordeal of drinking the bitter water or does not receive payment of her marriage-contract [*cf.* M. Sot. 4:3A, E].

5:4 A. A priest-girl, a Levite-girl, and an Israelite-girl, who married a priest, a Levite, or an Israelite,

B. a *Netinah*-girl married to a *Netin,* a *mamzeret*-girl married to a *mamzer,*

C. the wife of a proselyte, a freed slave, and a barren woman

D. either undergo the ordeal of drinking the bitter water or do not receive a marriage-contract.

E. R. Simeon b. Eleazar says, "A barren woman does not undergo the ordeal of drinking the bitter water and does not receive her marriage-contract,

F. "since it is said, *And she will be found guiltless and will conceive a child* (Num. 5:28)—in the case of a woman who is able to conceive,

"thus excluding this woman, who is not able to conceive."

G. But he who expresses jealousy to his betrothed or to the deceased childless brother's widow awaiting Levirate marriage with him—

H. [if] before he married her, she went in secret [with the man against whom she was warned], she does not undergo the ordeal of drinking the bitter water and does not collect a marriage contract [*cf.* M. Sot. 4:1A–C].

5:5 A. A young man who married a barren woman or a woman past menopause and who does not have another wife and children—

B. she does not undergo the ordeal of drinking the bitter water and does not collect a marriage-contract [*cf.* M. Sot. 4:3C–D].

C. *A woman who was pregnant by another husband [who died or divorced the woman] and a woman who was giving suck to a child by another husband do not undergo the ordeal of drinking the bitter water and do not receive the marriage-contract* [M. Sot. 4:3A].

D. R. Eleazar says, *"He has the power to set her apart and then to take her back after a while"* [M. Sot. 4:3B].

5:6 A. With any sort of man is a woman made unclean, except for a minor and for one who is not human [*cf.* M. Sot. 4:4C–E].

B. R. Yosé says, "He [the husband] may impose the ordeal of drinking the water on her,

C. "when the deaf-mute recovers his power of hearing and speech, the imbecile regains his senses, and the minor reaches maturity" [M. Sot. 4:5D–E].

D. Or if her husband went overseas,

E. or if her husband was imprisoned [*cf.* M. Sot. 4:5B].

5:7 A. A woman who commits lewdness with her minor son, who entered into the first stage of cohabitation with her—

B. the House of Shammai invalidate her from marriage into the priesthood.

C. And the House of Hillel declare her valid [*cf.* M. Sot. 4:4D].

5:8 A. *One witness says, "She was made unclean," and one witness says, "She was not made unclean,"—*

B. *a woman says, "She was made unclean," and a woman says, "She was not made unclean"* [M. Sot. 6:4]—

C. she either undergoes the ordeal of drinking the water or does not collect her marriage-contract.

D. R. Judah says, "One [such witness] has not got the power to deprive her of her marriage-contract.

E. "But [if] one witness says, 'She was made unclean,' and two say, 'She was not made unclean,'

F. "two say, 'She was made unclean,' and one says, 'She was not made unclean,'

G. "the single [witness's testimony] is nullified [because it is a] minority-[opinion]."

5:9 A. R. Meir would say, "Just as there are diverse tastes in regard to food, so there are diverse tastes in regard to women['s behavior].

B. "You can find a man on whose cup a fly flits by, and he will put it aside and won't even taste what's in that cup. This one is a bad lot for women, for he is [always] contemplating divorcing his wife.

C. "You can find a man in whose cup a fly takes up residence. So he tosses it out and does not drink what is in it. Such a one is like Pappos b. Judah, who used to lock his door to keep his wife inside when he went out.

D. "And you can find a man into whose cup a fly falls, and he tosses it away and drinks what is in the cup.

E. "This is the trait of the ordinary man, who sees his wife talking with her neighbors or with her relatives and leaves her be [*cf.* M. Sot. 4:4C].

F. "And you have a man into whose meal a fly falls, and he picks it up and sucks it [for the soup it absorbed] and tosses it away, and then eats what is on his plate.

G. "This is the trait of a bad man, who sees his wife going around with her hair in a mess, with her shoulders uncovered, shameless before her boy-servants, shameless before her girl-servants, going out and doing her spinning in the marketplace, bathing, talking with anybody at all.

H. "It is a commandment to divorce such a woman, as it is said, *When a man takes a wife and marries her, if then she finds no favor in his eyes because he has found some indecency in her, and he writes her a bill of divorce and puts it in her hand and sends her out of his house and she departs out of his house*" (Deut. 24:1).

I. *And if she goes and becomes another man's wife* (Deut. 24:2)—and Scripture calls him, "A different man," because he is not his match.

J. The first man put her away because of transgression, and this other one comes along and stumbles through her.

L. The second husband, if he has merit in Heaven, puts her away. And if not, in the end, she will bury him,

M. since it is said, *Or if the latter husband dies, who took her to be his wife* (Deut. 24:3)—

N. this man is deserving of death, for he received such a woman into his house.

5:10 A. He who hopes that his wife will die so that he will inherit her property, or that she will die so that he may marry her sister—in the end she will bury him.

B. And so in the case of a woman who hopes that her husband will die so that she marry someone else—in the end he will bury her.

5:11 A. He who betrothed a girl because he is shamed by her father or her brother or her relatives into doing so—in the end she will bury him.

B. And so she who is betrothed to a man because she is shamed into doing so by his father, brothers, or relatives—in the end he will bury her.

C. R. Meir did say, "He who marries a woman who is unworthy of him transgresses five negative rules.

D. "On the count of *not taking retribution,* and *not having vengeance,* and *not hating one's brother in his heart,* and *loving one's neighbor as himself,* and the count that *your brother should be able to live with you* (Lev. 19:18, 19:17, 19:18, 25:36).

E. "And not only so, but he stops procreation from happening in this world."

5:12 A. *She who says to her husband, "Heaven [knows] what is between me and you,"—they find a way to placate her* [M. Ned. 11:12].

B. For so we find in the case of the matriarch, Sarah, that the patriarch, Abraham, said to her, *"The Lord judge between me and you* (Gen. 16:5)."

C. But thus did she say to him, *"Send away this serving girl and her son"* (Gen. 21:10).

D. This teaches that the matriarch, Sarah, saw Ishmael building high places, hunting for locusts, offering them up, and burning them for idolatry. She said, "What if my son Isaac learns to do such things and goes and worships that way! The Name of Heaven will be profaned by such goings-on!"

E. He said to her, "After a decision is done *for* someone, do they exact a punishment from him? After we made her a queen, we made her a mistress, and we brought her to all this greatness, shall we throw her out of our house? What will people say about us? Will not the Name of Heaven be profaned by such a thing?"

F. She said to him, "Since you have said, 'There is a profanation of Heaven in such a thing,' and I say, 'There is a profanation of Heaven in such a thing,' let the Omnipresent decide between my view and your view."

G. The Omnipresent decided between her view and his, since it is said, *All which Sarah tells you hearken* (Gen. 21:12).

H. For does Scripture need to say, *All?* And why does Scripture say, *All?* This teaches that Heaven decided in favor of [Sarah] the second [time] just as it decided in her favor the first [time]. Just as in the second instance, in regard to Hagar, so in the first instance, in regard to Hagar, [Heaven was in accord with Sarah against Abraham].

5:13 A. Expounded R. 'Aqiba, *"And every earthen vessel whereinto any of them falls—whatsoever is in it conveys uncleanness* (Lev. 11:33). *It does not say, It is unclean, but, It conveys uncleanness—*

B. *"[teaching] that it conveys uncleanness to other things,*

C. and therefore teaching concerning *a loaf of bread which is unclean in the second remove that it imparts uncleanness in the third remove to another loaf of bread with which it comes into contact"* [M. Sot. 5:2A–B].

D. How so?

E. An oven is unclean in the first remove, and a loaf of bread [in contact with it] is unclean in the second remove, and that which is in contact with the loaf of bread is in the third remove.

F. Said R. Joshua, "Thus did Judah b. Patiri expound:

"'*And you shall measure without the city for the east side two thousand cubits* (Num. 35:5). And another Scripture states: *From the wall of the city and outward, a thousand cubits round about* (Num. 35:4).

G. "'*It is not possible to state that the required measure is two thousand amahs, for a thousand amahs already have been stated, and it is not possible to state that a thousand amahs are required, for already have two thousand amahs been required* [M. Sot. 5:3B–C].

H. "'So why have two thousand amahs been required?

I. "'*But a thousand amahs are the outskirts and two thousand amahs are the Sabbath limit'"* [M. Sot. 5:3E].

J. R. Eleazar b. R. Yosé the Galilean says, "Two thousand *amahs* form the limit of the cities of the Levites. Subtract from them a thousand *amahs* for the outskirts, and you turn out to have a quarter for outskirts and the rest for fields and vineyards" [*cf.* M. Sot. 5:3F].

6:1 A. R. Judah said in the name of Ben Patiri, "Lo, it says, *As God lives, who has taken away my right, and the Almighty, who has made my soul bitter* (Job 27:2)—

B. "thus teaching you that a man takes a vow by the life of the king only if he favors the king."

C. In the name of R. Nathan they say, "Lo, it says, *This will be my salvation, that a godless man shall not come before him* (Job 13:16)."

D. Rabbi says, "*God-fearing* is stated with reference to Abraham (Gen. 22:12), and *God-fearing* is stated with reference to Job (Job 1:1). Just as *God-fearing* stated with reference to Abraham means that Abraham did what he did out of love for God, so *God-fearing* stated with reference to Job means that Job did what he did out of love for God.

E. "And all the rest of the murmuring [against God] stated in that passage (Job 27) is stated only out of [need to relate] the events."

6:2 A. Expounded R. 'Aqiba: "When the Israelites came up from the sea, they wanted to proclaim a song.

B. "The Holy Spirit rested on them, and they thereby proclaimed their song.

C. "How did they say that song? Like a child who recites the *Hallel* in school.

D. "And they answered him [by repetition] at each and every phrase:

E. "Moses said, *'I shall sing unto the Lord'* (Ex. 15:1), and the Israelites answered him, *'I will sing unto the Lord.'*

6:3 A. "Moses said, *'My strength and my song is the Lord,'* (Ex. 15:2), and the Israelites said, *'My strength and my song is the Lord'*" [*cf.* M. Sot. 5:4A–F].

B. R. Eleazar b. R. Yosé the Galilean says, "They proclaimed the song like an adult who proclaims the *Hallel* in synagogue-worship, responding to him with the foregoing phrase, as follows:

C. "Moses said, *'I will sing to the Lord'* (Ex. 15:1), and the Israelites said, *'I will sing to the Lord.'*

D. "Moses said, *'My strength and song is the Lord,'* and the Israelites said, *'I will sing unto the Lord.'*

E. "Moses said, *'The Lord is a man of war'* (Ex. 15:3), and the Israelites said, *'I will sing unto the Lord.'*"

F. R. Neḥemiah says, "[They proclaimed the song] like men who recite the *Shema'* in synagogue-worship, as it is said, *And they said, saying* (Ex. 15:1).

G. "This teaches that Moses would open first with a given matter, and the Israelites would respond to him and complete saying [that same matter, thus:]

H. "Moses said, *'Then Moses sang,'* and the Israelites said, *'I shall sing unto the Lord.'*

I. "Moses said, *'My strength and song is the Lord,'* and the Israelites said, *'This is my God and I will glorify him.'*

J. "Moses said, *'The Lord is a man of war,'* and the Israelites said, *'The Lord is his name'*" [*cf.* M. Sot. 5:4G].

6:4 A. R. Yosé the Galilean says, "When the Israelites came up out of the sea and saw their enemies strewn as corpses on the seashore, they all burst out into song—even a child lying on his mother's lap and an infant sucking at its mother's breast.

B. "When they saw the Presence of God, the babe raised his head, and the infant took his mouth off his mother's teat and all responded in song, saying, *This is my God and I will glorify him* (Ex. 15:2)."

C. R. Meir says, "Even foetuses in their mothers' wombs broke out into song, as it is said, *Bless God in the great congregation, the Lord, O you who are of Israel's fountain* (Ps. 68:26).

D. "And even an infant took his mother's teat out of his mouth and broke into song, as it is said, *By the mouth of babes and infants thou hast founded a bulwark, because of thy foes* (Ps. 8:2)."

6:5 A. At that hour the ministering angels who had come together to cavil [against Israel] before the Holy One blessed be He, looked down.

When the Holy One blessed be He had created the first man, they had said before him, "Lord of the world, *What is man that thou art mindful of him, and the son of man that thou dost care for him? Yet thou hast made him little less than God, and dost crown him with glory and honor. Thou hast given him dominion over the works of thy hands; thou hast put all things under his feet all sheep and oxen, and also the beasts of the field, the birds of the air and the fish of the sea, whatever passes along the paths of the sea* (Ps. 8:5–8).

B. At that hour the Holy One, blessed be He, said to the ministering angels, "Come and behold the song which my children proclaim before me."

C. So they, when they beheld, proclaimed a song. What song did they proclaim? *O Lord, our Lord, how majestic is thy name in all the earth! Thou whose glory above the heavens is chanted by the mouth of babes and infants . . . O Lord, our Lord, how majestic is thy name in all the earth!* (Ps. 8:1–2, 9).

D. R. Simeon b. Menassia says, "This pericope was stated only with reference to Isaac, the son of Abraham, in the matter of the Binding."

6:6 A. Said R. Simeon b. Yoḥai, "Four lessons did R. 'Aqiba expound, and my lessons are better than his lessons."

B. R. 'Aqiba expounded, "*But Sarah saw the son of Hagar the Egyptian whom she had borne to Abraham, playing with her son Isaac* (Gen. 21:9). *Playing* stated here refers solely to idolatrous worship, since it is said, *And the people sat down to eat and drink and they arose to play* (Ex. 32:6). This teaches that the matriarch Sarah saw Ishmael building altars, hunting for locusts, and offering them up and sacrificing them for idolatry."

C. R. Eliezer b. R. Yosé the Galilean says, "*Playing* stated here refers only to fornication, as it is said, *The Hebrew servant whom you have brought among us came in to me to play with me* (Gen. 39:17).

D. "This teaches that the matriarch Sarah saw Ishmael ravish 'gardens' [maidens] and seduce married women."

E. R. Ishmael says, "The word *playing,* refers only to bloodshed, as it is said, *And Abner said to Joab, Let the young men, I pray thee, arise and play before us. . . . Then they arose and passed over by number . . . And each caught his opponent by the head and thrust his sword in his opponent's side; so that they fell down together* (II Sam. 2:14–16).

"This teaches that the matriarch Sarah saw Ishmael taking a bow and arrows and shooting toward Isaac, as it is said, *Like a madman who throws firebrands, arrows, and death, is the man who deceives his neighbor and says, 'I am only joking!'* (Prov. 26:18–19)."

F. "But I [Simeon b. Yoḥai] say, 'Heaven forefend that such a thing should take place in the home of that righteous man! Is it possible that there should be idolatry, fornication, and murder in the home of him concerning whom was said, *For I have chosen him, that he may charge his children and his household after him to keep the way of the Lord by doing righteousness and justice; so that the Lord may bring to Abraham what he has promised him* (Gen. 18:19).

G. "'But *playing* which is stated here refers only to the matter of inheritance."

"For when Isaac, the patriarch, was born to Abraham, the patriarch, everyone was happy and said, 'A son has been born to Abraham! A son has been born to Abraham! He will inherit the world and take two shares.'

"But Ishmael toyed with the thought, saying 'Don't be fools! Don't be fools! I am first-born and I am going to take two portions.'

"For in the reply to the matter you learn [what was at issue]: *For the son of this slave woman shall not be heir along with my son Isaac* (Gen. 21:10).

H. "And I [Simeon b. Yoḥai] prefer my opinion to the opinion of R. 'Aqiba."

6:7 A. R. 'Aqiba expounded: *"Shall the flocks and herds be slaughtered for them, to suffice them? Or shall all the fish of the sea be gathered together for them, to suffice them* (Num. 11:22)? This is by way of an example, as it is said, *And if she cannot afford a lamb* (Lev. 12:8). Which is more difficult? This, or *Hear, I pray you, you rebels! Shall we bring forth water for you out of this rock?* (Num. 20:10). You have to conclude that this is more difficult than *Hear . . . you rebels.*

"But (this shows) that one who profanes the Name of Heaven in secret—they overlook it. But if he does so out in the open, they exact punishment from him.

"This one which he committed in secret did the Omnipresent overlook."

B. R. Simeon b. Eleazar says, "Even this one which was done in secret did the Omnipresent not overlook, since it says, *Now you shall see whether my word will come true for you or not* (Num. 11:23)."

C. "But I [Simeon b. Yoḥai] say, 'Heaven forfend that into the mind of that righteous man such a thought should enter, that he should say, 'The Omnipresent cannot provide enough for us and our cattle!'

"It is not possible for him about whom it is said, *Not so with my servant Moses; he is entrusted with all my house* (Num. 12:7) to have in his mind the thought that the Omnipresent cannot provide enough for us and our cattle!

"And is it not so that when the Israelites were in Egypt, the Nile River provided sufficient fish for the Egyptians, and the cattle of the Egyptians supplied sufficient [meat] for the Egyptians?

"But the relevant matter is the following Scripture: *You shall not eat one day or two days or five days or ten days or twenty days, but a whole month* (Num. 11:19–20).

D. "Said Moses before the Holy One, blessed be He, 'Lord of the world, Is it proper for them that you should give them what they need and then put them to death? Do they say to a man, "Take a loaf of bread and go to hell"? Do they say to an ass, "Take a *kor* of barley and then we'll cut off your head"?'

"People will say about me and you, 'You will have no reward for tidings' [*cf.* II Sam. 18:22].

E. "He said to him, 'But is it proper for them to say, "The Omnipresent cannot provide sufficient food for us and our cattle? But let them and a thousand like them perish!"' But let your hand not be shortened before me even for a single moment, as it is said, *And the Lord said to Moses, Is the Lord's hand shortened? Now you shall see whether my word will come true for you or not* (Num. 11:23)."

6:8 A. Rabban Gamaliel son of R. Judah the Patriarch says, "It is not possible to stand against their foolishness!

"If you give them the meat of a large beast, they will say, 'But we wanted the meat of a small beast.'

"If you give them the meat of a small beast, they will say, 'We wanted the meat of a wild beast or a bird.'

"If you give them the meat of a wild beast or a bird, they will say, 'We wanted the flesh of fish and locusts,' since it is said, *Shall flocks and herds be slaughtered for them to suffice them? Or shall all the fish of the sea be gathered together for them to suffice them?* (Num. 11:22).

B. "The Holy Spirit replied, *'Now you shall see whether my word will come true for you or not'* (Num. 11:23)."

C. "And I [Simeon b. Yoḥai] prefer my opinion to the opinion of R. 'Aqiba."

6:9 A. Expounded R. 'Aqiba: "Lo, Scripture says, *Son of man, the inhabitants of these waste places in the Land of Israel keep saying, Abraham was only one man, yet he got possession of the land; but we are many; the land given surely is given us to possess* (Ez. 33:24).

B. "Now the matter yields an argument *a fortiori:* Now if Abraham, who served only one God, inherited the land, we, who serve many gods, surely should inherit the land."

C. R. Neḥemiah says, "Now if Abraham, who had only one son, whom he offered up, inherited the land, we, whose sons and daughters offer up [many sacrifices] to idolatry, surely should inherit the land."

D. R. Eliezer the son of R. Yosé the Galilean says, "Now if Abraham, who had no one [i.e., a distinguished ancestor] on whom to rely, inherited the land, we, who have one on whom to rely [namely, Abraham], surely should inherit the land."

E. "But I [Simeon b. Yoḥai] say, 'Now if Abraham, who had received only a few commandments, inherits the land, we, who have been commanded concerning all of the commandments, surely should inherit the land.

F. "You may know that [what I say is] so, for notice the answer which the prophet gave to them: *Therefore say to them, Thus says the Lord God: You eat flesh with the blood and lift up your eyes to your idols and shed blood. Shall you then possess the land? You resort to the sword, you commit abominations, and each of you defiles his neighbor's wife. Shall you then possess the land?* (Ez. 33:25–26)

"*You eat flesh with the blood*—this is chopping a limb from a living beast.

"*And you lift up your eyes to your idols*—this is idolatry.

"*And you shed blood*—this is murder.

"*You resort to the sword*—this is perversion of justice and thievery.

"*You commit abominations*—this is pederasty.

"*And eacy of you defiles his neighbor's wife*—this is fornication.

G. "Now the matter yields an argument *a fortiori:* Now if the seven commandments which have been issued to the children of Noah you have not observed in my presence, do you yet say, 'We shall inherit the land'?"

H. "And I [Simeon b. Yoḥai] prefer my opinion to the opinion of R. 'Aqiba."

6:10 A. Rabbi expounded, "Lo, Scripture says, *Thus says the Lord of hosts: The fast of the fourth, and the fast of the fifth, and the fast of the seventh, and the fast of the tenth, shall be to the House of Judah seasons of joy and gladness and cheerful feasts; therefore love truth and peace* (Zech. 8:19).

B. "*The fast of the fourth*— this is the seventeenth of Tammuz, on which the city was breached. And why is it called the fourth? Because it is the fourth among months.

"*The fast of the fifth*—this is the ninth of Ab, the day on which the sanctuary was burned. And why is it called the fifth? Because it is the fifth month.

"*The fast of the seventh*—this is the third of Tishre, the day on which Gedaliah b. Aḥiqam was murdered, killed by Ishmael b. Netaniah (teaching you, therefore, that the death of righteous men is as hard for the Omnipresent to take as is the destruction of the Temple).

"And why is it called the seventh? Because it is the seventh month.

"*The fast of the tenth*—this is the tenth of Tebeth, the day on which the king of Babylonia laid his hand on Jerusalem, as it is said, *In the ninth year, in the tenth month, on the tenth day of the month, the word of the Lord came to me: Son of man, write down the name of this day, this very day. The king of Babylonia has laid siege to Jerusalem this very day* (Ez. 27:1–2)."

6:11 A. "But I [Simeon b. Yoḥai] say, '*The fast of the tenth*—this is the fifth of Tebeth, on which the news reached the exiles, since it is said, *In the twelfth year of our exile, in the tenth month, on the fifth day of the month, a man who had escaped from Jerusalem came to me and said, The city has fallen* (Ex. 33:21). Now when they heard, they treated the day on which they heard the news as equivalent to the day on which the burning [of the Temple took place].

B. "'Now was this item not appropriate to be written first of all?

C. "'And why was it written at the end?

D. "'To arrange the months in accord with their proper order.

E. "'And I prefer my opinion to the opinion of R. 'Aqiba, for R. 'Aqiba lists the first [event] last and the last [event] first, but I list the first first and the last last.'"

7:1 A. The oath of witnesses and judges is said in any language [M. Sot. 7:1A5].

B. If one has imposed an oath upon them five times in any language which they understand, and they replied to him, "Amen,"

C. lo, they are liable.

7:2 A. The oath imposed by judges—how so?

B. Lo, he who is obligated to take an oath to his fellow—

C. they [Erfurt: the courts] say to him, "Know that the whole world trembled on the day on which it was said, *You shall not take the name of the Lord your God in vain* (Ex. 20:7)."

D. With reference to all the transgressions which are mentioned in the Torah, it is written, *And he shall be acquitted,* but with reference to this one, it is written concerning it, *And he shall not be acquitted.*

E. In regard to all the transgressions which are mentioned in the Torah, they exact retribution from the man himself. But with reference to this one, they exact retribution from the man and from the entire world, so that the transgression of the entire world is blamed on him,

F. since it is said, *Swearing and lying . . . therefore does the land mourn, and every one who dwells therein does languish* (Hos. 4:2–3).

G. In regard to all the transgressions which are mentioned in the Torah, they exact retribution from the man himself, but in this case, they exact retribution from him and from his relatives,

as it is said, *Suffer not your mouth to bring your flesh into guilt* (Qoh. 5:5), and *flesh* refers only to one's relative, as it is said, *From your flesh do not hide yourself* (Is. 58:7).

H. All transgressions which are mentioned in the Torah do they suspend punishment for two or three generations, but in this case, they impose punishment forthwith, since it is said, *I cause it to go forth, says the Lord of hosts, and it shall enter into the house of the thief and into the house of him who swears falsely by My name and it shall abide in the midst of this house and shall consume it with the timber thereof and the stones thereof* (Zech. 5:4).

I. *I cause it to go forth*—forthwith.

J. *And it comes into the house of the thief*—this is one who swears falsely, knowing that he does not have it, and who deceives [steals the mind of] people.

K. *And into the house of him who swears falsely by My name*—according to its plain meaning.

L. All transgressions which are mentioned in the Torah apply to one's property. But this one applies to his property and to his own person, as it is said, *And it will abide [spend the night].*

M. Come and see how things which fire cannot consume a false oath destroys.

7:(3)4 A. If one said, "I am not going to take an oath," they dismiss him forthwith.

B. If he said, "I am going to take an oath," they say to one another, *Depart, I pray you, from the tents of these wicked men* (Num. 16:26).

C. They impose upon him the oath which is stated in the Torah, as it is said, *And I will make you swear by the Lord, the God of heaven* (Gen. 24:3).

D. They say to him, "Know that it is not according to what is in your heart that we adjure you, but in accord with what is in our hearts. And so we find that when Moses adjured the Israelites in the plains of Moab, he said to them, 'Not according to what is in your hearts do I adjure you, but according to what is in my heart,'

E. "as it is said, *Nor is it with you only that I make this sworn covenant, but with him who is not here with us this day as well as with him who stands here with us this day before the Lord our God* (Deut. 29:13–14)."

7:5 A. Thus far we know that he spoke only with them. How do we know that he spoke also for generations to come after them, and to proselytes who would join them in time to come?

B. Since it is said, And not with you alone . . . but with him who is not here with us this day (Deut. 29:14).

7:6 A. I know only that this refers to the commandments which already had been commanded to the Israelites on Mount Sinai. How do we know that this included the reading of the *Megillah* [of Esther]?

B. Scripture says, *They confirmed and took upon them* . . . (Esther 9:27).

7:7 A. Blessings, *Hallel,* the *Shema',* [and] the Prayer are said in any language.

B. Rabbi says, "I say that the *Shema'* is said only in the Holy Language, as it is said, *And these words* (Deut. 6:6)."

C. *The blessing of the priests* [M. Sot. 7:2A4, 7:6A]—this refers to the blessing which is said when the priests stand on the steps of the *ulam.*

7:8 A. All are valid to go up onto the steps of the *ulam,* whether unblemished or blemished, whether it is the watch of that particular priest or whether it is not his watch,

B. except for a priest who has a blemish on his face, hands, or feet.

C. For he should not raise his hands (to bless the people) in the sanctuary, because the people look at him.

D. And just as there is a priestly blessing through the raising of the hands in the sanctuary, so there is a priestly blessing through the raising of the hands in the provinces.

7:9 A. M'ŚH B: R. Yoḥanan b. Beroqah and R. Eleazar Ḥisma came from Yabneh to Lud and they greeted R. Joshua in Peqi'in.

B. Said to them R. Joshua, "What was new in the school-house today?"

C. They said to him, "We are your disciples and we drink your water."

D. He said to them, "It is hardly possible that there should be nothing new in the school house today. Whose week was it?"

E. They said to him, "It was the week of R. Eleazar b. 'Azariah."

F. He said to them, "And whence was the narration?"

G. "*Assemble the people, men, women, and children, and the sojourner within your towns, that they may hear and learn to fear the Lord your God* (Deut. 31:12)."

H. He said to them, "And what did he explain in this connection?"

I. They said to him, "Rabbi, Thus did he explain in its connection: 'Now if the men came along to study, the women came along to listen, why did the children come along? To provide a reward to the people who brought them.'

7:10 A. "And yet another lesson did he expound:

B. *"You have declared this day concerning the Lord that he is your God, and that you will walk in his ways and keep his statutes and his commandments and his ordinances and will obey his voice; and the Lord has declared this day concerning you that you are a people for his own possession* (Deut. 26:17–18).

C. "Said the Holy One blessed be He to them, 'Just as you have made me the only object of your love in the world, so I shall make you the only object of my love in the world to come.'

7:11 A. "And yet another lesson did he expound:

B. *"The sayings of the wise are like goads, and like nails firmly planted are the collected sayings which are given by one shepherd* (Qoh. 12:11).

C. "Just as this goad leads the cow to bring life to the world, so the words of Torah are only life for the world, as it is said, *It is a tree of life* (Prov. 3:18).

D. "Or might one propose: Just as goads are movable, so also are the words of Torah? Scripture says, *And like nails firmly planted.*

E. "Or might one propose: They neither diminish nor increase? Scripture says, *Firmly planted.* Just as a plant flourishes and grows, so the words of Torah flourish and grow.

F. *"Collected sayings*—These are those who enter and come into session group by group, ruling for the unclean, 'Unclean,' and for the clean, 'Clean,' for the unclean in its place, and for the clean in its place.

7:12 A. "Perhaps a man might imagine, 'Since the House of Shammai declare unclean and the House of Hillel clean, Mr. So-and-so prohibits, and Mr. Such-and-such permits, why should I henceforward learn Torah?'

B. "Scripture says, *'Words . . . the words . . . These are the words . . .* (Deut. 1:1).

C. "All these words have been given by a single Shepherd, one God made them, one Provider gave them, the Lord of all deeds, blessed be He, has spoken it.

"So you, open many chambers in your heart and bring into it the words of the House of Shammai and the words of the House of Hillel, the words of those who declare unclean and the words of those who declare clean."

D. He said to him, "The generation in which R. Eleazar flourishes is not orphaned."

7:13 A. *They made him a platform of wood in the courtyard and he sits on it* [M. Sot. 7:8D–E).

B. R. Eliezer b. Jacob says, "It was on the Temple mount, as it is said, *And he read from it facing the square before the Water Gate from early morning until midday in the presence of the men and the women and those who could understand . . . And Ezra the scribe stood on a wooden pulpit which they had made for the purpose . . . And Ezra opened the book in the sight of all the people, for he was above all the people . . .* (Neh. 8:3–5)."

7:14 A. *And Ezra blessed the Lord, the great God, and all the people answered, "Amen, Amen," lifting up their hands, and they bowed their heads and worshiped the Lord with their faces to the ground* (Neh. 8:6).

B. And it says, *And when she looked, there was the king standing by his pillar at the entrance, and the captains and the trumpeters beside the king, and all the people of the land rejoicing and blowing trumpets* (II Chron. 23:13).

7:15 A. On that day [of assembly] the priests stand at the walls and at the gates, with golden trumpets in their hand, and they sound the trumpet with *teqi'ah*-sounds, *teru'ah*-sounds, and *teqi'ah*-sounds.

B. And any priest who does not have a trumpet in his hand feels as though he is no priest.

C. The Jerusalemites made a great profit from renting out trumpets for golden *denars*.

7:16 A. On that day [of assembly] did R. Ṭarfon notice a lame priest standing and blowing the trumpet. On that account he concluded that a lame man blows the trumpet in the sanctuary.

B. In the name of R. Nathan they said, "The Israelites became liable for destruction because they flattered Agrippa, the King" [*vs.* M. Sot. 7:8K].

7:17 A. *He reads from the beginning of, And these are the words* (Deut. 1:1) *up to Hear O Israel* (Deut. 6:4), *And it will come to pass if you hearken* (Deut. 11:13), *You will surely tithe* (Deut. 14:22), *And when you finish tithing* (Deut. 26:12) [M. Sot. 7:8L].

B. R. Judah says, "He did not have to begin at the start of the scroll, but from *Hear O Israel . . . And it will come to pass if you hearken . . . You will surely tithe . . . And when you finish tithing. . . .*

C. *"And the pericope of the king, until he finishes the entire passage* [M. Sot. 7:8L],

D. "and the pericope which is expounded that day (Deut. 31:10ff.], and he finishes down to the end."

E. *For the Lord your God is he that goes with you* (Deut. 20:4)—

F. This is the Name, which is put in the ark, as it is said *And Moses sent them to the war, a thousand from each tribe, together with Phinehas, the son of Eleazar the priest, with the vessels of the sanctuary and the trumpets for the alarm in his hand* (Num. 31:6).

G. This teaches that Phinehas was anointed for war.

H. *With the vessels of the sanctuary*—this is the ark, as it is said, *But they shall not go in to look upon the holy things even for a moment, lest they die* (Num. 4:20).

I. And there are those who say, These are the priestly garments, as it is said, *And the holy garments* (Ex. 29:29).

7:18 A. R. Judah b. Laqish says, "There were two arks, one which went out with them to battle, and one which stayed with them in the camp.

B. "In the one which went out with them to battle there was a scroll of the Torah, as it is said, *And the ark of the covenant of the Lord went before them three days' journey* (Num. 10:33).

C. "And this one which stayed with them in the camp, this is the one in which were the tablets and the sherds of the tablets, as it is said, *Neither the ark of the covenant of the Lord nor Moses departed out of the camp* (Num. 14:44)" [cf. M. Sot. 8:1R–S].

D. Two times does he go out and talk with them, once on the boundary [before invading the enemy's territory] and once on the battlefield.

E. On the boundary what does he say? "Hear the words of the priest['s war-regulations] and return [home]."

F. On the battlefield what does he say? *What man is there that has built a new house and has not dedicated it?* (Deut. 20:5)

G. [If] his house fell down and he built it up again, lo, this one goes home.

H. R. Judah says, "If he did something new in connection with the house, he goes home, but if not, he does not go home" [*cf.* M. Sot. 8:3G].

I. R. Eliezer says, "The men of the Sharon did not go home to their houses, because they do something new to their houses once in every seven years" [M. Sot. 8:3H].

J. *And what man is there that has planted a vineyard and has not enjoyed its fruit? Let him go back to his house, lest he die in the battle and another man enjoy its fruit* (Deut. 20:6).

K. All the same are the one who plants a vineyard and the one who plants five fruit-trees of five different kinds, even in five distinct rows—lo, such a one goes home [M. Sot. 8:2E–F].

L. R. Eliezer b. Jacob says, "I find implied in this Scripture only one who has planted a vineyard."

7:19 A. *And what man is there that has betrothed a wife and has not taken her? Let him go back to his house, lest he die in the battle and another man take her* (Deut. 29:7).

B. All the same is he who betrothes and he who enters into Levirate marriage, and even if there is a woman awaiting Levirate marriage with one of five brothers,

C. and even if there are five brothers who heard that their brother has died in battle, all of them return and come home [M. Sot. 8:2J–K].

7:20 A. I know only that the law applies to one who builds his house but has not dedicated it, planted a vineyard but has not eaten the fruit, betrothed a wife but has not taken her.

B. How do we know that if one has built a house and dedicated it, but has not lived in it twelve months, planted a vineyard and eaten its fruits, but has not had the use of it for twelve months, betrothed a wife and taken her, but has not dwelt with her for twelve months—how do we know that these [stay home and] do not move from their place [M. Sot. 8:4A–B]?

C. Scripture says, *When a man is newly married, he shall not go out with the army or be charged with any business; he shall be free at home one year, to be happy with his wife whom he has taken* (Deut. 24:5).

D. This matter was covered by the general principle, and why has it been explicitly stated? To allow for the imposition of an analogy on its basis, so teaching you:

Now just as this one is distinguished in having betrothed a wife and taken her but in not having lived with her for twelve months, that he does not move from his place, so all of them are subject to the same rule.

E. Torah thereby has taught a rule of conduct:

F. When a man gains a portion for his support, he buys himself a house. If he gains yet a further portion for his support, he takes a wife for himself, as it is said, *What man is there that has built a new house . . . And what man is there that has planted a vineyard . . . And what man is there that has betrothed a wife . . .* (Deut. 20:5,6,7).

G. And so did Solomon say in his wisdom, *Prepare your work without and make it ready for yourself in the field, and afterwards build your house* (Prov. 24:27)—

H. *Prepare yourself without*—this is a house.

I. *And make it ready for yourself in the field*—this is a field.

J. *And afterwards build your house*—this is a wife.

7:21 A. Another matter:

B. *Prepare yourself without*—this is Scripture.

C. *And make it ready for yourself in the field*—this is Mishnah.

D. *And afterward build your house*—this is Midrash.

E. Another matter:

F. *Prepare yourself without*—this is Mishnah.

G. *And make it ready for yourself in the field*—this is Midrash.

H. *And afterward build your house*—these are laws.

I. Another matter:

J. *Prepare yourself without*—this is Midrash.

K. *And make it ready for yourself in the field*—these are laws.

L. *And afterward build your house*—this are narratives.

M. Another matter:

N. *Prepare yourself without*—these are laws.

O. *And make it ready for yourself in the field*—these are narratives.

P. *And afterward build your house*—this is Talmud.

Q. R. Eliezer, son of R. Yosé the Galilean says, "*Prepare yourself without*—this is Talmud.

"*And make it ready for yourself in the field*—this is a good deed.

"*And afterward build your house*—come and collect your reward."

7:22 A. *And the officers shall speak further to the people, and say, What man is there that is fearful and fainthearted* (Deut. 20:8)—

B. "For he is afraid on account of the transgression which is in his hand, as it is said, *Why should I fear in bad days* (Ps. 49:6)," the words of R. Yosé the Galilean.

C. R. ʿAqiba says, "*What man is there that is fearful*—certainly.

"But why then does Scripture again say, *And fainthearted?* [To add:] even if he is the strongest of the strong men, the most powerful among the powerful men, if he is merciful, he should go home, as it is said, *Lest the heart of his fellows melt as his heart* (Deut. 20:8)."

D. R. Simeon says, "Whoever hears the speech of the priest before the battle lines and does not go home [if he should], in the end dies by the sword, and brings Israel down by the sword, and sends them out into exile from their land, so that others come and settle in their land, as it is said, *Lest another man take her* (Deut. 20:7).

E. "Might one think that this refers to his uncle or cousin?

F. "Here is *another* said, and further on, *another* is said. Just as *another,* stated below (Deut. 28:30), refers to a gentile, so *another,* stated here, refers to a gentile."

G. [If] he heard that his brother had died in battle, if this is before he is placed in the line of battle, he returns home. But if this is after he is placed on the line of battle, he does not go home [M. Sot. 8:2L].

7:23 A. There are those who go forth and return home, go forth and do not return home, and there are those who do not go forth at all [M. Sot. 8:4A].

B. All those of whom they have said that they go forth and return home pay their share of the taxes of the town and provide water and food for the battle.

C. And they repair the roads [M. Sot. 8:2/0].

D. And all the rest of them do not go home at all.

7:24 A. All those concerning whom they have said, "They do not go forth at all," for example, he who builds a house and dedicated it but has not lived in it for twelve months, planted a vineyard and eaten the fruit but not made use of it for twelve months, betrothed a wife and taken her in marriage and has not remained with her twelve months [M. Sot. 8:4B]—

B. these do not pay their share of the taxes of the town, and do not provide water and food for the battle.

C. And they do not repair the roads.

D. R. Judah did call a war fought by choice, a war imposed by religious duty.

E. *But in the case of a war imposed by obligation, everyone goes forth,*

F. *even a bridegroom from his chamber and a bride from her canopy* [M. Sot. 8:7f–G].

8:1 A. *The blessings and the curses* [M. Sot. 7:5A]—these are the ones which the Israelites spoke when the Israelites crossed the Jordan, as it is said, *And on the day you pass over the Jordan to the land which the Lord your God gives you, you shall set up large stones* (Deut. 27:2).

B. How did the Israelites cross the Jordan?

C. Every day the ark would journey behind two standards, but this day it journeyed first, as it is said, *Behold, the ark of the covenant of the Lord of all the earth passes over before you* (Josh. 3:11).

8:2 A. Every day the Levites would carry the ark, but this day the priests carried it, as it is said, *And it shall come to pass, when the soles of the feet of the priests that bear the ark of the Lord* (Josh. 3:13).

B. R. Yosé says, "In three places did the priests carry the ark: Once when the Israelites crossed the Jordan, once when they surrounded Jericho, and once when they brought it back to its place."

8:3 A. When part of the feet of the priests were dipped in the water, the water of the Jordan stood still, as it is said, *And the waters which came from above stood and rose up in one heap* (Josh. 3:15).

B. "Twelve *mils* by twelve *mils* was the height of the water," the words of R. Judah.

C. Said R. Eleazar b. R. Simeon, "And is man swifter, or is water swifter? You have to say that water is swifter than man.

"This teaches that the waters were continually driven backward and heaped up higher and higher, stacks by stacks, three hundred *mils,* until all the kings of the nations of the world saw them,

"as it is said, *And it came to pass, when all the kings of the Amorites which were beyond Jordan westward, and all the kings of the Canaanites, which were by the sea, heard how the Lord had dried up the waters, their heart melted, neither was there spirit in them any more, because of the children of Israel* (Josh. 5:1)."

8:4 A. And so did Rahab say to the messengers of Joshua, "*For we have heard how the Lord dried up the water of the Red Sea before you . . . And as soon as we heard it, our hearts did melt, neither did there remain any more* (Josh. 2:10,11)."

8:5 A. While they were still on the other side of the Jordan, Joshua said to them, "Know that you are entering the Land on condition that you will throw out its inhabitants,

"as it is said, *Then you shall drive out all the inhabitants of the land from before you* (Num. 33:52), *But if you do not drive out the inhabitants of the land from before you* (Num. 33:55), *Then I will do to you as I thought to do to them* (Num. 33:56).

B. "But if you do not accept [the task], the water will come and drown you."

8:6 A. While they were still in the Jordan, Joshua said to them, "*Take you up, every man of you, a stone upon his shoulder, according to the number of the tribes of the children of Israel* (Josh. 4:5), *And lay them down in the place where you lodge tonight* (Josh. 4:3), *in the place where the feet of the priests bearing the ark of the covenant had stood in the Jordan* (Josh. 4:9)."

B. This was a memorial for the children that their fathers had crossed the Jordan.

C. While they were still in the Jordan, Joshua said to them, "*Take twelve stones from here out of the midst of the Jordan from the very place where the priests' feet stood* (Josh. 4:3)."

D. R. Judah says, "R. Ḥalafta, Eleazar b. Matia, and Ḥananiah b. Kinai stood on those very stones and estimated that each one weighed forty *seahs*."

E. On this basis you may reckon how much is there in grapecluster.

F. And when the last person among the Israelites had gone up from the Jordan, the water of the Jordan went back to its place, as it is said, *The waters of the Jordan returned to their place and overflowed all its banks, as before* (Josh. 4:18).

G. It turned out that the ark and its bearers [Erfurt: *and the priests*] were on one side of the Jordan and the Israelites on the other.

H. So the ark carried its carriers and brought them across the Jordan.

I. You turn out to state, there are three sets of stones,

J. one which Moses set up on the shore of the Jordan in the plains of Moab, and one which he set under the place of the feet of the priests [in the Jordan], and one which they brought over with them.

K. R. Judah says, "They inscribed it [the Torah] on the stones of the altar."

L. They said to him, "[If so], how would the nations of the world learn the Torah?"

M. He said to them, "This teaches that the Omnipresent moved every nation and kingdom to send their scribes, and they translated what was written on the stones into seventy languages.

N. "At that moment the verdict against the nations of the world was sealed for destruction."

8:7 A. R. Simeon says, "They wrote it on plaster. How so? They laid it out and plastered it with plaster, and they wrote on it all the words of the Torah in seventy languages, and they wrote below, *That they teach you not to do after all their abominations* (Deut. 20:18):

B. "'If you repent, we shall receive you.'"

C. Come and see how many miracles were done for Israel!

On that day they crossed the water of the Jordan and came to Mount Gerizim and Mount Ebal in Samaria on the side of Shechem, near the oaks of Moreh, as it is said, *And are they not on the other side of Jordan, west of the road, toward the going down of the sun, in the land of the Canaanites who live in the Arabah, over against the Gilgal, beside the oak of Moreh* (Deut. 11:30)—[so traversing a distance of] more than sixty *mils.*

D. No man stood against them, and whoever stood against them was forthwith panic-stricken, as it is said, *I will send My terror before you, and will discomfort all the people to whom you shall come* (Ex. 23:27). And it says, *Terror and dread fall upon them . . . until your people pass over, O Lord* (Ex. 15:16).

E. *Until your people pass over*—this is the first passage.

F. *Until this people which you have acquired*—this is the second passage.

G. On this basis you must conclude: The Israelites ought to have had done for them at the Jordan what was done for them at the Sea, but they had [in the meantime] sinned.

8:8 A. And afterward they brought the stones and built an altar and offered up burnt-offerings and peace-offerings, and sat down and ate and drank.

B. And they took the stones and went and spent the night in their place, as it is said, *And carry them over with you and lay them down in the place where you lodge tonight* (Josh. 4:3).

C. Might one say, In any lodging place? Scripture says, *In the place in which you lodge tonight.*

D. And where did they lodge? In Gilgal.

E. And it says, *And those twelve stones, which they took out of the Jordan, Joshua set up in Gilgal* (Josh. 4:20).

F. Thus you learn that in Gilgal they set them up [M. Sot. 7:5P].

8:9 A. How did the Israelites say the blessings and the curses?

B. *Six tribes went up to the top of Mount Gerizim, and six tribes went up to the top of Mount Ebal. And the priests and the Levites and the ark of the covenant stood at the bottom in the middle* [M. Sot. 7:5C-D].

The priests surround the ark, and the Levites [surround] the priests, and all Israel are round about,

since it says, And all Israel and their elders and officers and judges stood on this side of the ark and on that (Josh. 8:33) [M. Sot. 7:5C–E].

C. What is the meaning of the Scripture, . . . *Half of them in front of Mount Gerizim and half of them in front of Mount Ebal* (Josh. 8:33)?

D. This teaches that the part which was before Mount Gerizim was greater than that before Mount Ebal, since the part of the tribe of Levi was below.

E. R. Eliezer b. Jacob says, "You cannot say that Levi was below, for it already has been said that Levi was above, and you cannot say that Levi was above, for already has it been stated that Levi was below.

"On this basis you must say that the elders of the priesthood and of the Levites were below, but the rest of the tribe was above."

F. Rabbi says, "Those who were appropriate for service stood below, and those who were not appropriate for service stood above."

G. *They turned their faces toward Mount Gerizim and began with the blessing: Blessed is the man who does not make a graven or molten image* [M. Sot. 7:5F–G]—an abomination to the Lord, the work of a craftsman, not put away in secret.

H. *And these and those answer, Amen.*

They turned their faces toward Mount Ebal and began with the curse: Cursed is the man who makes a graven or molten image (Deut. 27:15). *And these and those answer, Amen* [M. Sot. 7:5H–K].

I. They turn toward Mount Gerizim and began with blessings: Blessed is he who will carry out the teachings of the Torah,

toward Mount Ebal and began with curses, *Cursed is he who will not carry out* (Deut. 27:26).

8:10 A. There is a blessing in general and a blessing in particular, a curse in general and a curse in particular.

B. *To learn, to teach, to observe, and to do* (Deut. 5:1, 11:19)—four [duties with each commandment]. Four and four are eight, and eight and eight are sixteen [eight blessings and curses with the general commandment, and eight with the particular commandments],

C. with three covenants for each one—lo, forty-eight covenants for each commandment,

D. and so at Mount Sinai, and so in the plains of Moab.

8:11 A. R. Simeon excludes the one of Mount Gerizim and of Mount Ebal but includes the one of the Tent of Meeting.

B. You have none for which forty-eight covenants were not made.

C. R. Simeon b. Judah of Kefar Akko says in the name of R. Simeon, "You have nothing whatsoever in the Torah for which six hundred three thousand five hundred and fifty covenants were not made, equivalent to the number of people who went forth from Egypt."

D. Said Rabbi, "If matters are in accord with the view of R. Simeon of Judah of Kefar Ammos which he said in the name of R. Simeon, then you have nothing whatsoever in the Torah on account of which sixteen covenants were not made, and there is with each one of them six hundred three thousand five hundred and fifty."

9:1 A. If it [a neglected corpse] was found on the other side of the Jordan, they would go through the rite of breaking a heifer's neck, since it is said, *If in the land which the Lord your God gives you to possess, any one is found slain* (Deut. 21:1)—to include the other side of the Jordan.

B. R. Eleazar says, "In the case of all of them, if there was a corpse, they would go through the rite of breaking the heifer's neck [even if it was found hidden in a pile of rocks or hanging from a tree]."

C. Said to him R. Yosé b. R. Judah, "If it was only strangled and lying in a field, did they break a heifer's neck? On this account it is said, *Slain.* If so, why is it said, *Lying?* But even if it was slain and hanging in a tree, they did not break a heifer's neck" [*cf.* M. Sot. 9:2A–D].

D. [If] it was found in the entrance to a town, they nonetheless would measure. It is a religious duty to do the work of measuring.

E. How did they do it for him?

F. The agents of the court go forth and take markers, and they dig a hole and bury him, and they mark off his place, until they come to the high court in the hewn-stone chamber, and then they measure out.

G. [If] it is he is found nearer the frontier, to a town in which there are gentiles, or to a town in which there is no court, they do not measure [M. Sot. 9:2E].

H. They measure only for a town in which there is a court.

I. If there was a town of gentiles in between, or [if it was] near Jerusalem, they did not measure [M. Sot. 9:2E], but they left it and measured around it.

J. The area of its wine-press and its environs, lo, this is prohibited.

K. And how large is its environs? Forty *amahs.*

L. Rabbi says, "Fifty *amahs.*"

9:2 A. *The elders say, "Our hands have not shed this blood, and our eye did not see it"* (Deut. 21:7) [M. Sot. 9:6B].

B. *And the priests say, "Forgive, O Lord, your people, Israel whom you have redeemed"* (Deut. 21:8) [M. Sot. 9:6F].

C. And the Holy Spirit says, *"But let the guilt of blood be forgiven them"* (Deut. 21:8) [M. Sot. 9:6H].

D. In three passages [just now cited], the one who said one thing did not say another.

E. Similarly you say:

We came to the land to which you sent us, said Joshua.

Caleb said, *Let us now go up and inherit it.*

The spies said, *Yet the people who dwell in the land are strong* (Num. 13:27).

F. So you have three things side by side, and the one who said this one did not say that one, and whoever said that one did not say the other.

9:3 A. Similarly you say:

And she said, "Mark, I pray you, whose these are, the signet and the cord and the staff" (Gen. 38:25), so said Tamar.

B. Said Judah, *"She is more righteous than I"* (Gen. 38:26).

C. And the Holy Spirit says, *"And he did not lie with her again"* (Gen. 38:26).

D. So you have three things side by side, and the one who said this one did not say that one, and whoever said that one did not say the other.

9:4 A. Similarly you say:

And they said, Woe to us! Who can deliver us from the power of these mighty gods? (I Sam. 4:8)—so said the proper ones among them.

B. The evil ones among them said, *These are the gods who smote the Egyptians with every sort of plague in the wilderness* (I Sam. 4:8).

C. And the heroes among them said, *Take courage and acquit yourselves like men, O Philistines"* (I Sam. 4:9).

D. So you have three things side by side, just as before.

E. Similarly you say:

Out of the window she peered, she gazed (Jud. 5:28), said the mother of Sisera.

F. *Her wisest ladies make answer, . . . Are they not finding and dividing the spoil* (Jud. 5:29–30)—so said his wife and his daughters-in-law.

G. *So perish all thine enemies, O Lord! But thy friends be like the sun as he rises in his might* (Jud. 5:31)—so said the Holy Spirit.

H. Thus you have three things, side by side, just as before.

9:5 A. Similarly you say:

Micah of Moresheth prophesied in the days of Hezekiah, king of Judah (Jer. 26:18). "And what did he prophesy? *And he spoke to all the people of Judah, 'Thus says the Lord of Hosts: Zion shall be plowed as a field, Jerusalem shall become a heap of ruins, and the mountain of the house a wooded height.' Did Hezekiah king of Judah and all Judah put him to death? Did he not entreat the favor of the Lord, and did not the Lord repent of the evil which he had pronounced against them? But we are about to bring great evil upon ourselves* (Jer. 26:18–19)," so said the proper ones among them.

B. The evil ones among them said, "*There was another man who prophesied in the name of the Lord, Uriah the son of Shemaiah from Kiriath-jearim. He prophesied against this city and against this land in words like those of Jeremiah. And when King Jehoiakim with all his warriors and all the princes heard his words, the king sought to put him to death, but when Uriah heard of it, he was afraid and fled and escaped to Egypt . . . And they fetched Uriah from Egypt and brought him to King Jehoakim, who slew him with the sword* (Jer. 26:20–23)."

C. They said, "Just as Uriah prophesied and was killed, so Jeremiah is subject to the death-penalty," as it is said, *But the hand of Ahikam, the son of Shaphan was with Jeremiah, so that he was not given over to the people to be put to death* (Jer. 26:24).

D. This entire pericope is a mixture of the words of different parties, so that one who said one thing did not say the other.

9:6 A. Similarly you say:

An oracle concerning Nineveh. The book of the vision of Nahum of Elkosh. The Lord is a jealous God and avenging . . . The Lord is slow to anger and of great might . . . He rebukes the sea and makes it dry—(Nah. 1:1–4 *pass.*).

B. The entire pericope is a mixture of the words of different parties, so that the one who said one thing did not say the other.

9:7 A. Similarly you say:

To the choirmaster: according to Do-Not-Destroy, A Miktam of David. Do you indeed decree what is right, you gods? . . . Nay, in your hearts you devise wrongs, your hands deal out violence on earth. The wicked go astray from the womb, they err from their birth . . . They have venom like the venom of the serpent (Ps. 58:1–4, *pass.*).

B. The entire pericope is a mixture of the words of different parties, so that the one who said one thing did not say the other.

9:8 A. Similarly you say:

Under the apple tree I awakened you (Song 8:5), said the Holy Spirit.

B. *Set me as a seal upon your heart* (Song 8:6), said the congregation of Israel.

C. *For love is strong as death, jealousy is cruel as the grave* (Song 8:6), said the nations of the world.

D. Thus there are three things side by side, (just as before).

10:1 A. When righteous people come into the world, good comes into the world and retribution departs from the world.

B. And when they take their leave from the world, retribution comes into the world, and goodness departs from the world.

10:2 A. When bad people come into the world, retribution comes into the world, and goodness departs from the world.

B. And when they depart from the world, goodness comes back into the world, and retribution departs from the world.

C. How do we know that, when righteous people come into the world, goodness comes into the world, and retribution departs from the world? Since it is said, *And he called him Noah, saying, This one will comfort us in our work and in the toil of our hands* (Gen. 5:29).

D. And how do we know that, when they take their leave of the world, retribution comes into the world and goodness departs from the world? Since it is said, *The righteous man perishes and no one lays it to heart* (Is. 57:1), and it says, *He enters into peace, they rest in their beds who walk in their uprightness* (Is. 57:2)—He goes in peace to the grave. And it says, *But you, draw near hither, sons of the sorceress, offspring of the adulterer and the harlot* (Is. 57:3).

E. And how do we know that when bad people come into the world, retribution comes into the world and goodness departs from the world? Since it is said, *When the wicked comes, then comes also contempt, and with ignominy, reproach* (Prov. 18:3).

F. And how do we know that, when he departs from the world, goodness comes into the world and retribution leaves the world? Since it says, *And when the wicked perish, there is exultation* (Prov. 11:10). *And it says, So that the Lord may turn from the fierceness of his anger and show you mercy and have compassion on you* (Deut. 13:17).

10:3 A. So long as bad people are in the world, fierce anger is in the world.

When they perish from the world, retribution and fierce wrath depart from the world.

B. And it is not that the righteous people support the world when they are alive only, but even after death, as it says, *And after seven days the waters of the flood came upon the earth* (Gen. 7:10).

C. Now what is the meaning of these seven days? These are the seven days of mourning for Methuselah, the righteous man, which held back the retribution from coming upon the world.

D. Therefore it is said, *And after seven days.*

10:4 A. Another matter: What is the meaning of these seven days?

B. (Scripture thereby) teaches that the Omnipresent gave them seven days after the decree, so that they might repent, but they did not do so.

C. Therefore it is said, *And after seven days.*

D. Another matter: *And after seven days*—

E. This teaches that the Omnipresent changed the order of the world for them, so that the sun came up in the west and set in the east.

F. On that account it is said, *And it came to pass after seven days.*

10:5 A. Another matter: It teaches that the Omnipresent gave them food and drink, and they ate and drank, and he showed them a glimpse of the world to come. All this why? So they might understand and perceive and know what it is that they had lost.

B. All the time that Abraham was alive, there was plenty, since it says, *And Abraham was old, well advanced in years, and the Lord had blessed Abraham in all things* (Gen. 24:1).

C. But once Abraham had died, *There was famine in the land* (Gen. 26:1).

10:6 A. When Isaac came along, there was plenty, as it is said, *And Isaac sowed in that land and reaped in the same year a hundredfold* (Gen. 26:12).

B. So long as Abraham was alive, the wells gushed forth water. When Abraham had died, what does it say? *Now the Philistines had stopped and filled with earth all the wells which his father's servants had dug in the days of Abraham his father* (Gen. 26:15).

C. For they said, "Now that they do not gush forth water, they are only a hazard for travelers." They (therefore) went and stopped them up.

D. Isaac came along, and the wells gushed water, as it is said, *And Isaac dug again the wells of water which had been dug in the days of Abraham his father . . . And when Isaac's servants dug in the valley and found there a well of springing water . . .* (Gen. 26:18–19).

10:7 A. Before Jacob went down to Aram Naharaim, the house of Laban the Aramaean had not received a blessing, as it is said, *For you had little before I came, and it has increased abundantly, and the Lord has blessed you wherever I turned* (Gen. 30:30).

B. Once he came down, what does it say? *And the Lord has blessed you wherever I turned.*

C. And it says, *I have learned by divination that the Lord has blessed me because of you* (Gen. 30:27).

10:8 A. Before Joseph went down to Egypt, the house of Potiphar had not received a blessing. But once he went down, what does it say?

B. *From the time that he made him overseer in his house and over all that he had, the Lord blessed the Egyptian's house for Joseph's sake* (Gen. 30:5).

10:9 A. Before Jacob went down to Egypt, there had been famine, as it is said, *For the famine has been in the land these two years* (Gen. 45:6).

B. Once he came down there, what does it say? *Now here is seed for you, and you shall sow the land* (Gen. 47:23).

C. Said R. Yosé, "When Jacob our patriarch died, the famine came back where it had been, as it is said, *So do not fear; I will provide for you and for your little ones* (Gen. 50:21).

D. "*Providing* is stated here, and *providing* is stated later on. Just as in this context it is a situation of famine, so in the other context, it is a situation of famine."

10:10 A. So long as Joseph and the tribes were alive, the Israelites enjoyed greatness and honor, as it is said, *And the children of Israel were fruitful and multiplied* (Ex. 1:7).

B. When Joseph died, what does it say? *And Joseph died . . . , And a new king arose who knew not Joseph . . . , And he said to his people . . . , Come, let us take counsel against him* (Ex. 1:6, 8–10).

11:1 A. So long as Miriam was alive, the well provided ample water for all Israel. Once Miriam had died, what does it say? *And Miriam died there, and there was not enough water for the congregation* (Num. 20:1–2)—for the well dried up.

B. So long as Aaron was alive, a pillar of cloud led Israel. Once Aaron had died, what does it say? *When the Canaanite, the king of Arad, who dwelt in the Negeb, heard that Israel was coming* (Num. 21:1).

C. That bad man grew strong, and he came and made war against Israel. He said, "Where has their seer gone, who paved the way for them into the land?"

11:2 A. As long as Moses was alive, the manna came down to Israel. When Moses died, what does it say? *And the manna ceased on the morrow* (Josh. 5:12).

B. And it is not that the manna supported them while he was alive only, but also after he had died. For the manna which they had gathered on the day on which Moses had died did they eat from the seventh of Adar to the sixteenth of Nisan, thirty-nine days more.

C. Then they offered up the *'omer* in Gilgal, as it is said, *And the children of Israel ate the manna forty years, until they came to a habitable land; they ate the manna till they came to the border of the land of Canaan* (Ex. 16:35).

D. Now Scripture does not say only, *Until they came*. And why does Scripture say, *Until they came to the border of the land of Canaan?*

E. This is meant to teach that the manna which they had gathered on the day on which Moses died they ate from the seventh of Adar until the sixteenth of Nisan, thirty-nine days,

F. until they had offered the *'omer* in Gilgal.

G. For if the manna had not come to an end, they would not have wanted to eat from the natural produce of the land of Canaan.

11:3(4) A. R. Eleazar b. 'Azariah says, "To what is the matter likened? To a mortal king who said to his servant, 'Mix for me a cup of wine with warm water.'

"He said to him, 'We do not have warm water here.'

"'If not, mix it for me with cold water.'

B. "This tells you how good it was for the Israelites. For if manna had come down for the Israelites in Adar, they would not have eaten of the produce of the land of Canaan."

11:5 A. In the year in which the Israelites went forth from Egypt, on the sixteenth day of Iyyar the manna came down to Israel. On the seventh of Adar it ceased to come down. That day Moses died.

B. And on the sixteenth day of Nisan the manna which they had left was used up, as it is said, *And they ate of the produce of the land of Canaan that year* (Josh. 5:12).

C. Another matter: What is the meaning of Scripture's saying, *And the children of Israel ate the manna forty years* (Ex. 16:35)? But were not thirty days lacking (of those forty years)?

D. But they (then) ate unleavened cakes which they had brought forth with them from Egypt, which were as good for them as manna.

11:6 A. And how do we know that on the seventh of Adar Moses was born? As it is said, *And he said to them, I am a hundred and twenty years old this day* (Deut. 31:2).

B. Now does Scripture not say, *This day?* And why does Scripture say, *This day?* For on that day his years were brought to their fulness.

C. Another matter: Why does Scripture say, *This day?* It teaches that they were one hundred and twenty years exactly.

D. Another matter: Why does Scripture say, *This day?* It teaches that the Holy One blessed be He completes the years of the righteous with joy and happiness, as it is said, *The number of your days I will fulfill* (Ex. 23:26).

11:7 A. And how do we know that on the seventh of Adar Moses died? *And the people of Israel wept for Moses in the plains of Moab thirty days* (Deut. 34:8).

And it says, *And it came to pass, after the death of Moses the servant of the Lord, the Lord said to Joshua, the son of Nun, Moses' minister, Moses my servant is dead; now therefore arise, go over this Jordan* (Josh. 1:1–2).

Then Joshua commanded the officers of the people, saying, Pass through the camp and command the people, Prepare your provisions, for within three days you are to pass over this Jordan (Josh. 1:10–11).

And it says, *The people came up out of the Jordan on the tenth day of the first month* (Josh. 4:19).

B. Deduct from that date thirty-three days in retrospect, and you find that on the seventh of Adar Moses died.

11:8 A. R. Yosé b. R. Judah says, "When the Israelites went forth from Egypt, three good providers were appointed for them. These are they: Moses, Aaron, and Miriam.

B. "On their account were three gifts given to them: the pillar of cloud, manna, and the well—the well through the merit of Miriam, the pillar of cloud through the merit of Aaron, and the manna through the merit of Moses.

C. "When Miriam died, the well ceased, but it came back through the merit of Moses and Aaron.

"When Aaron died, the pillar of cloud ceased, but both of them came back through the merit of Moses.

"When Moses died, all three of them came to an end and never came back, as it is said, *In one month I destroyed the three shepherds*" (Zech. 11:8).

11:9 A. The hornet did not cross the Jordan, but it stood on the bank of the Jordan and spat poison at them.

11:10 A. As long as Joshua and the elders were alive, there was no Lie [of idolatry] among the Israelites, and the nations could do no harm to Israel, as it is said, *And the people served the Lord all the days of Joshua, and all the days of the elders who outlived Joshua, who had seen all the great work which the Lord had done for Israel* (Judges 2:7).

B. Once Joshua and the elders died, what does it say? *And the people of Israel served Cushan-rishathaim eight years* (Judges 3:8).

C. Now why was his name *Cushan-rishathaim?* For he committed two evil deeds, one that he subjugated the Israelites, and the other that he violated his oath.

11:11 A. As long as Samuel was alive, the Philistines fell at the hand of Israel, as it is said, *And the hand of the Lord was against the Philistines all the days of Samuel* (I Sam. 7:13).

B. After Samuel, what does it say? *And Samuel died* (I Sam. 25:1). *In those days the Philistines gathered their forces for war, to fight against Israel* (I Sam. 28:1).

11:12 A. One Scripture says, *And Samuel died,* and another Scripture says, *Now there died Samuel* (I Sam. 28:3, I Sam. 25:1).

B. *And Samuel died*—this surely refers to his death.

C. *Now there died Samuel*—this is with reference to the matter of Saul (who behaved as he did because Samuel had died).

D. R. Eleazar says, "Lo, it says, *He said to her, What is his appearance? And she said, An old man is coming up, and he is wrapped in a robe* (I Sam. 28:14).

E. "Now should it not enter your mind that Samuel had not died? For he had died, and it says, *Now Samuel had died, and all Israel had mourned for him and buried him in Ramah, his own city* (I Sam. 28:3).

F. "Now should we not have known that Ramah was his own city? But Scripture teaches you that all Israel mourned for him as they mourned for him in Ramah."

11:13 A. Similarly do you say:

When you depart from me today, you will meet two men of Rachel's tomb in the territory of Benjamin at Zelzah (I Sam. 10:2).

B. Now where do we find that Rachel was buried in the territory of Benjamin at Zelzah? Now was she not buried in Bethlehem, in the portion of Judah, as it is said, *And Rachel died and was buried on the road to Ephrat,* and Ephrat refers solely to the portion of Judah, since it is said, *But you, O Bethlehem Ephrathah, who are little to be among the clans of Judah* (Micah 5:2).

C. But he said to him, "At this time that I am speaking with you, lo, they are at the grave of Rachel. You will go toward them, and they will come toward you, and you will find them at the border of Benjamin, at Zelzah."

11:14 A. Similarly do you say:

Now Saul heard that David was discovered, and the men who were with him. Saul was sitting at Gibeah, under the tamarisk tree [in Ramah] with his spear in his hand (I Sam. 22:6).

B. If he was in Gibeah, he was not in Ramah, and if he was in Ramah, he was not in Gibeah.

C. But who upholds the foot of Saul in Gibeah? The court of Samuel of Ramah.

11:15 A. Similarly do you say:

Our feet have been standing within your gates, O Jerusalem (Ps. 122:2].

B. It is not possible to say so [that all of them were standing within the gates of Jerusalem].

C. But who supports our feet in war? It is the courts of David who are in session at the gates of Jerusalem.

11:16 A. Similarly do you say:

The whole land shall be turned into a plain from Geba to Rimmon, south of Jerusalem (Zech. 14:10). Now is the area south of Jerusalem not a plain? But Geba to Rimmon is a place of rocks and gulleys.

B. But just as Geba and Rimmon are destined to be a plain south of Jerusalem, so all the lands are destined to be a plain south of Jerusalem.

11:17 A. Similarly do you say:

And the five sons of Michal the daughter of Saul, whom she bore to Adriel the son of Barzillai the Meholathite (II Sam. 21:8). Now where do we find that Michal was given to Adriel the son of Barzillai the Meholathite? Was she not given only to Palti the son of Laish, who was of Gallim, as it is said, *And Saul had given Michal, his daughter, David wife, to Palti, the son of Laish, who was of Gallim* (I Sam. 25:44).

B. But Scripture thereby links the marriage of Merab to the marriage of Michal.

C. Just as the marriage of Michal to Palti the son of Laish was in transgression, so the marriage of Merab to Adriel was in transgression.

11:18 A. His disciples asked R. Yosé, "How did David marry the sister of his wife?"

B. He said to them, "After the death of Merab did he marry her."

11:19 A. R. Joshua b. Qorḥa says, "For his act of betrothal was not deemed a completely valid betrothal, as it is said, *Give me my wife, Michal, whom I betrothed at a price of a hundred foreskins of the Philistines* (II Sam. 3:14).

B. "Just as his act of betrothal was not a completely valid bethrothal, so his marriage was not a completely valid marriage."

11:20 A. One Scripture says, *And the five sons of Michal,* and another Scripture says, *And Michal, the daughter of Saul, had no offspring until the day of her death* (II Sam. 21:8, II Sam. 6:23).

B. Now how shall both of these Scriptures be confirmed?

C. On this basis you must conclude that they were the sons of Merab.

Merab gave birth to them, and Michal raised them, so they were called by her [Michal's] name, as it is said, *And the women of the neighborhood gave him a name, saying, A son has been born to Naomi* (Ruth 4:17).

D. And it says, *These are the generations of Aaron and Moses . . . And these are the names of the sons of Aaron* (Num. 3:1,2).

12:1 A. *In the thirty-sixth year of the reign of Asa, Baasha, king of Israel, went up against Judah and built Ramah* (II Chron. 16:1).

B. It is not possible to say so. For did not Asa bury Baasha in the twenty-sixth year of his reign? Why does Scripture say, *In the thirty-sixth year?*

C. It was the year that Solomon married into the family of the King of Egypt,

corresponding to the thirty-six years that a decree was issued against the royal house of David, that it be divided into two.

D. But in the end it is destined to return for them.

12:2 A. It corresponded to the thirty-six years that a decree was enacted against the kings of Aram, that they should be the enemies of Israel.

B. But at the end they are destined to fall by the hand of the son of David.

C. Therefore it is said, *In the thirty-sixth year of the reign of Asa* (II Chron. 16:1).

D. *So he died according to the word of the Lord which Elijah had spoken, and Jehoram, his brother, became king in his stead in the second year of Jehoram the son of Jehoshaphat, king of Judah* (II Kings 1:17).

E. It is not possible to say so. For did not Jehoshaphat rule five years after him?

F. But when Jehoshaphat, king of Judah, went with Ahab, king of Israel, to Ramoth Gilead, a decree was issued against Jehoshaphat for death, as it is said, *And when the captains of the chariots saw Jehoshaphat, they said, It is surely the king of Israel. So they turned to fight against him; and Jehoshaphat cried out* (I Kings 22:32).

G. He was worthy of being put to death at that hour, but it teaches that in reward for that cry, Scripture suspended (the decree) for him for seven years,and it counted them for his son.

12:3 A. *Jehoram was thirty-two years old when he became king, and he reigned eight years in Jerusalem* (II Kings 21:5).

B. And in the case of Ahaziah, his son, what does it say? *Ahaziah was forty-two years old when he began to reign, and he reigned one year in Jerusalem* (II Chron. 22:2).

C. Yet in another place it says, *Ahaziah was twenty-two years old when he began to reign* (II Kings 8:26).

D. Said R. Yosé, "Now how is it possible for a son to be two years older than his father? But when Asa, king of Judah, married off the daughter of Omri, king of Israel, to his son, Jehoshaphat, the decree was issued that the royal house of David will perish with the house of Ahab, as it is said, *But it was ordained by God that the downfall of Ahaziah should come about through his going to visit Joram* (II Chron. 22:7).

E. Both of them fell on the same day with one another.

12:4 A. Similarly: *All of these were enrolled by genealogies in the days of Jotham, king of Judah, and in the days of Jeroboam, king of Israel* (I Chron. 5:17).

B. It is not possible to say so. For did not Uzziah bury Jeroboam and yet three more kings after him?

C. But all those twenty-five years that Uzziah the king was afflicted with *ṣara'at,* Jotham his son was in charge of the royal palace, judging the people of the land.

12:5 A. Before Elijah was hidden away, the Holy Spirit was commonplace in Israel, as it is said, *And Elijah said to Elisha, Tarry here, I pray you, for the Lord has sent me to Beth El* (II Kings 2:2–3).

What does it then say? *And the sons of the prophets who were in Beth El came out to Elisha and said to him, Do you know that today the Lord will take away your master from over you? And he said, Yes, I know it; hold your peace* (II Kings 2:3).

Elijah said to him, "Elisha, tarry here, I pray you; for the Lord has sent me to Jericho (II Kings 2:4).

What does it then say? *The sons of the prophets who were at Jericho drew near to Elisha, and said to him, Do you know that today the Lord will take away your master from over you? And he answered, Yes I know it, hold your peace* (II Kings 2:5).

Then Elijah said to him, Tarry here, I pray you, for the Lord has sent me to the Jordan (II Kings 2:6).

What does it say? *And fifty men of the sons of the prophets also went and stood at a distance from them as they were both standing by the Jordan* (II Kings 2:7).

B. Now is it possible that it was because they were few in number? Scripture says, *Fifty men.*

C. Is it possible that they were of little weight? Scripture says, *And they said to him, Do you know that today the Lord will take away your master from over you?*

Our master they did not say, but *your master,* teaching that all of them were colleagues of Elijah, and they were just as weighty as Elijah.

D. And how do we know that the Holy Spirit then departed from them?

Since it is said, *And they said to him, Behold now, there are with your servants fifty strong men; pray, let them go, and seek your master; it may be that the Spirit of the Lord has caught him up and cast him upon some mountain or into some valley* (II Kings 2:16).

E. Now it is hardly possible for men that the night before one should say, *Do you know that today the Lord will take away your master from over you,* and now he should say, *Let them go and seek your master.*

F. But this tells us that the Holy Spirit had departed from them.

G. *But when they urged him till he was ashamed, he said, Send* (II Kings 2:17).

H. Why does Scripture say, *Until he was ashamed?* It teaches that he was embarrassed by them, that they not say that he does not want to greet his master.

12:6 A. So long as Elisha was alive, the bands of Arameans did not come into the frontiers of Israel, as it is said, *And the Arameans came no more on raids into the land of Israel* (II Kings 6:23).

B. When Elisha died, what does it say? *So Elisha died, and they buried him. Now bands of Moabites used to invade the land in the spring of the year* (II Kings 13:20).

13:1 A. After the first Temple was built, the Tent of Meeting was stored away, along with its boards, hooks, bars, pillars, and sockets.

B. Even so, they used only the the table which Moses had made, and the candlestick which Moses had made.

C. The candlestick which Moses made did not require oil of anointing, for the first act of sanctification had sanctified it for its time and for all time.

D. When the ark was stored away, with it were stored away the bottle of manna, the jar of oil for anointing, the staff of Aaron, its buds and flowers, and the chest in which the Philistines had placed wood for the God of Israel.

E. All of them were in the house of the Holy of Holies.

F. And when the ark was stored away, the Commandments were stored away.

G. Who stored it away?

H. Josiah the King stored it away.

I. Why did he do so?

J. When he saw written in the Torah, *The Lord will bring you and your king whom you set over you to a nation that neither you nor your fathers have known* (Deut. 28:36), he commanded the Levites and they hid it away, as it is said, *And he said to the Levites who taught all Israel and who were holy to the*

Lord, Put the holy ark in the house which Solomon, the son of David, king of Israel, built; you need no longer carry it upon your shoulders (II Chron. 35:3).

K. He said to them, "Hide it away [for future use], so that it will not be taken away into exile like the rest of the Temple utensils, so put it back in its place, as it is said, *Now serve the Lord your God and his people Israel* (II Chron. 35:3)."

L. Forthwith the Levites hid it away.

M. R. Eliezer says, "The ark was taken away in exile to Babylonia, as it is said, *Behold the days are coming, when all that is in your house and that which your fathers have stored up till this day shall be carried to Babylonia, no thing will be left, says the Lord* (II Kings 20:17). And *thing* refers only to the commandments which are in it."

N. R. Simeon says, "Lo, it says, *In the spring of the year King Nebuchadnezzar sent and brought him to Babylonia with the precious vessels of the house of the Lord* (II Chron. 36:10)—this refers to the ark."

O. R. Judah b. Laqish says, "The ark was hidden away in its place, as it is said, *And the poles were so long that the ends of the poles were seen from the holy place before the inner sanctuary; but they could not be seen from outside; and they are there to this day* (I Kings 8:8)."

13:2 A. When the first Temple was destroyed, the kingship was removed from the House of David.

B. The Urim and Thummim ceased [M. Sot. 9:12A].

C. The cities of refuge came to an end,

D. as it is said, *The governor told them that they were not to partake of the most holy food until there should be a priest to consult the Urim and Thummim* (Ezra 2:63).

E. This is like a man who says to his friend, "Until the dead will live," or, "Until Elijah will come."

13:3 A. When the latter prophets died, that is, Haggai, Zechariah, and Malachi, then the Holy Spirit came to an end in Israel.

B. But even so, they made them hear [Heavenly messages] through an echo.

C. M'ŚH Š: Sages gathered together in the upper room of the house of Guria in Jericho, and a heavenly echo came forth and said to them, "There is a man among you who is worthy to receive the Holy Spirit, but his generation is unworthy of such an honor."

They all set their eyes upon Hillel the elder.

D. And when he died, they said about him, "Woe for the humble man, woe for the pious man, the disciple of Ezra."

13:4 A. Then another time they were in session in Yabneh and heard an echo saying, "There is among you a man who is worthy to receive the Holy Spirit, but the generation is unworthy of such an honor."

B. They all set their eyes upon Samuel the Small.

C. At the time of his death what did they say? "Woe for the humble man, woe for the pious man, the disciple of Hillel the Elder!"

D. Also he says at the time of his death, "Simeon and Ishmael are destined to be put to death, and the rest of the associates will die by the sword, and the remainder of the people will be up for spoils.

"After this, great disasters will fall."

This he said in Aramaic.

E. Also concerning R. Judah b. Baba they ordained that they should say about him, "Woe for the humble man, woe for the pious man, disciple of Samuel the Small." But the times did not allow it.

13:5 A. Yoḥanan the High Priest heard a word from the house of the Holy of Holies: "The young men who went to make war against Antioch have been victorious," and they wrote down the time and the day.

B. And they checked, and the victory was at that very hour.

13:6 A. Simeon the Righteous heard a word from the House of the Holy of Holies: "Annulled is the decree which the enemy planned to bring against the sanctuary, and Gasqelges [Caligula] has been killed, and his decrees have been annulled."

And he heard [all this] in the Aramaic language.

13:7 A. So long as Simeon the Righteous was alive, the Western lamp remained permanently lit. When he died, they went and found that it had gone out.

B. From that time forward, sometimes they find it extinguished, and sometimes lit.

C. So long as Simeon the Righteous was alive, the altar-fire was perpetual. When they arranged it in the morning, it would flame up continually during the entire day. And they would offer on it daily whole-offerings and additional offerings and their drink-offerings. And they did not add to it more than two loads of wood with the daily whole-offering of twilight, solely so as to carry out the commandment of adding wood, as it is said, *The fire on the altar shall be kept burning on it, it shall not go out; the priest shall burn wood on it every morning* (Lev. 6:12).

D. After Simeon the Righteous died, however, the power of the altar-fire grew weak. For even after they had laid it out in the morning, they did not refrain from adding wood to it all day long.

E. So long as Simeon the Righteous was alive, the Two Loaves and the

Show-Bread were blessed. The Two Loaves were divided on *Aṣeret* [Pentecost] to the priests, and the Show-Bread on the festival to all the watches [delete: and to the men of that watch]. And some of them ate and were sated, while others ate and left bread over. And no one got more than an olive's bulk.

F. But when Simeon the Righteous died, the Two Loaves and the Show-Bread were no longer blessed. So the modest priests kept their hands off the bread, and while the gluttons divided it up among themselves, (but) each did not receive more than a bean['s lump of bread].

13:8 A. M'ŚH B: A priest of Sepphoris took his share and the share of his fellow. But even so, he did not receive more than a bean['s bulk of bread].

B. And they called him, "Grabber," until this very day.

C. In the year in which Simeon the Righteous died, he said to them, "This year I am going to die."

D. They said to him, "How do you know?"

E. He said to them, "On every Day of Atonement there was a certain elder, dressed in white and cloaked in white, who would go in with me and come out with me. This year, however, while he went in with me, he never came out."

F. After the festival he fell ill for seven days and then died.

G. After Simeon the Righteous died, his brethren refrained from blessing the people with the Divine Name.

13:9 A. *The awakeners* [M. Sot. 9:10B]—these are the Levites who say on the platform, *Rouse yourself! Why do you sleep, O Lord* (Ps. 44:23).

B. Said to them (Rabban) Yoḥanan (ben Zakkai), "Now is there such a thing as sleep before Him? And has it not already been said, *Lo, the Guardian of Israel neither slumbers nor sleeps* (Ps. 121:4).

C. "But so long as Israel is immersed in pain and the nations of the world are wallowing in prosperity, as it were, *Rouse yourself! Why do you sleep.*"

13:10 A. *The knockers* [M. Sot. 9:10B]—these are those who knock the calf between its horns, just as they stun a beast to be sacrificed for idolatry.

B. Said to them Yoḥanan the high priest, "How long are you going to feed *ṭerefah*-meat to the altar?"

C. Until his time a hammer did strike in Jerusalem [M. Sot. 9:10C] on the intermediate days of the festival.

D. Also: he decreed concerning the confession [concerning tithes] and annulled [the rules of] doubtfully-tithed produce.

E. For he sent to all the towns of Israel and found that they were separating only the great heave-offering alone. As to first tithe and second tithe, some of them separated these tithes, and some of them did not.

F. He said to them, "Just as the great heave-offering, if neglected, is a transgression punishable by death, so tithing the heave-offering, if neglected, is a transgression analogous [in regard to heave-offering] to certainly untithed produce [and punishable by death].

G. "So let people designate heave-offering *and* heave-offering of the tithe and hand them over to the priest, and [let them designate] second tithe and render it unconsecrated in exchange for coins. And as to the rest of the tithes, e.g., poorman's tithe, let him who wants to collect from his fellow produce evidence in behalf of his claim" [so now people do not have to ask, as at M. Sot. 9:10D].

14:1 A. Rabban Yohanan b. Zakkai says, "*When murderers became many, the rite of breaking the heifer's neck was annulled* [M. Sot. 9:9A],

B. "for the heifer whose neck is to be broken is brought only in a case of doubt.

C. "But now there are many who commit murder in public.

14:2 A. "When adulterers became many, the ordeal of the bitter water was annulled,

B. "for the ordeal of the bitter water is performed only in a case of doubt.

C. "But now there are many who see [their lovers] in public."

14:3 A. When hedonists became many, fierce wrath came upon the world, and the glory of Torah ceased.

B. When those who went about whispering in judgment multiplied, conduct deteriorated, the laws were perverted, and the Holy Spirit ceased in Israel.

14:4 A. When those who displayed partiality in judgment multiplied, the commandment, *You shall not respect persons in judgment* (Deut. 1:17) was annulled, and *You shall not be afraid of anyone* (Deut. 1:17) ceased.

B. And they removed the yoke of Heaven from themselves, and accepted the authority of the yoke of mortal man.

14:5 A. When they compelled people to be their business agents, bribing became commonplace, and justice was perverted, *And they went backward and not forward* (Jer. 7:24).

B. And about them is said what is said about the sons of Samuel, *Yet his sons did not walk in his ways, but turned aside after gain; they took bribes and perverted justice* (I Sam. 8:3).

14:6 A. R. Meir says, "They openly demanded their portions [personally demanding the tithes, as Levites]."

B. R. Judah says, "They forced goods on private people [compelling people to serve as their business agents]."

C. R. 'Aqiba says, They seized the gifts [of the shoulder, cheek, and maw given to priests] by force."

D. R. Yosé says, "They took a basket of tithes by force."

E. Now even though Eli cursed Samuel only conditionally, see how the curse stuck to him!

14:7 A. When there multiplied [judges who say,] "I accept your favor," and "I appreciate your favor," there was a multiplication of: *Every man did that which was right in his own eyes* (Judges 17:6).

B. And the whole kingdom went rotten, declining more and more.

C. And when there multiplied: *Every man did that which was right in his own eyes,* common sorts became exalted, and people of stature became humbled.

D. And the whole kingdom went rotten, declining more and more.

E. When envious men and plunderers multiplied [—they are those who shed blood—] those who hardened their heart multiplied, everybody closed his hand and transgressed that which is written in the Torah, *Take heed lest there be a base thought in your heart . . . and your eye be hostile to your poor brother and you give him nothing* (Deut. 15:9).

14:8 A. When those who draw out their spittle multiplied, the disciples became few in number, and the glory of the Torah was annulled.

B. When there were multiplied *Their heart goes after their gain* (Ezek. 33:31), there multiplied *Those who call evil good and good evil* (Is. 5:20).

C. When there multiplied *Those who call evil good and good evil,* the whole world was filled with people saying, "Woe, woe."

D. When arrogant people increased, Israelite girls began to marry arrogant people,

E. because in our generation people see only the outward appearance.

14:9 A. When there multiplied those *who stretched forth necks and wanton eyes* (Is. 3:16), the ordeal of the bitter water became common.

B. But it was suspended.

C. When the haughty of heart became many, contentiousness increased in Israel [—they are those who shed blood].

D. When those who accept gifts became many, days became few, and years were shortened.

E. When disciples of Shammai and Hillel who had not served the masters sufficiently well became many, disputes became many in Israel, and [the Torah was] made into two Torahs.

14:10 A. When those who accept charity from gentiles became many—as it were—did the gentiles begin to become smaller and the Israelites to become exalted?

B. Quite the opposite: it is not easy for Israel in the world.

15:1 A. *When the Temple was destroyed, the shamir-worm ceased, and the honey of supim* [M. Sot. 9:12B].

B. Said R. Judah, "What is the character of this worm? It is a creature from the six days of Creation. When they put it on stones or on beams, they are opened up before it like the pages of a notebook. And not only so, but when they put it on iron, [the iron] is split and falls apart before it. And nothing can stand before it.

C. "How is it kept? They wrap it in tufts of wool and put it in a lead tube full of barley-bran."

D. "And with it Solomon built the Temple, as it is said, *There was neither hammer, nor axe, nor any tool of iron heard in the house, while it was being built* (I Kings 6:7)," the words of R. Judah.

E. R. Neḥemiah says, "They sawed with a saw outside, as it is said, *All these were of costly stones . . . sawed with saws in the house and outside* (I Kings 7:9).

F. "Why does Scripture say, *Inside the house and outside?* Inside the house they were not heard, for they prepared them outside and brought them inside."

G. Said Rabbi, "The opinion of R. Judah seems to me preferable in regard to the stones of the sanctuary, and the opinion of R. Neḥemiah in regard to the stones of [Solomon's] house."

15:2 A. Rabban Simeon b. Gamaliel said, "You should know that the dew has been cursed [M. Sot. 9:12E]:

B. "In olden times, when the dew came down on straw and on stubble, it would turn white, as it is said, *And when the dew had gone up, there was on the face of the wilderness a fine, flake-like thing, fine as hoar-frost on the ground* (Ex. 16:14].

C. "But now it turns black.

D. "In olden times, any city which got more dew than its neighbors produced a larger harvest. Now it produces less."

E. *Rabban Simeon b. Gamaliel says in the name of R. Joshua, "From the day on which the Temple was destroyed, there is no day on which there is no curse, and dew has not come down as a blessing, and the good taste of produce is gone* [M. Sot. 9:12E].

F. "And the first curse endures [even when the later curse comes]."

G. *R. Yośe says, "Also: the fatness of produce is gone"* [M. Sot. 9:12F].

H. *R. Simeon b. Eleazar says, "[When] purity [ceased], it took away the taste and scent.*

"[When] tithes [ceased], they took away the fatness of corn" [M. Sot. 9:13].

15:3 A. When R. Eliezer died, the glory of the Torah ceased.

B. When R. Joshua died, men of counsel ceased, and reflection ended in Israel [*cf.* M. Sot 9:15D].

C. When R. 'Aqiba died, the arms of Torah were taken away, and the springs of wisdom ceased [*cf.* M. Sot. 9:15G].

D. When R. Eleazar b. 'Azariah died, the crown of wisdom ceased, for, *The crown of the wise is their riches* (Prov. 14:24) [*cf.* M. Sot. 9:15D].

15:4 A. *When Ben 'Azzai died, conscientious students ceased* [M. Sot. 9:15B].

15:5 A. *When Ben Zoma died, exegetes died* [M. Sot. 9:15C].

B. *When R. Ḥanina b. Dosa died, wonder-workers died out in Israel* [M. Sot. 9:15H].

C. When Abba Yosé b. Qiṭnit of Qaṭanta died, piety became small in Israel.

D. (Why was he called a man of Qaṭanta? Because he was the very essence of piety.)

E. *When Rabban Simeon b. Gamaliel died, locusts came and troubles increased* [M. Sot. 9:15E].

F. When Rabbi died, troubles were doubled.

15:6 A. Rabban Simeon b. Gamaliel says, "You have not got a single sort of trouble which comes upon the community, on account of which the court does not annul some form of rejoicing."

15:7 A. *When the Sanhedrin was terminated, singing in banquet-halls was terminated* [M. Sot. 9:11].

B. And what good was the Sanhedrin for Israel? But it was for this matter, concerning which it is said, *And if the people of the land do at all hide their eyes from that man, when he gives one of his children to Molech, and do not put him to death, then I will set my face against that man and against his family* (Lev. 120:4–5).

C. At first, when a man would sin, if there was a Sanhedrin in operation, they would exact punishment from him. Now [that there is no Sanhedrin], punishment is exacted both from him and from his relatives, as it is said, *Then I will set my face against that man and against his family.*

D. They have compared the matter to one who went bad in a town, so they gave him over to strap-bearer, and he strapped him.

He was too hard for the strap-bearer.

They gave him over to a rod-officer, and he beat him. He was too hard for the rod-officer.

They gave him over to a centurion and he put him in prison, but he was too hard for the centurion.

They gave him over to a magistrate, and he threw him into a furnace.

E. So is Israel: the latter tribulations make them forget the former tribulations.

15:8 A. *In the war against Vespasian they decreed concerning the wearing of wreaths by bridegrooms* [M. Sot. 9:14A].

B. And what are the sorts of bridegroom's wreaths [against which they decreed]? Those made of salt or brimstone. But those made of roses and myrtles they permitted.

C. In the war against Titus [better: Quitus] they made a decree against crowns for brides.

D. And what are the sorts of crowns for brides against which they made their decree? Gold-embroidered silks. But she may go forth in a cap of fine wool.

E. *And that a man should not teach Greek to his son* [M. Sot. 9:14C].

F. They permitted the household of Rabban Gamaliel to teach Greek to their sons, because they are close to the government.

15:9 A. And that a man should not plaster his house with plaster—

B. that is with the egg of plaster. But if he put straw or sand into the mixture, it is permitted.

C. R. Judah says, "[If] he mixed sand in it, lo, this is binding cement, and it is prohibited. [But if] he put straw into it, it is permitted."

D. *After the last war, they made a decree* against the marriage-canopy of bridegrooms.

E. Against what sort of marriage-canopy of bridegrooms did they make such a decree? It is against those made of gold. But he may make a framework of laths and hang on it anything he wants.

F. And *that a bride should not go forth in a palanquin in the town.*

G. *But our rabbis permitted a bride to go forth in a palanquin in the town* [M. Sot. 9:14D, E].

H. Even against *pholiaton* [a spiced oil] did R. Judah b. Baba make a decree, but sages did not concur with him.

15:10 A. Said R. Ishmael, "From the day on which the Temple was destroyed, it would have been reasonable not to eat meat and not to drink wine.

B. "But a court does not make a decree for the community concerning things which the community simply cannot bear."

C. He did say, "Since they are uprooting the Torah from our midst, let us make a decree against the world, that it be left desolate—

D. "that no one should marry a wife and produce children, or have the week of celebration for a son,

E. "until the seed of Abraham will die out on its own."

F. They said to him, "It is better for the community to behave in error and not do so deliberately."

15:11 A. After the last Temple was destroyed, abstainers became many in Israel, who would not eat meat or drink wine.

B. R. Joshua engaged them in discourse, saying to them, "My children, on what account do you not eat meat?"

C. They said to him, "Shall we eat meat, for every day a continual burnt-offering [of meat] was offered on the altar, and now it is no more?"

D. He said to them, "Then let us not eat it. And then why are you not drinking wine?"

E. They said to him, "Shall we drink wine, for every day wine was poured out as a drink-offering on the altar, and now it is no more."

F. He said to them, "Then let us not drink it."

G. He said to them, "But if so, we also should not eat bread, for from it did they bring the Two Loaves and the Show-Bread.

"We also should not drink water, for they did pour out a water-offering on the Festival.

"We also should not eat figs and grapes, for they would bring them as First Fruits on the festival of Aṣeret [Shabu'ot]."

H. They fell silent.

15:12 A. He said to them, "My children, to mourn too much is not possible.

B. "But thus have the sages said: A man puts on plaster on his house but he leaves open a small area, as a memorial to Jerusalem.

15:13 A. "A man prepares what is needed for a meal but leaves out some small things, as a memorial to Jerusalem.

15:14 A. "A woman prepares her ornaments, but leaves out some small thing, as a memorial to Jerusalem,

B. "since it is said, *If I forget you, O Jerusalem, let my right hand wither! Let my tongue cleave to the roof of my mouth, if I do not remember you, if I do not set Jerusalem above my highest joy!* (Ps. 137:5–6)."

15:15 A. And whoever mourns for her in this world will rejoice with her in the world to come,

B. as it is said, *Rejoice with Jerusalem and be glad for her, all you who love her; rejoice with her in joy, all you who mourn over her* (Is. 66:10).

GITTIN

1:1 A. He who delivers a writ of divorce by boat is equivalent to him who delivers it from abroad [M. Git 1:1A].

B. He has to state, "In my presence it was written, and in my presence it was signed."

C. [He who delivers a writ of divorce] from Transjordan is equivalent to one who delivers a writ of divorce in the Land of Israel,

D. and he does not have to state, "In my presence it was written and in my presence it was sealed" [M. Git. 1:3A].

E. *He who delivers a writ of divorce from overseas [and] cannot state, "In my presence it was written, and in my presence it was signed,"*—if he can confirm it through its signatures, it is valid.

F. And if not, it is invalid [M. Git. 1:3C–E].

G. One must conclude: They have ruled, He must state, "In my presence it was written, and in my presence it was signed," not to impose a stringent ruling, but to provide for a lenient ruling.

H. He who delivers a writ of divorce from overseas, and it was not written in his presence, and it was not signed in his presence, lo, this one sends it back to its place, and he calls a court in session for that matter, and has it confirmed through its signatures. Then he delivers it again, and states, "I am an agent of a court."

I. In the Land of Israel an agent appoints another agent.

J. Rabban Simeon b. Gamaliel says, "An agent does not appoint another agent in the case of writs of divorce."

K. At first they would rule, "[He who brings a writ of divorce must testify that in his presence it was written and in his presence it was signed, if he brought it] from one province to another.

L. "Then they ruled, 'From one neighborhood to another.'"

M. *Rabban Simeon b. Gamaliel says, "Even from one jurisdiction to another"* [M. Git. 1:1G].

1:2 A. A more strict rule applies to [writs of divorce deriving from] overseas than to [writs of divorce deriving from] the Land of Israel, and to [writs of divorce deriving from] the Land of Israel then to [writs of divorce deriving from] overseas.

B. For he who delivers a writ of divorce from overseas must state, "In my presence it was written, and in my presence it was signed."

C. Even though there are disputants [against its validity], it is valid.

1:3 A. He who brings a writ of divorce from the Land of Israel [and] cannot state, "In my presence it was written, and in my presence it was signed,"—if there are witnesses, it is confirmed through its signatures [M. Git. 1:3B–E].

B. In what way have they ruled, "Let it be confirmed through its signatures?"

C. Witnesses who stated, "This is our handwriting"—it is valid.

D. [If they said], "It is our handwriting, but we do not know either the man or the woman," it is valid.

E. [If they said], "This is not our handwriting," but others give testimony concerning them, that it is their handwriting,

F. or if an example of their handwriting was forthcoming from some other source,

G. it is valid.

H. R. Meir says, "*Akko* and its neighborhood are *equivalent to the Land of Israel so far as writs of divorce are concerned*" [M. Git. 1:2D].

I. And sages say, "Akko and its neighborhood are equivalent to foreign territory so far as writs of divorce are concerned."

J. M'ŚH B: A man from Kepar Sasi delivered a writ of divorce for a woman in the presence of R. Ishmael.

K. R. Ishmael said to him, "Where do you come from?"

L. He said to him, "Rabbi, From Kepar Sasi, at the border of the Land."

M. He said to him, "Also you must state, 'In my presence it was written, and in my presence it was signed,' so that we shall not be in need of witnesses."

N. After he left, R. Le'i said before him, "Rabbi, Kepar Sasi is within the border of the Land of Israel, nearer to Sepphoris than to Akko."

O. He said to him, "Since the matter has gone forth subject to a ruling in favor of permitting [the validity of the writ of divorce], it is done with."

1:4 A. R. Judah says, "Even though both of its witnesses are Samaritans, it is valid" [M. Git. 1:5A–B].

B. Said R. Judah, "M'ŚH W: *They brought before Rabban Gamaliel in Kepar 'Otenai the writ of divorce of a woman, and its witnesses were Samaritans, and he declared it valid*" [M. Git. 1:5C].

C. *All documents which come forth from gentile registries, even though their signatories are gentiles* [M. Git. 1:5D]—

D. R. 'Aqiba declares valid in the case of all of them.

E. But sages declare invalid in the case of writs of divorce from women and writs of emancipation for slaves [=M. Git. 1:5E].

F. Said R. Eleazar b. R. Yosé, "Thus did they say to sages in Ṣidon: 'R. 'Aqiba and sages did not differ concerning documents which come forth from gentile registries, that even though their signatories are gentiles, they are valid.

G. "'Concerning what did they differ?

H. "'Concerning those prepared by unauthorized people.

I. "'For R. 'Aqiba declares valid in the case of all of them.

J. "'And sages declare invalid in the case of writs of divorce for women and writs of emancipation for slaves.'"

K. Rabban Simeon b. Gamaliel says, "Also writs of divorce for women and writs of emancipation for slaves are valid,

L. "in a situation in which there is no Israelite to sign [the document as a signatory]."

1:5 A. R. Eleazar said, "We stated to R. Meir, 'On what account do they act to the advantage of a slave not in his presence?'

B. "He said to us, 'It is only a disadvantage for him. For if it was the slave of a priest, he turns out to invalidate him from eating heave-offering' [*cf.* M. Git. 1:6E].

C. "We said to him, 'But is it not so that if he wanted not to support him and not to provide for him, he has the right to do so' [M. Git. 1:6E]?

D. "He said to us, 'But is it not so that the slave of a priest who fled, or the wife of a priest who rebelled against him—lo, these continue to have the right to eat food in the status of heave-offering.

E. "'But in the case of a woman [being divorced] it is not so.

F. "'But it is to her disadvantage with regard to support,

G. "'and she is invalidated from eating heave-offering.'"

1:6 A. He who says, "Give this *maneh* to So-and-so, which I owe him,"

B. "Give this *maneh* to So-and-so, a bailment which he has in my hands,"

C. "Take this *maneh* to So-and-so, a bailment which he has in my hands,"—

D. if he wanted to retract, he may not retract.

E. And he is responsible to replace it should it be lost, up to that point that he [to whom it is owing] receives that which belongs to him.

1:7 A. [He who says], "Take this *maneh* to So-and-so," "Give this *maneh* to So-and-so,"—

B. if he wanted to retract, he may retract.

C. [If] he went and found him dead, let him return the money to the one who gave it.

D. If he [the one to whom the money is given] should die, let him hand over the money to the heirs [of the one who originally gave it].

1:8 A. [He who said,] "Receive this *maneh* in behalf of So-and-so,"

B. "Acquire this gift in behalf of So-and-so,"

C. "Receive this writ of gift for So-and-so,"

D. "Acquire this writ of gift for So-and-so,"—

E. if he wanted to retract, he may not retract.

F. [If] he went and found him dead, let him give it to the heirs.

G. But if after the death of the donee he made acquisition, he should restore it to the heirs [of the donor],

H. for they do not acquire an advantage for a deceased person once death has taken place.

1:9 A. [If he said], "Carry this *maneh* to So-and-so,"

B. "Take this to So-and-so,"

C. "Let this *maneh* for So-and-so be in your hand,"

D. and he died,

E. if the heirs [of the sender] wanted to force him [not to deliver it], they cannot do so.

F. And one need not say, in the case of one who says, "Acquire possession for him," or who says, "Receive it for him" [that the rule is the same].

2:1 A. He who delivers a writ of divorce from overseas and gave it over to the woman, but did not say to her, "In my presence it was written and in my presence it was signed,"

B. lo, this one takes it back from her even after three years, and then goes and gives it to her, saying to her, "In my presence it was written, and in my presence it was signed."

2:2 A. A woman is believed to state, "This is the writ of divorce which you gave to me."

B. [If] it was torn, it is valid.

C. [If] it was ripped up [torn in many places], it is invalid.

D. [If] there is in it a tear made by a court, it is invalid.

E. R. Simeon b. Eleazar says, "One seals up the tears [in the document] and delivers it to her, and says to her, 'In my presence it was written, and in my presence it was signed.'"

F. *[If] one says, "In my presence it was written," and one says, "In my presence it was sealed," it is invalid.*

G. *[If] two say, "In our presence it was written," and one says, "In my presence it was sealed,"*

H. *R. Judah declares valid* in this case [M. Git 2:1F, H].

I. R. Simeon says, "Even if he wrote it today and sealed it on the morrow, it is valid" [M. Git. 2:2].

J. If one wrote it in this town, he should not sign it in another town.

K. But if he signed it [elsewhere], it is valid.

L. [If] he wrote it in the Land and signed it abroad, he must state, "In my presence it was written, and in my presence it was signed."

M. [If] one wrote it abroad and signed it in the Land of Israel, he does not have to say, "In my presence it was written, and in my presence it was signed."

2:3 A. If he wrote it with nut shells or pomegranate husks,

B. with congealed blood or congealed milk,

C. on olive leaves or pumpkin leaves,

D. on carob leaves,

E. or on anything which lasts,

F. it is valid [cf. M. Git. 2:3A–G].

G. [If he wrote it] on leaves of lettuce or onion, on leaves of fenugreec or on vegetables' leaves, on anything which does not last, it is invalid.

H. This is the general principle: [If] he wrote it in anything which lasts on something which does not last, or in something which does not last on something which lasts, it is invalid.

I. [It is not valid] unless he wrote it with something which lasts on something which lasts.

2:4 A. He who traces something like the shape of writing on hide—it is invalid.

B. He who makes a mark on hide like the shape of writing—it is valid.

C. R. Yosé the Galilean says, "Just as a *scroll* [Deut. 24:1] is something which is not animate, so it excludes anything which is animate" [*cf.* M. Git. 2:3L].

D. R. Judah b. Patira says, "Just as a scroll is distinctive in that it is plucked up from the ground, so something which is attached to the ground is excluded" [M. Git. 2:4A].

E. "[If] he wrote it on the horn of a deer and cut if off, signed it, and gave it to her, it is invalid, since it says, *And he will write and he will give* (Deut. 24:1)—

F. "Just as the giving must be of something which is not attached, so the writing [to begin with] must be on something which is not attached" [M. Git. 2:4].

G. [If] he wrote it for her on the horn of a cow and gave her the cow,

H. or on the hand of a slave and gave her the slave,

I. she has acquired possession of these [*cf.* M. Git. 2:3H–K].

J. [If] he then said to her, "Lo, this is your writ of divorce," and the rest of it [the cow, the slave] is in compensation for the marriage-contract," she has received her writ of divorce, and she has received her payment of her marriage-contract.

K. [If he said to her], "Lo, this is your writ of divorce, on condition that you give me back the paper," lo, this one is deemed to have been divorced.

L. " . . . On condition that the paper is mine," or if he gave her the paper itself [so that the paper was hers to being with], or if she wrote it on her hand,

M. she is not deemed to have been divorced.

2:5 A. All are valid to receive a woman's writ of divorce [in her behalf],

B. except for a deaf-mute, an idiot, and a minor.

2:6 A. All are believed to deliver a woman's writ of divorce, even her son, even her daughter,

B. *and even the five women who are in such a relationship to her that they are not believed to testify that her husband has died are believed to deliver her divorce:*

C. *her mother-in-law, the daughter of her mother-in-law, her co-wife, her husband's brother's wife, and the daughter of her husband [by another marriage]* [M. Git. 2:7A–B].

D. R. Simeon b. Eleazar says in the name of R. 'Aqiba, *"A woman herself delivers her own writ of divorce* [M. Git. 2:7E].

E. "[This is] on the basis of an argument *a fortiori:* Now if her co-wife, who is not believed to testify that her husband has died, is believed to deliver her writ of divorce, she, who is believed to testify that her husband has died, surely should be believed to deliver her writ of divorce."

F. [The reply to D–E:] It is sufficient for that which is produced through reasoning to be equivalent to that on the basis of which one has reasoned:

Now if the co-wife has to say, "In my presence it was written, and in my presence it was signed," so, [also] she has to testify, "In my presence it was written and in my presence it was signed."

G. He himself who delivered a writ of divorce to his own wife does not have to state, "In my presence it was written, and in my presence it was signed."

2:7 A. The writ of divorce for a woman which one wrote not for her own name is invalid [*cf.* M. Git. 3:1A],

B. since it says, *And he shall write for her* (Deut. 24:1)—for her in particular.

C. The writ of emancipation of a slave which one wrote not for his own name is invalid,

D. since it says, *And not yet ransomed or given her freedom* (Lev. 19:20). And below it says, *And he shall write to her* (Deut. 24:1).

Now just as *to her* stated elsewhere means that it must be for her in particular, so *to her* stated here must mean that it must be for her in particular.

E. The scroll for a woman accused of adultery which one wrote not for her own name is invalid,

F. since it says, *And the priest shall prepare for her this entire Torah* (Num. 5:30)—that is all the rites concerning her must be [done] for her sake in particular.

G. [If] the scribe wrote it for her sake, and the witnesses signed it for her sake [in particular], even though they wrote it and signed it and gave it to him and he gave it to her, it is invalid.

H. It is valid only if he [the husband] will say to the scribe, "Write," and to the witnesses, "Sign."

2:8 A. And not only so, but even if he wrote it in his own hand to the scribe, saying, "Write," and to the witnesses, "Sign,"

B. even though they wrote it and signed it and gave it to him and he gave it to her, it is invalid.

C. It is valid only if they hear his [the husband's] voice saying to the scribe, "Write," and to the witnesses, "Sign."

2:9 A. [If] one borrowed from him a thousand *denars* with a bond of indebtedness and paid him back,

B. and he now proposes to borrow from him a second time,

C. he should not give him back the first bond of indebtedness,

D. for he weakens the claim of the purchasers.

2:10 A. [If he] mortgaged a house to him [or] mortgaged a field to him, and he paid him back and proposes to borrow from him a second time—

B. lo, this one should not return him the first bond of mortgage, because he weakens the claim of those who follow him.

C. Said R. Judah, "M'ŚH B: "Ben Qedara was writing out sample copies of writs of divorce in the evening.

D. "And the case came before sages, and they declared all of them invalid."

E. *R. Eliezer declares all of them valid, except for writs of divorce for women, as it is said, "And he shall write for her* (Deut. 24:1)—for her own name."

2:11 A. A writ of divorce which one lost, and which he found after a while,

B. even though he recognizes its distinguishing traits,

C. is invalid.

D. since distinguishing traits do not apply to writs of divorce.

E. What is the meaning of "after a while"?

F. Sufficient time for someone else to come to that same location.

G. But [if] he handed it over to him in a box, chest, or cupboard, and he locked the door thereof, and then the key was lost,

H. even though he found it only after a while,

I. it [the writ of divorce] remains valid.

2:12 A. And three more [cases] did they add [to M. Git. 3:4]:

B. [if] a wild beast was mauling him, or a river was sweeping him away, or a house fell on him,

B. they apply to him the strict rulings applicable to the living and the strict rulings applicable to the dead.

C. *An Israelite girl married to a priest, or a priest-girl married to an Israelite does not eat heave-offering* [M. Git. 3:4F].

D. The slave of a priest who fled, and the wife of a priest who rebelled against him [and ran away],

E. lo, these continue to eat heave-offering [in the assumption that the master or husband is yet alive].

F. A person guilty of manslaughter should not go outside of the frontier of a city of refuge,

G. but should assume that the high priest is yet alive.

2:13 A. [If the husband said to] bring this writ of divorce to his wife on condition that she give "to my father, or to my brother, two hundred *zuz*,"

B. He [the messenger] has the power to appoint a [messenger].

C. [If he said,] ". . . on condition that she give *you* two hundred *zuz*," he cannot appoint an agent.

D. For he has relied upon none except this one.

E. [If] he said to him, "Bring this writ of divorce to my wife,"

F. he has the power to appoint an agent.

G. [If he said,] "*You* bring this writ of divorce to my wife," then he does not have the power to appoint an agent,

H. [for the husband] has relied upon no one except this particular man [*cf.* M. Git. 3:5].

3:1 A. He who lends money to a priest and a Levite and a poor man *and they died*

B. *has to get permission from the heirs* [of the man to whom he lent the money to continue to collect what is owing to him from heave-offering, tithe, or poorman's tithe] [M. Git. 3:7D].

C. Now who are these heirs?

D. Rabbi says, "Anyone who [actually] inherits his estate."

E. R. Eliezer b. Jacob says, "He who lends money to a priest or to a Levite in the presence of a court, and one of them died, separates [tithes and heave-offering] on their account with the permission of that tribe" [*cf.* M. Git. 3:7E].

F. He who lends money to a poor man, who died—

G. [he falls] into the domain of all the poor.

H. R. Aḥa says, "Into the domain of the poor only of Israel."

I. He who lends money to a poor man who got rich—they do not separate poorman's tithe on his account,

J. for they do not set apart poorman's tithe from that which is lost.

K. The poor man has acquired that [loan] which is in his possession.

L. He who lends money to a priest, to a Levite, or to a poor man, separates crops on their account at the lowest price.

M. And the Seventh Year does not abrogate the debt.

N. If he wanted to retract, he cannot retract.

O. If they despaired of [raising a crop that year], they do not separate tithes on their account,

P. for they do not separate tithe for that which is lost.

Q. He who says, "Here is this *maneh* for you, and give it to Mr. So-and-so, the son of Levi, from my share," if he wanted to retract, he cannot retract.

R. [If he said,] "Take this *maneh* from the money set aside for tithe which you have in my possession and here is its value for you,"

S. lo, this one does not consider the matter of heave-offering of tithe.

T. "A *kor* of tithe belonging to you is in my possession, here is its value"—

U. lo, this one does take account of the heave-offering of tithe.

V. "A *kor* of tithe for you is in my possession," and he went and gave it to someone else—

W. he has only a complaint against him.

3:2 A. *[If] he put aside produce so that he may set apart heave-offering and tithes on its account [reckoning that it will serve for these purposes],*

B. *coins so that he may set apart second-tithe on its account,*

C. *he designates produce [as unconsecrated] relying upon them in the assumption that they remain available* [M. Git. 3:8A–C].

D. He does not take account of the possibility that the produce has rotted, that the wine has turned into vinegar, that the coins have gotten rusty.

E. [If] he went and found them rotted, turned into vinegar, or rusted, lo, this one then does take into account that fact.

F. He takes into account the possibility of grain's having rotted during a time sufficient that it rot, for wine, during a time sufficient that it turn into vinegar, for money, during a time sufficient that it rust.

G. "*[If] they were lost, lo, this one takes account of that fact for the period of the preceding twenty-four hours," the words of R. Eleazar* [M. Git. 3:8D].

H. R. Judah says, "At three seasons of the year they examine the condition of wine" [M. Git. 3:8E].

3:3 A. *[If the husband] got to his wife first,*

B. *or sent a messenger to her* [M. Git. 4:1E–F],

C. [and] said to her, "as to the writ of divorce which I sent you, I don't want you to be divorced with it,"

D. *lo, this is null* [M. Git. 4:1G–H].

E. *At first [the husband] would set up a court in another place and declare it null* [M. Git. 4:2A].

F. "If they declared it null, it was null," the words of Rabbi.

G. Rabban Simeon b. Gamaliel says, "He has not got the power to nullify it or to add to any condition found in it."

H. "If he said to two men, 'Give this writ of divorce to my wife,' he has the power to annul it in the presence of one of them and in the absence of the other," the words of Rabbi.

I. Rabban Simeon b. Gamaliel says, "He has the power to nullify it only in the presence of both of them.

J. "If he said to this one by himself and that one by himself [that he wished to send the writ of divorce], then he has got the power to nullify it even in the presence of one of them and in the absence of the other" [*cf.* M. Git. 4:1].

3:4 A. *A slave who is taken captive, and they redeemed him as a slave is to be subjugated,* and his master is to pay his value.

B. *[If he was redeemed,] as a free man, he is not to be subjugated,* and his master does not pay his value.

C. *Rabban Simeon b. Gamaliel says, "One way or the other, he is to be enslaved, and his master is to pay his cost* [M. Git. 4:4A–D].

D. "Just as Israelites are commanded to redeem free men, so they are commanded to redeem their slaves."

3:5 A. R. Eleazar says, "Even in this case [M. Git. 4:7F] he should not remarry her, on account of the good order of the world" [M. Git. 4:7G].

B. What is the sort of vow which requires the examination of a sage?

C. If one said "*Qonam* be what my wife enjoys of mine, for she has stolen my wallet," ". . . for she has beaten up my son,"

D. [if] he found out that she had not hit him or that she has not stolen it, [he must undergo the examination of a sage for the absolution of his vow].

E. Under what circumstances?

F. In a case in which he vowed and then divorced her.

G. But if he divorced her and afterward took the vow, he is permitted [to remarry her].

H. [If] he took a vow to divorce her and changed his mind, he is permitted [to remarry her].

I. [If] he took a vow to be a Nazirite, or by an offering [*Qorban*], or by an oath, he is permitted [to remarry her].

J. On what account did they rule, "*He who puts away his wife because of her having a bad name may not remarry her*" [M. Git. 4:7A]?

K. For if one puts away his wife because of her having a bad name, and then she is married to someone else and produces a child, and afterward the things said about the first wife turn out to be a joke—

L. if he said, "If I had known that these things were a joke, even if someone had given me a hundred *manehs,* I should never have divorced her,"

M. [then, if he has the power to nullify the divorce and remarry her] the writ of divorce turns out to be invalid, and the offspring [of the second marriage] to be a *mamzer.*

N. And on what account did they rule, "*He who puts away his wife because of a vow may not remarry her*" [M. Git. 4:7B]?

O. For, if one puts away his wife because of a vow, and she is married to someone else and she produces a child,

P. and then the vow should turn out to be null,

Q. [if] he said, "If I had known that the vow was null, if someone had given me a hundred *manehs,* I should never have divorced her,"

R. it will turn out that the writ of divorce is invalid, and the offspring a *mamzer.*

S. R. Eleazar b. R. Yosé says, "On what account did they rule, *He who puts his wife away because of her having a bad name may not remarry her?* So that Israelite girls should not be sexually promiscuous.

T. "They will say to her, 'You should know that he who puts away his wife because of her having a bad name—she cannot go back to him!'

U. "On what account did they rule, *He who puts away his wife because of a vow may not remarry her?*

V. "So that the Israelite girls should not be promiscuous in taking vows.

W. "They will say to her, "You should know that he who puts away his wife because of her taking a vow—she cannot go back to him!'"

X. *He who divorces his wife by reason of sterility, and she was married to someone else and had children by him, and she then claims payment for her marriage-contract* from the first husband—

Y. in the name of *R. Judah they said, "[They say to her] 'Your silence is better for you than your speech'"* [M. Git. 4:8A, D–E].

Z. R. Eleazar b. R. Yosé says, "He who divorces his wife by reason of sterility—they pay off her marriage-contract,

AA. "in the assumption that she is suitable [and that the fault is not hers, but that she may have children by some other man]."

3:6 A. They do not swallow gold denars in wartime [as a way of hiding them from the enemy],

B. on account of the danger to life.

C. *Rabban Simeon b. Gamaliel says, "They do not help captives to escape, because of the good order of captives"* [M. Git. 4:6F,H].

3:7 A. At first they ruled, *He who causes uncleanness to the clean things of someone else, and he who mixes heave-offering in the produce of someone else—*

B. they reverted to rule, Also: *he who mixes wine used for idolatrous purposes [in acceptable wine of his fellow]—*

C. *if he did so inadvertently, he is exempt.*

D. *If he did so deliberately, he is liable* [M. Git. 5:4G–I],

E. for the good order of the world.

3:8 A. *Priests who made a sacrifice refuse* [by their improper intention, at the time of slaughtering it, to eat it at the wrong time or in the wrong place],

B. *[if they did so] inadvertently, are exempt* [M. Git. 5:4J].

C. [If they did so] deliberately, they are liable,

D. for the good order of the world.

E. A messenger of a court who inflicted a blow by the authority of the court and did bodily harm,

F. [if he did so] inadvertently, he is exempt.

G. [If he did so] deliberately, he is liable,

H. for the good order of the world.

I. An expert physician who prescribed a cure by the authority of a court and did damage,

J. [if he did so] inadvertently, he is exempt.

K. [If he did so] deliberately, he is liable,

L. for the good order of the world.

3:9 A. He who cuts up the foetus in the womb of the mother did damage—

B. doing so by the authority of the court,

C. [if he did so] inadvertently, he is exempt.

D. [if he did so] deliberately, he is liable,

E. for the good order of the world.

3:10 A. The law concerning the usurping occupant does not apply to the Land of Judah,

B. for the sake of securing the settlement of the province [by permitting purchasers freedom from claims against their title to the land bought from a usurper].

C. Under what circumstances?

D. In the case of those who were slain before the war and in the time of the war [of Bar Kokhba].

E. But *in the case of those who were slain from the war and onward the law of the usurping occupant does apply* [M. Git. 5:6B].

F. As to Galilee, it is always subject to the law of the usurping occupant.

G. *He who purchases a field from a usurping occupant and went and purchased it afterward from the householder—*

H. his purchase is valid [*vs.* M. Git. 5:6D–E].

I. *[If he first purchased it] from the householder and then went and purchased it from the usurping occupant,* his purchase is null [*vs.* M. Git. 5:6F].

J. If the householder made him responsible for it, his purchase is valid.

K. *This is the first Mishnah.*

L. *The court which was after them ruled: He who purchased [a property] from a usurping occupant pays to the owner a quarter* [M. Git. 5:6I–J]—

M. a quarter [of the value, to be paid] in real estate, a quarter in ready money—

N. and the claim of the owner is uppermost [to decide which he prefers].

O. *If he has sufficient funds to purchase the field, he takes precedence over anyone else.*

P. *Rabbi called a court into session, and they voted that, if the field had remained in the possession of the usurping occupant for twelve months, then whoever comes first has the right to purchase it.*

Q. *[Nonetheless the purchaser] pays the owner a quarter of the value* [M. Git. 5:6N–O], [either] a quarter in land, [or] a quarter in ready money.

R. And the claim of the owner is uppermost.

S. If he [the one from whom the field was seized] has sufficient funds to purchase the field he takes precedence over anyone else.

3:11 A. Share-croppers, tenant-farmers, and guardians are not subject to the law of the usurping occupant.

B. He who takes over a field in payment of a debt, [or] in payment of a tax-debt payable in installments—they are not subject to the law of the usurping occupant.

C. As to the collection of the tax itself: they wait for the owner [to redeem it] for twelve months.

D. R. Simeon b. Eleazar says, "He who purchases a field from a woman for the value of her marriage-contract and then goes and purchases it from the husband—his purchase is valid.

E. "[If he went and bought it first] from the husband and afterward went and bought it from the wife, his purchase is null.

F. "If the wife had made the husband responsible for it in her marriage-contract, his purchase is valid" [*cf.* M. Git. 5:6G–H].

3:12 A. *As to children: their purchase is valid, and their sale is valid*

B . *in the case of movables* [M. Git. 5:7D–E], but not in the case of real estate.

C. Rabban Simeon b. Gamaliel says, "They referred to children only because of prevailing circumstances."

3:13 A. A poor man who takes them [olives which he gleans from a tree] in his hand and throws them down one by one—

B. what is under it [the tree] is wholly subject to the prohibition against thievery [*cf.* M. Git. 5:8I–K].

C. A city in which Israelites and gentiles live—

D. the collectors of funds for the support of the poor collect equally from Israelites and from gentiles,

E. for the sake of peace.

F. They provide support for the poor of the gentiles along with the poor of Israel,

G. for the sake of peace.

3:14 A. They make a lament for, and bury, gentile dead,

B. for the sake of peace.

C. They express condolences to gentile mourners,

D. for the sake of peace.

4:1 A. [The woman who said to a messenger], "Receive my writ of divorce in my behalf," and [the messenger said to the husband], "Your wife said, 'Receive my writ of divorce in my behalf,'"

B. "Bring [my writ of divorce to me]," and, [the messenger reported to the husband that she had said,] " Bring it to her,"

C. "Receive it for her," and, "Make acquisition of it for her"—

D. if he wanted to retract, he may not retract [*cf.* M. Git. 6:1].

E. "Bring me my writ of divorce," and, "Your wife said, 'Bring me my writ of divorce,'"

F. "Take it," and, "Take it to her,"

G. "Give it to her,"

H. "Receive it for her," and "Acquire it for her"—

I. "if he wanted to retract, he may not retract," the words of Rabbi.

J. Rabban Simeon b. Gamaliel says, "[If] he said], 'Bring it to her,' and, 'Give it to her,' if he wanted to retract, he may retract. [If he said,] 'Receive it for her,' 'Make acquisition in her behalf,' if he wanted to retract, he may not retract."

K. Rabbi says, "In the case of all of them, he may not retract, unless he states, '*I do not want you to receive it for her* [M. Git. 6:1F], but merely bring it to her and deliver it to her.'"

4:2 A. [If the wife said], "Receive my writ of divorce for me," and "Your wife said, 'Receive my writ of divorce for me,'"

B. "Receive it for me," and, "Your wife said, 'Bring me my writ of divorce.'"

C. "Take it," "Carry it," and, "Give it to her,"

D. "Receive it in her behalf," and "Make acquisition of it in her behalf,"

E. if he wanted to retract, he may retract.

F. [If she said], "Carry my writ of divorce to me," "Take my writ of divorce to me,"

G. "Let my writ of divorce be in your hand for me,"

H. it is equivalent to her saying, "Receive my writ of divorce in my behalf."

I. [He who says], "Bring a writ of divorce of your wife," " . . . a writ of divorce of your daughter," ". . . a writ of divorce of your sister," and he [to whom it is said] went and gave it to her, it is invalid [*cf.* Lieberman, p. 260, to Is. 10–12].

J. [If] they said to him, "Shall we write a writ of divorce for your wife," "Here is a writ of divorce for your wife," ". . .a writ of divorce for your daughter," ". . .a writ of divorce for your sister,"

K. and he went and delivered it to her, it is valid.

L. *Even if the first witnesses are the same as the last ones,*

M *or there was one of the first and one of the last*

N. even if they are brothers,

O. *and a third party joins together with them* [M. Git. 6:2E–F].

P. A minor who knows who to take care of her writ of divorce, lo, this one may be divorced [cf. M. Git. 6:2K].

Q. But she does not [have the power to] appoint a messenger until she produces two pubic hairs.

4:3 A. What is the sort of minor who knows how to take care of her writ of divorce [M. Git. 6:2K]?

B. This is any girl to whom they give her writ of divorce or some other object and who returns it after a while.

4:4 A. *The woman who said, "Receive my writ of divorce for me in such and such a place," and he received it for her in some other place—*

B. *it is invalid.*

C. *R. Eleazar declares it valid.*

D. *"Bring me my writ of divorce from such and such a place," and he brought it to her from some other place—*

E. *it is valid* [M. Git. 6:3K–O].

F. But in the case of all of them she is divorced, unless [the husband said], "I want you to receive it for her only in such-and-such a place."

4:5 A. He who says, "Banish my wife,"—they write and hand over to her a writ of divorce.

B. [If he said], "Lo, this is your writ of divorce," and she said, "Hand it over to so-and-so," —she is not divorced.

C. [If she added,] ". . .so that he may receive it in my behalf," lo, she is divorced.

4:6 A. *[If] he said to two, "Give a writ of divorce to my wife,"*

B. *or to three, "Write a writ of divorce and give it to my wife,"*

C. "Write and give a writ of divorce to my wife,"

D. *they write and hand it over to her* [M. Git. 6:7A–C].

E. If they do not know how to write it, let them learn how to do so.

4:7 A. [If] they know the man but do not know the wife, they write and hand it over.

B. [If] they know the wife and do not know the man, they write it but do not hand it over.

C. [If] he said, "Write it," but did not say, "Give it over," even though they know both of them, they write it but do not hand it over.

4:8 A. [If a man] was afraid and shouting from the top of a mountain, saying, "Whoever hears my voice—let him write a writ of divorce to my wife," lo, these should write it and hand it over [*cf.* M. Git. 6:5–6].

B. *A healthy man who said, "Write a writ of divorce for my wife," and who went up to the roof-top and fell down—*

C. they write and hand it over to her so long as he is yet breathing.

D. Rabban Simeon b. Gamaliel says, "*If he fell on his own, lo, this is a writ of divorce* [M. Git. 6:6E–F].

E. "If after a while he fell, they write it but do not hand it over,

F. "For I say, 'The wind knocked him off the roof.'"

4:9 A. [If] he said to two men, "Give a writ of divorce to my wife on condition that she wait for me two years [without remarrying],"

B. and then he went and said to two others, "Give a writ of divorce to my wife on condition that she pay me two hundred *zuz*,"

C. the instructions which he gave at the end do not nullify the instructions he gave at the outset.

D. But the choice is hers: If she wanted, she may wait two years, and if she wanted, she may pay off the two hundred *zuz* [*cf.* M. Git. 7:5A–B].

4:10 A. [If] he said to two men, "Give a writ of divorce to my wife on condition that she wait for me two years," and then he went and said to two others, "Give a writ of divorce to my wife on condition that she wait for me three years,"

B. the instructions which he gave at the end do nullify the instructions he gave at the outset.

C. And one of the former group and one of the latter group do not join together to deliver her writ of divorce to her.

D. [If he said], "Lo, this is your writ of divorce, on condition that you not have sexual relations with so-and-so," lo, this is a valid writ of divorce, and he does not have to take account of the possibility that she will go and have sexual relations with him.

E. [If he said, "Lo, this is your writ of divorce] on condition that you will marry and have sexual relations with father," or, "with my brother," lo, this one should not remarry, [but if she did remarry], she should not go forth.

F. ". . . on condition that you have sexual relations with so-and-so," if she had sexual relations with him, lo, this is a valid writ of divorce, and if not, it is not a valid writ of divorce.

4:11 A. "Lo, this is your writ of divorce on condition that you eat pork,"

B. and, if she was a non-priest, "On condition that you eat heave-offering,"

C. and, if she was a Nazirite-girl, "On condition that you drink wine,"

D. if she ate or drank [what he specified] lo, this is a valid writ of divorce.

E. And if not, it is not a valid writ of divorce.

4:12 A. He who says to his wife, "Lo, here is your writ of divorce [effective] one hour before his [my] death,"

B. and so, he who says to his servant-girl, "Lo, here is your writ of emancipation [effective] one hour before his [my] death,"

C. lo, these women [if married to or owned by a priest] should not eat food in the status of heave-offering,

D. lest the man die an hour later.

4:13 A. [If] he said to ten men, "Give a writ of divorce to my wife,"

B. one of them takes it in behalf of all of them.

C. [If he said,] "All of you take it,

D. one of them hands it over in the presence of all of them.

E. Therefore if one of them died, lo, this is an invalid writ of divorce [M. Git. 7:7G–I].

5:1 A. [If a man] was crucified or hacked up, and he gave a sign to write a writ of divorce to his wife,

B. they write and hand it over to her,

C. so long as he is breathing [*cf.* M. Git. 6:6].

D. [If] he was ill and struck dumb, *and they said to him "Shall we write a writ of divorce for your wife,"*

E. *[and] he nodded his head,*

E. *they test him three times.*

G. *If he said for no, "No," and for yes, "Yes"* [M. 7:1D–F],

H. his words are valid.

I. Just as they test him as to a writ of divorce, so they test him as to purchases, gifts, inheritances, and statements of testimony.

5:2 A. *"This is your writ of divorce, effective today, if I die from this illness"* [M. Git. 7:3H],

B. "If I die from this illness, lo, this is your writ of divorce effective today,"

C. his statement is confirmed [M. Git. 7:3E].

D. "This is your writ of divorce effective today if I die from this illness,"

E. if a house fell on him, or a snake bit him,

F. it is not a writ of divorce.

G. For he did not die of that particular ailment.

H. [If he said, "Lo, this is your writ of divorce], if I do not arise from this ailment,"

I. if the house fell on him, or a snake bit him,

J. lo, this is a valid writ of divorce.

K. For in point of fact he did not arise from that illness.

5:3 A. He who says to his wife, "Lo, this is your writ of divorce effective today, after death"—

B. Rabbi says, "It is a writ of divorce."

C. And sages say, "It is not a writ of divorce.

D "And if he dies, she performs the rite of *ḥaliṣah* and does not enter into Levirate marriage" [M. Git. 7:3F].

E. And so he who says to his slave-girl, "Here is your writ of emancipation effective today, after death"—

F. Rabbi says, "It is a valid writ of emancipation."

G. And sages say, "Writs of emancipation for slaves are equivalent to writs of divorce for women."

H. He who says, "Make so-and-so, my slave, a free man, effective today, after death," has said nothing.

I. But they force the heirs to carry out the statement of the deceased.

5:4 A. "This is your writ of divorce, effective today, if I die from this ailment"—

B. "during the intervening days [between the statement and the man's death] he acquires what she finds and has possession of the fruit of her labor and the right of abrogation of her vows," the words of R. Judah [M. Git. 7:4E].

C. R. Meir says, "It is a matter of doubt."

D. R. Yosé says, "Their punishment for having intercourse is suspended" [M. Git. 7:4F].

E. And sages say, "She is divorced in every respect—

F. "on condition that he die."

G. *She should not continue to live with him* [M. Git. 7:4A], even in the presence of her minor son,

H. for she is not ashamed to have sexual relations in his presence.

I. [If] they saw that she continued with him alone in the dark, or that she slept with him at the foot of the bed,

J. even if he was awake and she was asleep, he was asleep and she was awake,

K. they do not take account of the possibility that they did some other sort of business,

L. but they do take account [solely] of the possibility of their having had sexual relations.

M. And they do not take account of the possibility of [sexual relations for] betrothal.

N. R. Yosé b. R. Judah says, "Also: They do take account of the possibility of a betrothal."

O. [But if] two people saw her continue alone with him,

P. she does require a second writ of divorce from him.

Q. [If only] one person saw it, she does not require a second writ of divorce from him.

R. [If one saw it] in the morning and one at twilight—

S. this was an actual case, and R. Eleazar b. Tadai came and asked sages, who ruled, "It is only a single witness [at a time], and she does not require a second writ of divorce from him."

5:5 A. [If the husband said,] *"Lo, this is your writ of divorce, on condition that you pay me two hundred zuz"* [M. Git. 7:5A],

and he died,

B. if she paid the money, she is not subject to the Levir.

C. And if not, she is subject to the Levir.

D. Rabban Simeon b. Gamaliel says, "Let her pay the money to his father or his brother or to one of the heirs."

E. *"Lo this is your writ of divorce, on condition that you pay me two hundred zuz,"*

and the writ of divorce was ripped up or lost—

F. lo, this is a valid writ of divorce.

G. For he who says, "On condition . . .," is equivalent to one who says, "Effective immediately."

H. But she should not remarry before she pays the money.

I. ". . .when you will pay me two hundred *zuz,*" and the writ of divorce was ripped up or lost,

J. if she had paid over the money, lo, this is a valid writ of divorce.

K. And if not, it is not a valid writ of divorce.

L. [If he said,] "Lo, this is your writ of divorce on condition that you pay me two hundred *zuz,*" and he went and said to her, "Lo, this is your writ of divorce effective immediately," he has said nothing whatsoever.

M. What should he do?

N. Let him take it back from her and go and hand it over to her again and say to her, "Lo, this is your writ of divorce effective immediately."

5:6 A. *"Lo, this is your writ of divorce, on condition that you serve father,"* [M. Git. 7:6A–B], *or ". . . on condition that you give suck to my son,"*

B. [if] she served him a single hour or gave suck to him a single hour, lo, this is a valid writ of divorce.

C. ". . .on condition that you give suck to my son,"—

D. "Twenty-four months," the words of R. Meir [M. Git. 7:6D].

E. R. Judah says, "Eighteen months" [M. Git. 7:6E].

F. Rabban Simeon b. Gamaliel says, "They count for the infant from the time that he was born."

G. ". . .on condition that you serve father," and "on condition that you give such to my son," lo, this woman is divorced forthwith,

H. "unless he said to her, 'If you do not serve, and if you do not give suck,'" the words of R. Meir.

I. And sages say, "If the condition is carried out, she is divorced. And if not, she is not divorced."

J. Rabban Simeon b. Gamaliel says, "No condition stated in a document is valid which is not stated twice."

K. ". . . 'On condition that you serve father, and on condition that you serve my son,' and he died, since the condition has not been met, it is not a writ of divorce," the words of R. Meir.

L. And sages say, "She has the power to say to him, 'Bring over father, and I'll serve him.' 'Bring over your son, and I'll give him suck.'"

M. ". . . on condition that you serve father," but the father said, "I don't want her to serve me," since the condition has not been met, it is not a writ of divorce.

N. Rabban Simeon b. Gamaliel says, "If he said it of his own free will, lo, this is a valid writ of divorce. If he said it because of [her] provocation, it is not a writ of divorce."

O. ". . . Lo, this is your writ of divorce, on condition that you serve father for two years," and "on condition that you give suck to my son for two years,"

P. and the writ of divorce was torn up or lost,

Q. even if this was during the two years, lo, this is a valid writ of divorce.

R. For whoever says, "On condition," is like him who says, "Effective immediately."

S. ". . . when you will have served father for two years," and the writ of divorce was torn up or lost,

T. [if this happened] during the two years, it is not a valid writ of divorce.

U. [If it happened] after two years, lo, this is a valid writ of divorce.

V. ". . . on condition that you serve father for two years," and "on condition that you give suck to my son for two years,"

W. the condition is to be met, even after the man's death [within the two year period].

5:7 A. Kepar 'Otenai is in Galilee. Antipatris is in Judah.

B. As to the area between them, they assign it to its more stringent status:

C. she is divorced and not divorced.

D. If he said, "For I am going from Judah to Galilee," if he reached Antipatris and went back, his condition is null.

E. ". . . I am going from Galilee to Judah," and he reached Kepar 'Otenai and went back, his condition is null.

F. ". . . I am going overseas," and he reached Akko and came back his condition is null.

G. ". . .I am sailing on the Great Sea," and he reached the place at from which the ships sail and went back, his condition is null [*cf.* M. Git. 7:7].

5:8 A. *"Lo, this is your writ of divorce, if I am apart from your presence for thirty days,"*

B. *[if] he was coming and going, coming and going,*

C. *since he did not continue with her,*

D. *lo, this is a writ of divorce* [M. Git. 7:7M–P].

E. But she should not remarry until he is absent for thirty days.

5:9 A. *"Lo this is your writ of divorce if I do not come back in twelve months," and he died during the twelve months* [M. Git. 7:8A–B]—

B. she should not remarry [without dealing with the levir].

C. And our rabbis instructed her to remarry.

D. But if the writ of divorce was torn up or lost during the twelve-month-period, it is not a writ of divorce.

E. [If this happened] after the twelve month period, lo, this is a valid writ of divorce.

5:10 A. *"Lo this is your writ of divorce, on condition that you give me two hundred zuz,"*

and then he went and said to her, "Lo, they are forgiven you,"

he has said nothing.

B. What should he do?

C. He should take them from her and then go and return them to her, and at that point he should say to her, "Lo, they are forgiven to you."

5:11 A. "Lo, this is your writ of divorce, on condition that you never again go to your father's house,"

"On condition that you never again drink wine,"—

it is not a writ of divorce,

B. for she might go to her father's house or drink wine.

C. " . . . On condition that you not go to your father's house for thirty days,"

"On condition that you not drink wine for thirty days,"—

lo, this is a valid writ of divorce.

D. And one does not take account of the possibility that she might go or might drink.

E. "Lo, this is your writ of divorce on condition that you not climb this tree,"

and " . . . on condition that you not go over this wall,"

F. if the tree was cut down or the wall torn down, lo, this is a valid writ of divorce.

G. " . . . on condition that you climb this tree," or, "that you climb over this wall,"

H. if the tree was cut down or the wall torn down, lo, this is not a valid writ of divorce.

5:12 A. " . . on condition that you not fly in the air," ". . .on condition that you not cross over the Great Sea by foot,"

lo, this is a writ of divorce.

B. ". . . on condition that you cross the Great Sea by foot,"

C. it is not a valid writ of divorce.

D. R. Judah b. Tema says, "In this case it is a writ of divorce."

E. A general principle did R. Judah b. Tema state, "Any condition which it is not possible for her to carry out, and which he stated as a condition to her, he has intended only by way of exaggeration—

F. "whether he said it orally or in a document.

G. "Any condition which is confirmed when stated orally is confirmed when stated in a document, and any condition which is not confirmed when stated orally is not confirmed when stated in a document."

6:1 A. R. Eliezer says, "Even if it is nearer to her than to him,

B. "if a dog came along and took it [the writ of divorce],

C. "she is not divorced.

D. "But if not, she is divorced" [*cf.* M. Git. 8:2H–K].

E. [If] he is inside [the house] and she is outside, and he threw it to her,

F. once it has passed from the threshhold outward, lo, she is divorced.

G. [If] he is outside and she is inside, and he threw it to her,

H. once it has passed inside the threshhold, lo, she is divorced.

I. *If he said to her, "Collect this writ of indebtedness," or if she found it behind him, and lo, it is her writ of divorce* [M. Git. 8:2A–B],

J. and afterward he said to her, "This is your writ of divorce,"

K. Rabbi says, "It is a valid writ of divorce."

L. R. Simeon b. Eleazar says, "It is not a writ of divorce,

M. "unless he said to her at the moment of giving it over, 'It is your writ of divorce.'"

N. [If] he put it into her hand while she was sleeping, [and] she awoke, read it, and lo, it is her writ of divorce,

O. and afterward he said to her, "It is your writ of divorce,"

P. Rabbi says, "It is a valid writ of divorce."

Q. R. Simeon b. Eleazar says, "It is not a valid writ of divorce,

R. "unless he says to her at the moment at which he hands it over to her, 'It is your writ of divorce.'"

6:2 A. *If she was standing on the roof-top and he threw it to her,*

B. *once it has reached the airspace of the roof, lo, she is divorced.*

C. *[If] he is above and she is below, and he threw it to her,*

D. *once it has gone forth from the domain of the roof,*

E. [*if it should be*] *blotted out or burned,*

F. *lo, she is divorced* [M. Git. 8:3G–L].

G. [If he said to her,] "Lo, this is your writ of divorce," and she took it from his hand and tossed it into the sea or a river,

H. and he then went and said to her, "It really was an invalid writ," "It was blank paper,"

I. he has not got the power to prohibit her [from remarrying].

6:3 A. *The House of Hillel say, "A man does not dismiss his wife with an old writ of divorce,*

B. "so that her writ of divorce should not be older than her son" [M. Git. 8:4A].

C. [If] he wrote it in accord with the date of a province, in accord with the dating of a hyparchy,

D. or if there were two kings in power, and he wrote the writ of divorce bearing the date of only one of them, it is valid.

E. [If he wrote it in accord] with the date of the father of his [the reigning emperor's] father, it is valid.

F. If he wrote it in accord with the date of the founder of the dynasty [e.g., Arsaces], it is invalid.

G. If they were called by the same name as the founder of the dynasty [e.g., Arsaces IX], it is valid.

6:4 A. A male convert who changed his [Israelite] name for a gentile name—it is valid.

B. And so you rule in the case of a female convert.

C. Writs of divorce which come from abroad, even though the names written in them are gentile names, are valid,

D. because Israelites overseas use names which are gentile names [*cf.* M. Git. 8:5R].

6:5 A. [If] a man has two wives, one in Judah and one in Galilee, and he has two names, one used in Judah and one used in Galilee,

B. [if] he divorced his wife in Judah by the name he uses in Galilee, and his wife in Galilee by the name he uses in Judah, it is invalid.

C. If [however] he said, "I, Mr. So and so, from Judah, with the name I use in Galilee, and married to a woman in Galilee,"

D. or if he was somewhere else [than Judah or Galilee] and wrote it in the name [used in either one of them],

E. it is valid.

F. R. Simeon b. Gamaliel says, "Even if he wrote his name as used in

Judah when in Galilee, and his name as used in Galilee when in Judah, it is valid."

6:6 A. *"All those prohibited relationships of whom they have said that their co-wives are permitted to remarry [without a Levirate connection],*

B. *"[if] these co-wives went and got married, and they [the prohibited relationships] turned out to be barren,*

C. *"she goes forth* [M. Git. 8:6A–C], and the thirteen rulings [listed at M. Git. 8:5F–Q] apply to her," the words of R. Meir, which he said in the name of R. 'Aqiba.

D. And sages say, "*Mamzerim* are not produced in the violation of the laws of Levirate marriage."

6:7 A. *"He who consummates marriage with his deceased childless brother's widow,*

B. *"and her co-wife went and married someone else,*

C. *"and this one turned out to be barren—*

D. *"she goes forth from this one and from that one* [M. Git. 8:7A–D].

E. "And the thirteen rulings apply to her," the words of R. Meir, which he said in R. 'Aqiba's name.

F. And sages say, "*Mamzerim* are not produced in the violation of the laws of Levirate marriage."

6:8 A. He who gives a writ of divorce to his wife, but did not have it witnessed—

B. The House of Shammai say, "He has invalidated her from marriage into the priesthood" [*cf.* M. Git. 8:8J–L, M. Git. 8:9H–J].

C. [If] he brought his wife over to a scribe and took her writ of divorce and handed it to her, but he did not say to her, "It is your writ of divorce,"

D. R. Yosé says, "If they were engaged in that very matter, she is divorced. And if not, she is not divorced" [*cf.* M. Git. 8:2].

E. Said R. Simeon b. Eleazar, "The House of Shammai and the House of Hillel did not differ concerning the case *of him who divorces his wife and spent the night with her in an inn,* that she does not require from him a second writ of divorce.

F. "Concerning what did they differ?

G. "Concerning a case in which he actually has sexual intercourse" [*cf.* M. Git. 8:9A–C].

6:9 A. "An unfolded writ of divorce containing a single witness,

B. "a folded writ of divorce containing [only] two witnesses,

C. "or with its witnesses on the inside [folds]—

D. "she goes forth and the thirteen rules apply to her," the words of R.

Meir, which he said in the name of R. 'Aqiba [*cf.* M. Git. 8:9H–J].

E. And sages say, "The witnesses sign a writ of divorce only for the good order of the world."

F. What is a "bald" [defectively-witnessed] writ of divorce?

G. Any [folded writ of divorce] with seven folds and six witnesses, six folds and five witnesses, five folds and four witnesses, four folds and three witnesses, three folds and two witnesses [M. Git. 8:10D–E].

H. As to less than that number: *Only they complete it who are relatives suitable to give testimony under some other circumstance* [M. 8:10C].

7:1 A. *He who divorces his wife and said to her, "Lo, you are permitted [to marry] any man except for so-and-so"—*

B. *R. Eliezer permits* her to marry any man except for that particular person [M. Git. 9:1A–B].

C. R. Eliezer concedes that if she married someone else and was widowed or divorced, that she is permitted to marry this person to whom she [originally] was forbidden.

D. After the death of R. Eliezer, four elders came together to reply to his rulings: R. Ṭarfon, R. Yosé the Galilean, R. Eleazar b. 'Azariah, and R. 'Aqiba.

E. Said R. Ṭarfon, "[If] she went and married his brother [that is, the brother of the man whom she was forbidden by the terms of the writ of divorce to marry], and he [the second husband] died childless—how is this woman going to enter into Levirate marriage with him [to whom she was forbidden by the terms of her writ of divorce]? It will turn out that he has made a stipulation contrary to what is written in the Torah, [and] his condition is null. Thus have we learned that this is not a *cutting off* [Deut. 24:1]."

7:2 A. Said R. Yosé the Galilean, "Where do we find a relationship of marriage in the Torah in which a woman is permitted to one and prohibited to another?

B. "But if she is permitted, she is permitted to every man, and if she is prohibited, she is prohibited to every man. Thus have we learned that this is not a *cutting off*."

7:3 A. R. Eleazar b. 'Azariah says, "*Cutting off* (Deut. 24:1)—something which severs the relationship between him and her. Thus have we learned that this is not a *cutting off*."

B. Said R. Yosé, "I prefer the opinion of R. Eleazar b. 'Azariah."

C. R. Simeon b. Eleazar answered and said, "Lo, [if] she went and married someone else and he divorced her, and he said to her, 'Lo, you are permitted [to marry] any man,'—how will this [second husband] permit what the first [husband] has prohibited?

D. "Thus you have learned that this is not a *cutting off*."

7:4 A. R. 'Aqiba says, "[If] this one to whom she was prohibited was a priest, and the one who divorced her died,—she would turn out to be a widow [in respect] to this one but a divorcee [in respect] to all others of his brethren, the priests.

B. "Thus we have learned that this is not a *cutting off*.

C. "Another matter: To whom has the Torah applied a more stringent rule [so far as priests' marriage-partners are concerned], the category of divorcees or the category of widows? A divorcee is subject to a more strict rule than a widow.

D. "Now if the widow, who is subject to a less stringent rule, is prohibited from marrying someone who is permitted to her, a divorcee, who is subject to a more stringent rule, surely should be prohibited from marrying someone who is permitted to her! [B. Git. 83A: "Seeing then that she would be forbidden to the priest *qua* divorcee, though this involves but a minor transgression, should she not all the more as a married woman, which is more serious, be forbidden to all men!] Thus we have learned that this is not *cutting off*.

7:5 E. "Another matter: [if] she went and married someone else and had children from him and he died,

F. "[then] if she goes back and marries this one to whom she had been forbidden [as Eliezer has conceded she may do, T7:1C], will it not turn out that the children of the first husband [whom she married after her divorce] are *mamzerim* [retroactively, since the original divorce is now nullified]? Thus we have learned that this is not *cutting off*."

G. R. Simeon b. Eleazar says, "[If] she went and married someone else, who divorced her, and who said to her, 'Lo, you are permitted [to marry] any man,' how will this one permit what the first husband prohibited? Thus we have learned that this is not *cutting off*."

7:6 A. A writ of divorce which has no date [M. Git. 9:4E]—

B. Abba Saul says, "Even if it is written in it, 'I this day divorce you'—it is valid."

C. [If] they wrote, "On the day on which Mr. So-and-so tore up his deeds," it is valid.

7:7 A. A writ which has no witnesses, but which they gave to her in the presence of witnesses, is valid.

B. In the name of R. Eleazar they said, "She brings his witnesses to court and does not have to bring the writ of divorce, and she collects [the payment of the marriage-contract even] from mortgaged property [M. Git. 9:4J–M]."

7:8 A. A writ of divorce on which there is an erasure or an interlinear insertion, [if this was in] the body of the document, is invalid.

B. [If this is] not in the body of the document, it is valid.

C. If one restores [the erasure] at the bottom, even in the body of the document, it is valid.

7:9 A. A writ of divorce on which the witnesses signed after an interval sufficient to inquire after one's welfare is invalid.

B. For they have signed only concerning the asking after their welfare.

C. [If] one replied a word or even two words relating to the writ of divorce, it is valid.

7:10 A. [If] one wrote it on one side of the page, and the witnesses signed on the other side of the page, it is invalid [*cf.* M. Git. 9:7A–B].

B. [If] one restored to it some one thing or two things dealing with a writ of divorce, it is valid.

7:11 A. [If] the names of the witnesses were separated from the body of the writ of divorce by a distance of two lines, it is invalid.

B. [If the space between the body of the writ and the signatures of the witnesses is] less than this, it is valid [*cf.* M. Git. 9:6].

C. How much may the names of the witnesses be distant from the body of the writ for the writ to be valid?

D. "Sufficient so that they may be read with it [the body of the text]," the words of Rabbi.

E. R. Simeon b. Eleazar says, "The space of a single line."

F. R. Dosetai b. R. Yannai says, "The space taken up by the signatures of two witnesses."

G. A writ of divorce on which five witnesses signed and of which the first three turn out to be invalid—the testimony [of the document] is confirmed by the remainder of the witnesses.

H. A writ of divorce which was written in five languages, and which five witnesses signed in five languages, is invalid.

I. [If] it was torn, it is valid.

J. [If] it was torn with the sort of tear made by a court, it is invalid.

7:12 A. [If] it was eaten by moths or rotted or was made as full of holes as a sieve, it is valid.

B. [If] it was erased or faded but its impression remains,

C. [if] one can read it, it is valid.

D. If not, it is invalid.

7:13 A. "I witness it," "I signed it as a witness,"

B. if an example of their handwriting is available from some other source, it is valid.

C. And if not, it is invalid.

D. Rabban Simeon b. Gamaliel says, "It was a great ordinance which they ordained, that witnesses should place their names on writs of divorce."

QIDDUSHIN

1:1 A. *A woman is acquired [as a wife] in three ways, and acquires herself [to be a free agent] in two ways. She is acquired through money, a writ, and sexual intercourse* [M. Qid. 1:1A–B].

B. *By money*—how so?

C. [If] he gave her money or something worth money, saying to her, "Lo, you are consecrated to me,"

"Lo, you are betrothed to me,"

"Lo, you are a wife to me,"

lo, this one is consecrated.

D. But [if] she gave him money or something worth money and said to him, "Lo, I am betrothed to you,"

"Lo, I am sanctified to you,"

"Lo, I am a wife to you,"

she is not consecrated.

1:2 A. *By a writ* [—how so?]

B. Must one say it is a writ which has a value of a *peruṭah*?

C. But even if one wrote it on a sherd and gave it to her,

on waste paper and gave it to her,

D. lo, this one is consecrated.

1:3 A. *By sexual intercourse* [—how so?]

B. By any act of sexual relations which is done for the sake of betrothal is she betrothed.

C. But if it is not for the sake of betrothal, she is not betrothed.

1:4 A. A man should not marry a wife until the daughter of his sister grows up or until he will find a mate suitable for himself,

B. since it is said, [*Do not profane your daughter by making her a harlot*] *lest the land fall into harlotry and the land become full of wickedness* (Lev. 19:29).

C. R. Eleazar says, "This is an unmarried man who has sexual relations with an unmarried woman not for the sake of effecting a marriage."

D. R. Eleazar says, "How do we know that he is punished before the Omnipresent as is he who has sexual relations with a woman and her mother?

E. "Here it is said *wickedness*, and elsewhere it is said, *If a man takes a wife and her mother also, it is wickedness* (Lev. 20:14)."

F. R. Eliezer b. Jacob says, "Since he has sexual relations with many girls and does not know with which one he has had sexual relations, and she has received sexual relations from many men and does not know from which ones she has received sexual relations, this man turns out to marry his daughter, and that one marries his sister, and the whole world is turned into *mamzerim.*

G. "On that account it is said, *And the land became full of wickedness* (Lev. 19:29)."

H. R. Judah b. Betera says, "Lo, it says, *Lest the land fall into harlotry* (Lev. 19:29)—The produce turns into weeds: What is this child? Neither a priest, nor a Levite, nor an Israelite [since no one knows]."

I. Sages voted to support the opinion of R. Judah,

J. since it is said, *Lift up your eyes to the bare heights and see! Where have you not been lain with? You have polluted the land with your vile harlotry. Therefore the showers have been withheld, and the spring rain has not come* (Jer. 3:2–2).

1:5 A. How does [he redeem himself] by deduction from the purchase price [at his outstanding value] [M. Qid. 1:2B]?

B. [If] he wanted to redeem himself during these years, he reckons the value against the years [left to serve] and pays off his master.

C. And the hand of the slave is on top [in estimating the sum to be paid].

D. How is usucaption [established in the case of] real estate?

E. [If] he locked, made a fence, broke down a fence, in any measure at all,

F. lo, this is usucaption.

G. How is usucaption [established in the case of] slaves?

H. [If] he [the slave] tied on his [the master's] sandal, or loosened his sandal, or carried clothing after him to the bathhouse, lo, this is usucaption.

I. [If] he lifted him up [e.g., the slave lifted the master up on a horse]—

J. R. Simeon says, "You have no act of usucaption more effective than that!"

1:6 A. And he [the slave] acquires himself through [the loss, through the master's tort] of the major limbs.

B. "*And he acquires himself through money paid by others and through a writ of indebtedness taken on by himself* [M. Qid. 1:3B],

C. "because it is as if the left hand pays over to the right hand," *the words of R. Meir.*

D. *And sages say, " By money paid by himself and by a writ taken on by others, on condition that the money belong to others* [M. Qid. 1:3C–D],

E. "and he says to him, 'On condition that you have permission only to use the funds to redeem him.'"

F. R. Simeon b. Eleazar said in the name of R. Meir, "Also: through a writ of indebtedness taken on by others, but not taken on by himself" [*vs.* M. Qid. 1:3C].

1:7 A. A boat is acquired through drawing.

B. R. Nathan says, "A boat and documents are acquired through drawing and through a writ."

C. What is the meaning of *drawing* [M. Qid. 1:4B]?

D. Whether one drew [the animal], or led it, or called it and it came after him, lo, this is an effective act of drawing.

1:8 A. What is an act of *delivery* [M. Qid. 1:4A]?

B. Any act in which he handed over to him the bit or the bridle—lo, this is an act of delivery.

C. Under what circumstances did they rule, Movables are acquired through drawing? In the public domain or in a courtyard which does not belong to either one of them.

D. But if it is the domain of the purchaser, once he has taken upon himself [to pay the agreed upon sum], he has acquired the thing.

E. [And if it is] in the domain of the seller, once he has raised up the object or after he has taken it out from the domain of the owner [it has been acquired].

F. In the domain of this one in whose hands the bailment is located, an act of acquisition is carried out when he [the owner] will have taken it upon himself [to allow the buyer a portion of the premises to effect an acquisition] or when he [the purchaser] will have rented their place for himself.

1:9 A. If one exchanged with another person real estate for other real estate, movables for other movables, real estate for movables, movables for real estate,

B. *once this one has made acquisition, the other has become liable for what is given in exchange* [M. Qid. 1:6B–C].

C. *The right of the Most High is effected through money* [M. Qid. 1:6G] —how so?

D. The Temple-treasurer who paid over coins of the Sanctuary for movables—the Sanctuary has made acquisition wherever [the movables] may be located.

E. But an ordinary person has not made acquisition until he will have drawn [the object].

F. *One's word of mouth [dedication of an object] to the Most High is equivalent to one's act of delivery to an ordinary person* [M. Qid. 1:6H]—how so?

G. "This ox is sanctified," "This house is sanctified"—even if it is located at the end of the world, the Sanctuary has made acquisition wherever it is located.

H. But in the case of an ordinary person, he makes acquisition only when he will effect usucaption.

1:10 A. *What is a positive commandment dependent upon the time* [of year, for which men are liable and women are exempt (M. Qid. 1:7C)]?

B. For example, building the *Sukkah,* taking the *lulab,* putting *tefillin.*

C. What is *a positive commandment not dependent upon the time [of year* (M. Qid. 1:7D)]?

D. For example, restoring lost property to its rightful owner, sending forth the bird, building a parapet, and putting on *ṣiṣit.*

E. R. Simeon declares women exempt from the requirement of wearing *ṣiṣit,* because it is a positive commandment dependent upon time.

1:11 A. What is *a commandment pertaining to the son concerning the father [to which men and women are equally liable* (M. Qid. 1:7B)]?

B. Giving him food to eat and something to drink and clothing him and covering him and taking him out and bringing him in and washing his face, his hands, and his feet.

C. All the same are men and women. But the husband has sufficient means to do these things for the child, and the wife does not have sufficient means to do them,

D. for others have power over her.

E. What is *a commandment pertaining to the father concerning the son* [M. Qid. 1:7A]?

F. To circumcize him, to redeem him [if he is kidnapped], and to teach him Torah, and to teach him a trade, and to marry him off to a girl.

G. And there are those who say, "Also: to row him across the river."

H. R. Judah says, "Whoever does not teach his son a trade teaches him to be a mugger."

I. Rabban Gamaliel says, "Whoever has a trade, to what is he compared? To a vineyard surrounded by a fence, to a furrow surrounded by a border.

J. "And whoever does not have a trade—to what is he compared? To a vineyard not surrounded by a fence, to a furrow not surrounded by a border."

II K. R. Yosé says in the name of Rabban Gamaliel, "Whoever has a trade—to what is he compared? To a woman who has a husband. Whether she pretties herself or does not pretty herself, people don't stare at her. And if she doesn't pretty herself, he curses her.

L. "And whoever does not have a trade—to what is he compared? To a woman who does not have a husband. Whether she pretties herself or does not pretty herself, everybody stares at her. And if she doesn't pretty herself, he doesn't curse her."

III M. R. Yosé b. R. Eleazar said in the name of Rabban Gamaliel, "Whoever has a trade—to what is he compared? To a fenced-in vineyard, into which cattle and beasts cannot enter. And people who go back and forth don't trample in it. And people don't see what's in it.

N. "And whoever does not have a trade—to what is he compared? To a vineyard with a broken-down fence, into which cattle and beasts can enter, and people who go back and forth trample through it. And everybody sees what's in it."

1:12 A. R. Eleazar b. R. Simeon says, "Every commandment for which the Israelites became liable before they entered the Land applies in the Land and outside of the Land, and [every commandment] for which the Israelites became liable only after they came into the Land applies only in the Land [*cf.* M. Qid. 1:9A–C],

B. "except for the forgiveness of debts, the redemption of fields which have been sold, and the sending forth free of the Hebrew slave [in the Seventh Year].

C. "For even though they became liable to them only after they had come into the Land, they apply in the Land and outside of the Land."

1:13 A. *Whoever does a single commandment—they do well for him and lengthen his days* and his years *and he inherits the Land* [M. Qid. 1:10A–B].

B. And whoever commits a single transgression—they do ill to him and cut off his days, and he does not inherit the Land.

C. And concerning such a person it is said, *One sinner destroys much good* (Qoh. 9:18).

D. By a single sin this one destroys many good things.

E. A person should always see himself as if he is half meritorious and half guilty.

F. [If] he did a single commandment, happy is he, for he has inclined the balance for himself to the side of merit.

G. [If] he committed a single transgression, woe is he, for he has inclined the balance to the side of guilt.

H. Concerning this one it is said, *One sinner destroys much good.*

I. By a single sin this one has destroyed many good things.

1:14 A. R. Simeon b. Eleazar says in the name of R. Meir, "Because the individual is judged by his majority [of deeds], the world is judged by its majority.

B. "And [if] one did one commandment, happy is he, for he has inclined the balance for himself and for the world to the side of merit.

C. "[If] he committed one transgression, woe is he, for he has inclined the balance for himself and for the world to the side of guilt.

D. "And concerning such a person it is said, *One sinner destroys much good—*

E. "By the single sin which this one committed, he destroyed for himself and for the world many good things."

1:15 A. R. Simeon says, "[If] a man was righteous his entire life but at the end he rebelled, he loses the whole, since it is said, *The righteousness of the righteous shall not deliver him when he transgresses* (Ez. 33:12).

1:16 A. "[If] a man was evil his entire life but at the end he repented, the Omnipresent accepts him,

B. "as it is said, *And as for the wickedness of the wicked, he shall not fall by it when he turns from his wickedness [and the righteous shall not be able to live by his righteousness when he sins*] (Ez. 33:12)."

1:17 A. Whoever occupies himself with all three of them, with Scripture, Mishnah, and good conduct,

B. concerning such a person it is said, *And a threefold cord is not quickly broken* (Qoh. 5:12) [*cf.* M. Qid. 1:10E–G].

2:1 A. Just as a man does not effect a betrothal for his son, either on his own or through his agent,

B. so a woman does not effect a betrothal for her daughter, either on her own or through her agent [*cf.* M. Qid. 2:1C].

2:2 A. He who says to a woman, "Lo, you are betrothed to me, on condition that I am [called] Joseph,"

B. and he turns out to be [called] Joseph and Simeon,

C. ". . . on condition that I am a perfumer," and he turns out to be a perfumer and a tanner,

D. ". . . on condition that I am a town-dweller," and he turns out to be a town-dweller and a villager [M. Qid. 2:3E–F],

E. lo, this woman is betrothed.

F. [If he said, "Lo, you are betrothed to me, on condition that] I am only Joseph,"

G. and he turned out to be Joseph and Simeon,

H. ". . . that I am only a perfumer," and he turned out to be a perfumer and a tanner,

I. ". . . that I am only a town-dweller," and he turned out to be a town-dweller and a villager,

J. she is not betrothed.

2:3 A. "Be betrothed to me with this and this," and she was eating [the pieces of fruit] one by one [M. Qid. 2:1H–I],

B. if there remained in his possession produce worth a *peruṭah,* she is betrothed, and if not, she is not betrothed.

C. "Be btrothed to me with this cup," if the value of the cup and of what is in it is a *peruṭah,* she is betrothed, and if not, she is not betrothed.

D. And she has acquired both it and what is in it.

E. "With what is in this cup,"

F. if what is in it is worth a *peruṭah,* she is betrothed, and if not, she is not betrothed.

G. And she has acquired only what is in it alone.

2:4 A. [If a man said to a woman, "Be betrothed to me] on condition that I am poor," and he was poor but got rich,

B. ". . . on condition that I am rich" and he was rich and became poor,

C. ". . . on condition that I am a perfumer," and he was a perfumer but became a tanner,

D. ". . . on condition that I am a tanner," and he was a tanner but became a perfumer,

E. ". . . on condition that I am a town-dweller," and he was a town-dweller but he moved to a village,

F. ". . . on condition that I am a villager," and he was a villager, but he moved to a town,

G. ". . . on condition that I have children," and he had children, but then they died,

H. ". . . on condition that I have no children," and he had no children, and afterward children were born to him—

I. lo, this woman is betrothed.

J. [If he said, however,] that he was only poor, and he was rich and became poor,

K. that he was only rich, and he was poor and became rich,

L. ". . .that I am only a perfumer," and he was a tanner and became a perfumer,

M. ". . . that I am only a tanner," and he was a perfumer and became a tanner,

N. ". . . that I am only a town-dweller," and he was a villager and became a town-dweller,

O. ". . . that I am only a villager," and he was a town-dweller and became a villager,

P. that he had no children, and he had children, but afterward they died,

Q. that he had children, and he did not have any, but afterward children were born to him,

R. she is not betrothed.

S. This is the principle: In the case of any condition which is valid at the moment of betrothal, even though it was annulled afterward, lo, this woman is betrothed.

T. And in the case of any condition which is not valid at the moment of betrothal, even though it was validated afterward, lo, this woman is not betrothed.

2:5 A. "Be betrothed with a *sela,*" and after she took it from his hand, she said, "I was thinking that you were a priest, but you are only a Levite,"

B. ". . . that you were rich, but you are only poor,"

C. lo, this woman is betrothed.

D. This is the principle: Once the tokens of betrothal have fallen into her hand, whether he deceived her or she deceived him, lo, this one is betrothed.

E. *R. Simeon says, "If he deceived her to her advantage in the* case of money, *lo, this woman is betrothed* [M. Qid. 2:2H].

F. "How so?

G. "'. . . with this silver *denar,*' and it turned out to be gold—she wants the gold one more than the silver one.

H. "'. . . a poor man,' and he turned out to be a rich man—she wants the rich man more than she did the poor man."

I. R. Simeon concedes that if he deceived her to her advantage in a matter of genealogy, she is not betrothed.

2:6 A. "Be betrothed to me with this *sela,* with this cow, with this cloak,"

B. once she has taken the *sela,* and drawn the cow, and made use of the cloak, lo, this woman is betrothed.

2:7 A. "Collect this *sela* for me,"

B. and at the moment at which it was given over, he said to her, "Lo, you are betrothed to me,"

C. lo, this woman is betrothed.

D. [If this happened] after she has taken it from his hand, [however,] if she agrees, then she is betrothed, but if she does not agree, she is not betrothed.

E. "Here is this *sela* which I owe you,"

F. [if] at the moment of giving it over, he said to her, "Lo, you are betrothed to me,"

G. if she concurs, she is betrothed, and if she does not concur, she is not betrothed.

H. [If this happened] after she has taken it from him, even though both of them concur, she is not betrothed.

I. "Be betrothed to me with the *sela* of mine which is in your hand"—she is not betrothed.

J. What should he do?

K. He should take it from her and then go and give it back to her and say to her,"Lo you are betrothed to me."

2:8 A. "Be betrothed to me with this *sela,*"

B. [if] after she took if from his hand, she tossed it into the ocean or into the river—

C. she is not betrothed.

D. "Be betrothed to me with this *maneh,*" and she said to him, "Give it to so-and-so"—

E. she is not betrothed.

F. ["Give it to Mr. So-and-so,] who will receive it for me,"

G. lo, she is betrothed.

H. [If] he gave her her tokens of betrothal but did not say to her, "Lo, you are betrothed unto me,"

I. R. Judah says, "She is not betrothed."

J. Rabbi says, "If they were occupied with that very matter [when he gave over the tokens], she is betrothed, but if not, she is not betrothed."

K. "Be betrothed to me with this *maneh,*" and it turns out to be a *maneh* lacking a *denar*—she is not betrothed.

L. [If] it was a bad *denar,* let him exchange it for a good one.

2:9 A. [If] he was counting out and putting into her hand one by one,

B. she has the power to retract up to the time that he completes [counting out the specified sum].

C. [If in a dispute about how much was specified for a betrothal,] this one says, "With a *maneh,*" [a hundred *zuz*] and this one says, "With two hundred *zuz,*" and this one went home and that one went home,

D. and afterward they laid claim against one another and effected betrothal,

E. if the man laid claim against the woman,

F. let the claims of the woman be carried out.

G. And if the woman laid claim against the man, let the claim of the man be carried out.

H. And so in the case of him who sells an object, and he was counting out [the objects] into the hand of the buyer, he has the power to retract.

I. [If] this one claims, "[You sold it for] a *maneh,*" and that one claims, "[You bought it for] two hundred *zuz,*" and this one went home and that one went home, and afterward they laid claim against one another,

J. if the purchaser laid claim against the seller, let the claim of the seller be done,

K. and if the seller laid claim against the purchaser, let the claim of the purchaser be done.

3:1 A. He who says to a woman, "Lo, you are betrothed to me through the bailment which I have in your hand,"

B. [if] she went off and found that it had been stolen or had gotten lost,

C. if [of that bailment] there was left in her possession something worth a *peruṭah,*

D. she is betrothed, and if not, she is not betrothed.

E. But [if it concerned] a loan, even though there was something worth a *peruṭah* left in her possession, she is not betrothed.

F. R. Simeon b. Eleazar says in the name of R. Meir, "A loan is equivalent to a bailment. If there remained in her hand something worth a *peruṭah,* she is betrothed. And if not, she is not betrothed."

3:2 A. *He who says to a woman, "Lo, you are betrothed to me on condition that I speak in your behalf to the government," "That I work for you as a laborer"* [M. Qid. 3:6H]—

B. and he gave her something worth a *peruṭah* [on the spot],

C. "lo, this woman is betrothed forthwith,

D. "unless he should say, 'I did not speak in your behalf, and I did not do the work,'" the words of R. Meir.

E. And sages say, "[If] the condition is carried out, she is betrothed, and if not, she is not betrothed."

F. Rabban Simeon b. Gamaliel says, "A condition in documents which is not stated twice is not valid" [*cf.* M. Qid. 3:4].

G. [If he said,] "On condition that I speak in your behalf to the government," if he spoke in her behalf as people generally do it, she is betrothed, and if not, she is not betrothed.

H. ". . . through the value of my speaking in your behalf to the government," if he spoke in her behalf to the value of a *peruṭah,* she is betrothed, and if not, she is not betrothed.

I. ". . . through the act of labor which I shall do in your behalf," if he worked in her behalf to the value of a *peruṭah,* she is betrothed, and if not, she is not betrothed.

J. ". . . on condition that I shall work with you," ". . . on condition that I shall labor with you tomorrow,"

K. if he did work in her behalf value to the extent of a *perutah,* she is betrothed, and if not she is not betrothed.

L. ". . . *on condition that I have two hundred zuz," lo, this woman is betrothed* [M. Qid. 3:2E], for he may have that sum on the other side of the world.

M. ". . . on condition that I have two hundred *zuz* in such-and-such a place,"

N. if he has the money in that place, she is betrothed, and if not, she is not betrothed.

3:3 A. ". . . on condition that I have [money] in the hand of Mr. so-and-so,"

B. even though [the other party] said, "He has no money in my hand,"

C. she is betrothed.

D. For they might have conspired to defraud her.

E. ". . . until he will say that he has the money in my hand,"

if he said, "He has money in my hand," she is betrothed, and if not, she is not betrothed.

F. ". . . *on condition that I show you two hundred zuz," if he showed her the money on the table [of a money-changer], she is not betrothed* [M. Qid. 3:2F, H].

G. For he stated that he would show her only what in fact belonged to him.

3:4 A. ". . .*on condition that I have a kor of land," lo, this woman is betrothed* [M. Qid. 3:3A–B],

B. for he might have such land on the other side of the world.

C. ". . . *on condition that I have it in this place," if he has it in that place, she is betrothed, and if not, she is not betrothed.*

D. ". . .*on condition that I show you a kor of land" if he showed it to her in a plain [of public property], she is not betrothed* [M. Qid. 3:3E–G].

E. For he stated that he would show her only what in fact belonged to him.

3:5 A. ". . . on condition that So-and-so will concur," even though he said, "I do not concur," she is betrothed.

B. For he may concur a while later.

C. ". . . unless he will say, 'I concur,'" if he says, "I concur," she is betrothed, and if not she is not betrothed.

3:6 A. ". . . *on condition that father agrees"* [M. Qid. 3:6D], even though his father did not agree, she is betrothed.

B. Perhaps he may agree some other time.

C. *[If] the father died, lo, this woman is betrothed.*

D. *[If] the son died*—this was a case, and they came and *instructed the father to say, "I do not concur"* [so that the woman is exempt from the Levirate connection] [M. Qid. 3:6F–G].

3:7 A. *Any condition that is dependent on an antecedent act is void [And any condition that can in the end be fulfilled and was laid down as a condition from the beginning—such a condition is valid*] [M. B.M. 7:11].

B. How so?

C. "Lo, I shall perform the rite of *ḥaliṣah* with you, on condition that father concurs,"

D. even though the father did not concur, lo, this woman is divorced.

E. "Lo, I have sexual relations with you on condition that father approves," even though the father did not approve, she is betrothed.

F. R. Simeon b. Eleazar says in the name of R. Meir, "If the father approved, she is betrothed. If the father did not approve, she is not betrothed.

G. "For the act of sexual relations was only on account of the prior betrothal."

H. A principle did R. Simeon b. Eleazar lay down: "Any condition which it is possible for either her or her agent to do, and which he made with her—his condition is valid.

I. "And any condition which it is possible only for her herself to do, and which he made with her—his condition is null.

J. How so?

L. "'Lo, I divorce you on condition that father approves,' if the father approved, she is divorced. If the father did not approve, she is not divorced.

M. "'*Lo, I betroth you on condition that father approve,' if the father approved, she is betrothed, and if the father did not approve, she is not betrothed,* [M. Qid. 3:6D–E].

N. "On condition that you not be subjected to Levirate marriage"—lo, this girl is betrothed, but his condition is null.

O. For he has made a stipulation contrary to what is written in the Torah, and whoever makes a stipulation contrary to what is written in the Torah—his stipulation is null.

P. ". . . on condition that you have no claim against me for food, clothing and sex," lo, this woman is betrothed, but his condition is null.

3:8 A. This is the general principle:

B. Whoever makes a stipulation contrary to what is written in the Torah governing a matter of property—his stipulation is valid.

C. [If it concerns] something which is not a matter of property, his stipulation is null.

D. ". . . on condition that I am rich,"—they do not mean that he has to be the richest of the rich, but only as rich as people in his town generally regard as rich.

3:9 A. ". . . on condition that I am a disciple of a sage,"—they do not mean that he has to be like Simeon b. 'Azzai or Simeon b. Zoma,

B. but only the sort of person people in his town generally regard as a disciple of a sage.

3:10 A. ". . . with this silver *denar*," and it turns out to be gold,

B. she is not betrothed [*cf.* M. Qid. 2:2].

C. What should he do?

D. He should take it back from her and go and give it to her again and say to her, "Lo, you are betrothed to me."

4:1 A. He who gives permission to three men to effect an act of betrothal for him with a woman—

B. R. Nathan says, "The House of Shammai say, 'Two may serve as witnesses, and one as an agent.'

C. "And the House of Hillel say, 'All three of them are agents, and they have not got the power to serve as witnesses.'"

4:2 A. *He who says to his agent, "Go and betroth for me Miss So-and-so in such-and-such a place," and he went and betrothed her in some other place—*

B. *she is not betrothed.*

C. *". . . lo, she is in such and such a place,"*

D. *and he went and betrothed her in some other place,*

E. *lo, this woman is betrothed* [M. Qid. 2:4].

F. R. Eleazar says, "In the case of all of them, lo, this woman is betrothed,

G. "unless he should say, 'I want you to be betrothed to me only in such and such a place.'"

H. *And he who says to his fellow, "Go and betroth for me Miss So-and-so," and he went and betrothed her for himself,*

I. *she is betrothed* [M. Qid. 3:1A–B] to the second man.

4:3 A. [*He who says, "Lo, you are betrothed to me retroactively] from now after thirty days,"*

B. *and a second party came along and betrothed her during the thirty days—*

C. she is betrothed [M. Qid. 3:1F–G] to the second party [or: to both of them].

D. How should they arrange matters?

E. One gives a writ of divorce, and the other marries her.

F. If they were two brothers, she is invalidated from marrying the one or the other.

4:4 A. He who betrothes a woman in error, *or with something of less than the value of a peruṭah,*

B. *and so a minor who effected an act of betrothal—*

C. *even though he sent along presents afterward,*

D. *she is not betrothed.*

E. *For it was on account of the original act of betrothal that he sent the gifts* [M. Qid. 2:6].

F. But if he had an act of sexual relations, he has acquired [the woman as his wife].

G. R. Simeon b. Judah says in the name of R. Simeon, "Even though he had sexual relations, he has not acquired her.

H. "For the act of sexual relations was only on the strength of the original act of betrothal [which was null]."

4:5 A. He who effects an act of betrothal by means of something which is stolen, or with a bailment,

B. or who grabbed a *sela'* from her and betrothed her with it—

C. lo, this woman is betrothed.

D. [If] he said to her, "Be betrothed to me with the *sela'* which is in your hand,"

E. she is not betrothed.

F. What should he do?

G. He should take it from her and go and give it back to her, and say to her, "Lo, you are betrothed to me."

4:6 A. He who betrothes a woman with meat of cattle of tithe, even if it is after slaughter—she is not betrothed.

B. [If he does so] with its bones, sinews, horns, hooves, blood, fat, hide, or shearings, lo, this woman is betrothed.

4:7 A. *He who betrothes a woman, whether with Most Holy Things or Lesser Holy Things—she is not betrothed* [M. Qid. 2:8A–B].

B. *[If he did so with] something which had been dedicated to the Temple,*

C. "*if he did so deliberately, he has betrothed her,*

D. "because he has committed an act of sacrilege.

E. "*If he did so inadvertently* [M. Qid. 2:8F], he has not committed an act of sacrilege [and therefore the object, not being available for ordinary use by retaining its character as something holy, is not suitable for this purpose]," the words of R. Meir.

F. R. Judah says, "If there is in the object [of a] the value of enjoyment [to a priest] to the extent of a *peruṭah,* she is betrothed. And if not, she is not betrothed."

G. Said Rabbi, "The opinion of R. Judah appears to me preferable on the case of that which is dedicated [M. Qid. 2:8F–H], and the opinion of R. Meir in the case of food in the status of second tithe [M. Qid. 2:8C–E]."

4:8 A. He who betrothes a woman by means of libation-wine, an idol, a city and its inhabitants which are slated for destruction [for rebellion], hides with a hole cut out at the heart, an *asherah* and its produce, a high place and what is on it, a statue of Mercury and what is on it, and any sort of object which is subject to a prohibition by reason of deriving from idolatry—

B. in the case of all of them, even though he sold them and betrothed a woman with their proceeds—

C. she is not betrothed [*cf.* M. Qid. 2:9A–C].

D. [If he did so] with purification-water and with purification-ash, she is betrothed [*cf.* M. Qid. 2:10A].

E. R. Judah says, "If there is in the object the value of enjoyment [to a priest] to the extent of a *peruṭah,* she is betrothed. And if not, she is not betrothed."

4:9 A. *He who says to a woman, "Lo, you are betrothed [to me] after I convert,"*

". . . after you convert,"

". . . after I am freed,"

". . . after you are freed,"

". . . after your husband will die,"

". . . after your sister will die,"

". . . after your Levir will perform the rite of ḥaliṣah with you,"

B. even though the condition is met,

C. *she is not betrothed* [M. Qid. 3:5I].

4:10 A. *"I betrothed my daughter, but I do not know to whom I betrothed her,"*

B. *and someone came along and said, "I betrothed her"—*

C. *he is believed* [M. Qid. 3:7A–C] to consummate the marriage.

D. [If] after he has consummated the marriage, someone else came along and said, "I betrothed her,"

E. he has not got the power to prohibit her [from remaining wed to the husband who got there first].

4:11 A. [If a man said], "I betrothed my daughter," the minors are subject to his statement, but the adults are not subject to his statement.

B. "My daughter has been betrothed,"—the adults are subject to his statement, but the minors are not subject to his statement.

C. "I received the writ of divorce for my daughters"—the minors are subject to his statement, but the adults are not subject to his statement.

D. "My daughter has been divorced"—

E. the minors are not subject to his statement [*cf.* M. Qid. 3:8K].

4:12 A. *"She was taken captive and I redeemed her"* [M. Qid. 3:8G],

B. or, "She was invalidated by one of those who are invalid" [for marriage with a priest]—

C. he has not got the power to prohibit her [from marrying a priest].

D. [If he said], "I have betrothed my daughter," and he had ten daughters, all of them are prohibited by reason of doubt [from remarrying without a writ of divorce].

E. If he said, "The oldest one," only the oldest one is deemed to have been betrothed.

F. If he said, "The youngest," only the youngest is deemed to have been betrothed [*cf.* M. Qid. 3:9].

G. And so two brothers who betrothed two sisters—

H. this one does not know which one of them he betrothed, and that one does not know which one of them he betrothed—

I. both of them are prohibited by reason of doubt.

J. But if they were engaged in the betrothal of the older girl to the older man, and the younger girl to the younger man,

K. [if] the older one says, "I was betrothed only to the older brother," then the younger sister has been betrothed only to the younger brother.

4:13 A. *"I have betrothed you,"*

but she says, "You have betrothed only my daughter,"

B. *he is prohibited to marry the relatives of the older woman, and the older woman is prohibited to marry his relatives.*

C. *And he is permitted to marry the relatives of the younger woman, and the younger woman is permitted to marry his relatives.*

4:14 A. *"I betrothed your daughter,"*

and she says, "You betrothed only me,"

B. *he is prohibited from marrying the relatives of the younger girl, and the younger girl is permitted to marry his relatives.*

C. *And he is permitted to marry the relatives of the older woman, and the older woman is prohibited from marrying his relatives* [M. Qid. 3:10F–I, 3:11].

4:15 A. A priest-girl, a Levite-girl, and an Israelite-girl who were married to a proselyte—

B. the offspring is in the status of a proselyte.

C [And if they married] a freed slave, the offspring is in the status of a freed slave [*cf.* M. Qid. 3:12].

4:16 A. A gentile, or a slave who had sexual relations with an Israelite girl, and she produced a son—the offspring is a *mamzer.*

B. R. Simeon b. Judah says in the name of R. Simeon, "A *mamzer* derives only from a woman who is prohibited by reason of the Scriptural statements on prohibited sexual unions, and on account of whom they are liable to extirpation."

5:1 A. "Converts and freed slaves, *Mamzers* and *Netins,* 'silenced ones,' and foundlings, and all those who are prohibited to enter into the congregation are permitted to marry one another," the words of R. Meir [*cf.* M. Qid. 4:1D, 4:3A].

B. R. Judah says, "There are four congregations: the congregation of priests, the congregation of Levites, the congregation of Israelites, and the congregation of proselytes. And the rest are permitted to intermarry with one another."

C. And sages say, "There are three congregations: the congregation of priests, the congregation of Levites, and the congregation of Israelites."

D. *R. Eliezer says, "All those who are prohibited from entering into the congregation:*

E. *"Those who are of certain status with those who are of doubtful status, those who are of doubtful status with those who are of certain status, and those who are of doubtful status and those who are of doubtful status, are prohibited* from marrying one another.

F. "*Which are those who are of doubtful status? 'Silenced ones,' foundlings and Samaritans*" [M. Qid. 4:3C–G].

G. And so did R. Eliezer say, "A *mamzer* should not marry a Samaritan woman, and a Samaritan should not marry a *mamzer*–girl. And a Samaritan should not marry a Samaritan girl, and so is the rule for a 'silenced one,' a foundling, and others of the same sort."

5:2 A. "A proselyte and a freed slave are permitted to marry a *mamzer*-girl, and the offspring is in the status of a *mamzer,*" the words of R. Yosé.

B. R. Judah says, "A proselyte may not marry a proselyte-girl."

C. A proselyte, a freed slave, and a man of impaired priestly stock are permitted to marry a priest-girl.

D. What is a *mixture* [of proselytes or people of impaired priestly stock, which produces a girl suitable for marriage to an Israelite, but invalid for marriage into the priesthood]?

E. Any girl in whom is no trace of ancestry of a *Netin* or a *mamzer* or servants of the kings.

F. R. Meir says, "I heard that any girl who bears no trace of ancestry of a *Netin,* a *mamzer,* or a servant of the kings, do they marry right up into the priesthood."

G. R. Simeon b. Eleazar says in the name of R. Meir, and so did R. Simeon b. Menassia say in accord with his opinion, "On what account did they declare a *mixture* to be invalid for marriage into the priesthood?

H. "Because of the possibility of impaired priestly ancestry which is mixed in her genealogy.

I. "They are able to discern the Israelites, *Netins*, and *Mamzers* who are among her ancestors. But they are not able to discern the ancestors of impaired priestly stock which are among them."

5:3 A. *The daughter of a father of impaired priestly stock is invalid for marrying into the priesthood for all time.*

B. *R. Judah says, "The daughter of a male proselyte is equivalent to the daughter of a male of impaired priestly stock* and is invalid for marrying into the priesthood" [M. Qid. 4:6A, D].

C. A girl of *mixed stock* is invalid for marriage into the priesthood.

D. [If] she was married to an Israelite, her daughter is valid for marrying into the priesthood.

E. A female convert and a woman of impaired priestly stock are invalid for marriage into the priesthood.

F. [If] she was married to an Israelite, her daughter is valid for marriage into the priesthood.

G. A girl taken captive is invalid for marriage into the priesthood.

H. [If] she was married to an Israelite, her daughter is valid for marriage into the priesthood.

I. A slave-girl is invalid for marriage into the priesthood.

J. [If] she was married to an Israelite, her daughter is valid for marriage into the priesthood.

K. It turns out that Israelites are a [genealogical] purification-pool for priests, and a slave-girl is a purification-pool for all those who are invalid.

5:4 A. "*Netins* and *Mamzers* will be clean in the world to come," the words of R. Yosé.

B. R. Meir says, "They will not be clean."

C. Said to him R. Yosé. "But has it not truly been said, *I will sprinkle clean water upon you, and you shall be clean* (Ez. 36:25)."

D. Said to him R. Meir, "*And you shall be clean from all your uncleannesses, and from all your idols I will cleanse you* (Ez. 36:25)."

E. Said to him R. Yosé, "Why then does Scripture say, 'I shall clean you'? It means, Even from the *Netins* and the *Mamzers*."

F. An Egyptian man who married an Egyptian woman, an Edomite man who married an Edomite woman—the first generation and the second are prohibited from entering the congregation, but the third is permitted.

G. Said R. Judah, "Benjamin, an Egyptian proselyte, had a companion from among the disciples of R. 'Aqiba.

"He said, 'I am an Egyptian proselyte, and I married a woman who was an Egyptian proselyte. Lo, I am planning to arrange a marriage for my son with a woman who is the daughter of an Egyptian proselyte woman, so that the son of my son will be permitted to enter into the congregation,

H. "'since it is said, *[You shall not abhor an Edomite, for he is your brother; you shall not abhor an Egyptian, because you were a sojourner in his land.] The children of the third generation that are born to them may enter the congregation of the Lord* (Deut. 23:7–8).'

I. "Said to him. R. 'Aqiba, 'Benjamin, you have erred in this law. After Sennacherib came up and made a mixture of all the nations, the Ammonites and Moabites no longer are found in their original location, and the Egyptians and the Edomites are no longer found in their original location [cf. M. Yad. 4:4].

"'But an Ammonite man marries an Egyptian woman, and an Egyptian man marries an Ammonite woman, and any one of all these marries any one of all the families of the earth, and any one of the families of all the earth marries any one of these.

J. "'All follows the status of the offspring.'"

K. *As to a Levite-girl or Israelite-girl, they add on to them [examination of] yet another [generation]* [M. Qid. 4:4C].

L. Lo, they are then twelve [mothers].

M. [If] one made inquiry of the mother, he does not have to make inquiry concerning the children.

N. [If] he made inquiry concerning the children, he does not have to make inquiry concerning the mother.

O. [If] he made inquiry concerning the adults, he does not have to make inquiry concerning the minors.

P. [If] he made inquiry concerning the minors, he does not have to make inquiry concerning the adults.

Q. Under what circumstances?

R. In the case of one wife.

S. But in the case of two wives [if] one has made inquiry concerning the mother, he must make inquiry concerning the children.

T. [If] he has made inquiry concerning the children, he has to make inquiry concerning the mother.

U. [If] he has made inquiry concerning the adults, he has to make inquiry concerning the minors.

V. [If] he has made inquiry concerning the minors, he has to make inquiry concerning the adults.

5:5 A. *He who says, "This man, my son, is a mamzer," is not believed* [M. Qid. 4:8A].

B. "'This man, my son, is the son of a divorcee," or 'the son of a woman who has undergone the rite of *ḥalisah,*'

C. "concerning a minor, he is believed.

D. "concerning an adult, he is not believed," the words of R. Judah [*cf.* M. Qid. 3:8].

E. And sages say, "*Even if both of them say concerning the foetus in her womb that it is a mamzer, they are not believed*" [M. Qid. 4:8B].

5:6 A. *He who went, along with his wife, overseas, and he came along with his wife and children, and said, "The woman who went overseas with me, lo, this is she, and these are her children," does not have to bring proof concerning her or concerning the children.*

B. *[If he said], "She died, and these are her children," he brings proof concerning the children, but he does not have to bring proof concerning the woman* [M. Qid. 4:10].

5:7 A. [For] a woman is believed to say, "These are my children."

B. *And [he who says], "A woman whom I married overseas, lo, this is she, and these are her children," has to bring proof concerning the woman, but does not have to bring proof concerning the children* [M. Qid. 4:11].

5:8 A. [For] a woman is believed to say, "These are my children."

5:9 A. *A woman remains alone with two men* [M. Qid. 4:12A],

B. even if both of them are Samaritans,

C. even if both of them are slaves,

D. even if one of them is a Samaritan and one a slave,

E. except for a minor,

F. for she is shameless about having sexual relations in his presence.

5:10 A. As to his sister and his sister-in-law and all those women in a prohibited relationship to him which are listed in the Torah—he should not be alone with them [M. Qid. 4:12A] except before two [witnesses].

B. But she should not be alone even with a hundred gentiles.

C. R. Eleazar says, "Also: He who has a wife and children, but they are not living with him, should not teach scribes" [M. Qid. 4:13C].

D. *R. Judah says, "An unmarried man should not shepherd* small *cattle.*

E. *"And two unmarried men should not sleep in a single cloak"* [M. Qid. 4:14A–B].

F. And sages say, "Israelites are not suspect in such a matter."

5:11 A. R. Meir did say, "There is a husband and a wife who produce five castes.

B. "How so?

C. "A gentile man who has a slave-boy and a slave-girl, and they have two children, and one of them converted—

D. "Lo, [1] one is a proselyte, and [2] one is a gentile.

E. "[If] their master converted and converted the slaves, and they then produced a son, then [3] the offspring is a slave.

5:12 A. "[If] the slave-girl is freed, and that slave-boy had sexual relations with her, and they produced a son, the son is [4] a *mamzer.*

B. "And [if] both of them are freed,

C. "and they produced a son.

D. "then the son is [5] a freed slave.

5:13 A. "There is he who sells his father and pays her marriage-contract to his mother.

B. "How so?

C. "He who has a slave-boy and a slave-girl, and they produced a son—

D. "he freed his slave-girl and married her, and wrote over his property to her son—

E. "then it is he who sells his father and pays his mother her marriage-contract."

5:14 A. *Whoever has business with women should not be alone with women* [M. Qid. 4:14D]—

B. for example, goldsmiths, carders, [handmill] cleaners, peddlars, wool-dressers, barbers, launderers, and mill-stone chisellers.

C. R. Meir says, "You have no trade which has ever disappeared from the world.

D. "Yet woe is the man who sees his parents in a mean calling" [*cf.* M. Qid. 4:14F].

5:15 A. *Rabbi says, "A man should always* endeavor to *teach his son a trade which is clean* of thievery *and easy.*

B. "*And he should pray to Him to whom belongs all wealth.*

C. "For you have no trade in which is not found poverty,

D. "to inform you that wealth and poverty are not derived from a particular trade" [M. Qid. 4:14F–I].

E. R. Simeon b. Eleazar says, "In your whole life, did you ever see a lion working as a porter, a deer working as a fruitpicker, a fox working as a storekeeper, a wolf selling pots, a domestic beast or a wild beast or a bird who had a trade?

F. "Now these are created only to work for me, and I was made only to work for my Master.

G. "Now is there not an argument *a fortiori:* Now if these, who were created only to work for me, lo, they make a living without anguish, I who have been created to work for my Master, is it not reasonable that I too should make a living without anguish!

H. "But my deeds have ruined things, and I have spoiled my living" [*cf.* M. Qid. 4:14J].

5:16 A. *R. Nehorai says, "I should leave every trade there is in the world and teach my son only Torah.*

B. *"For they eat the fruit of labor in Torah in this world, but the principal lasts for the world to come.*

C. "For every sort of trade which there is in the world serves a man only when he is young, when he yet has his strength.

D. *"But when he falls ill or grows old or has pains, and does not work any more, in the end he dies of hunger.*

E. *"But Torah keeps a man from all evil when he is young and gives him a future and a hope when he is old. When he is young, what does it say? They who wait upon the Lord shall renew their strength* (Is. 40:31). *And concerning his old age, what does it say? They shall still bring forth fruit in old age"* (Ps. 92:14) [M. Qid. 4:14N–T].

5:17 A. *And so you find with regard to the patriarch, Abraham, that the Omnipresent blessed him in his old age more than in his youth, as it is said, And Abraham was old and well along in years and the Lord blessed Abraham in all things* (Gen. 24:1) [M. Qid. 4:14U].

B. R. Meir says, "That he had no daughter."

C. R. Simeon says, in the name of R. Judah, "That he did have a daughter."

D. R. Eleazar the Modite says, "Abraham possessed an astrological instrument, on account of which everybody came to him."

E. R. Simeon b. Yoḥai says, "This was a fine gem, which was hung around the neck of the patriarch, Abraham.

F. "And whoever stared at it was cured forthwith.

G. "When Abraham the patriarch died, the Omnipresent took it and hung it around the orb of the sun."

5:18 A. Another point: That Esau did not rebel during his lifetime.

5:19 A. A third measure: That Ishmael repented during his lifetime.

5:20 A. Others say, "Abraham did have a daughter, and her name was, *In all things.*"

5:21 A. And the Omnipresent blessed when in his old age more than in his youth.

B. And why all this?

C. *Because he kept the entire Torah even before it had come, since it says, Since Abraham obeyed my voice and kept my charge, my commandments, my statutes and my Torahs* (Gen. 26:5)—

D. *My Torah* is not said, but rather, *my Torahs*—

E. this teaches that to him were revealed the mysteries of the Torah in all their details.

INDEX TO BIBLICAL AND TALMUDIC REFERENCES

by Arthur Woodman, Canaan, New Hampshire

BIBLE

MISHNAH

TOSEFTA

BABYLONIAN TALMUD

GENERAL INDEX